Teaching Guide

BOOK 1 • LESSONS 1 – 30

Reading Eggs Teaching Guide – Book 1

ISBN: 978-1-76020-084-8

Published by Blake Education Pty Ltd
ABN 50 074 266 023
Locked Bag 2022
Glebe NSW 2037

Ph: (02) 8585 4085
Fax: (02) 8585 4058

Email: info@blake.com.au
Website: www.blake.com.au

Publisher: Katy Pike
Series editor: Sara Leman and Megan Smith
Editors: Sandra Iannella and Stacey Belgre
Designed and typeset by The Modern Art Production Group
Printed by Green Giant Press

Introduction

Reading Eggs

Since the launch of the website in 2008, Reading Eggs has grown to be an integral part of how children learn to read in many schools and homes across Australia and the world. Millions of children have successfully used the program and it's a key learning tool in more than 10 000 schools worldwide. The program has continued to grow and improve with many additional lessons, features, books and teaching resources. The Reading Eggs website now has a vast range of literacy resources including teaching tools, posters, lesson plans, worksheets and more than 2000 e-books, making it the most comprehensive reading program on the web.

Reading Eggs Teaching Guide

The four books in this series cover the 120 Reading Eggs lessons that are the core of the learn-to-read program. Each lesson has now been fully cross-referenced to all other components in the program and to the Australian Curriculum. Whether it's handwriting lessons for the Interactive Whiteboard, apps for student practice on their iPads, whole class alphabet activities, comprehension teaching posters, memorable songs, flashcards or more books to read, you will find a vast range of resources to use in your classroom. Every lesson comes with four student worksheets that focus on a specific skill including phonemic awareness, phonics, sight words, vocabulary, comprehension and handwriting.

Reading Eggs Lessons 1 - 30

This book covers lessons 1 – 30. Each lesson is supported by two pages of teaching notes with learning objectives, curriculum links, classroom activities and a Reading Eggs lesson sequence that links to the four student worksheets. Also included for each lesson are the related Reading Eggs activities, interactives, songs, apps and e-books that can be used to reinforce the content and skills covered in each lesson.

My program

From lesson 11 onwards, the additional *My Program* books appear, with four books for every lesson. These carefully levelled books are a balance of fiction and nonfiction titles, each with their own short comprehension quiz. *My Program* books provide students with the real reading practice they need to improve their reading fluency, vocabulary and comprehension skills. In later lessons, other parts of the program including the Skills Bank spelling lessons, Driving Tests and Storylands appear as part of each student's *My Program* board.

Contents

Reading Eggs Teaching Guide Books 1 to 4 Overview

Lesson	Phonic Letters and Sounds	Phonically Decodable Words	High Frequency Sight Words
Reading Eggs Teaching Guide Book 1 Overview			
1 - the letter m	m		
2 - the letter s	s		
3 - words I and am, and the letter i	a, m, am, i	Sam	I, am
4 - the letter t	t		
5 - the word and sound at	a, t, at	bat, cat, fat, pat, rat, sat, mat, hat	at, a, I, am
6 - the letter b	b	bat	
7 - the letter c	c	cat	
8 - the letter f	f, at	cat, bat, fat, mat, sat	
9 - the word a	a, m, t, at, am	am, Sam, cat, bat, fat, mat	I, a, am
10 - Review	a, b, c, f, i, m, s, t, am, at	am, Sam, at, bat, cat, fat, mat, sat	I, am, at, a
11 - the letter n	n	cat, sat, bat	I
12 - the letter p	p, am	pat	am
13 - the sound ap	a, p, ap	Sam, pats, cat, bat, fat, sat, zap, map, cap, tap, nap, rap, lap, gap	I, am, a
14 - the letter h	h	hat, ham	
15 - the letter r	r	rat, ram, rap	
16 - the sound an	a, n, an	ran, fan, can, van, pan, ant, Sam, bat, cat, rat	I, am, a, an, can, man
17 - the letter z	z	zap	
18 - the letter e, the sound ee	e, ee	bee, tree, see, seed, weed, Zee, three, tee	see
19 - the words see and the	s, ee	Sam, can, see, man, fan, pan, tap, cap, hat, bat, cat, sat, rat, mat, fat, zap, map	see, the, I, can, man, at, am
20 - Review	n, p, h, r, z, e, ap, an, ee	see, can, hat, man, bee, bat, Sam	see, the, can, man, you, I
21 - the letter v	v	van	see, the
22 - and		see, ant, band, rat, hat, sand, hand, land, mat, bee, bat, cat, Sam	and, see, the
23 - the letter d	d	Dan, dad	you
24 - the words in and had		rat, cat, hat, sat, fat, map	in, had, I, can, see, the, a
25 - the letter j	j	jam	see, you, the, can
26 - the sound ad	ad	dad, bad, had, pad, mad, sad, cats, rats, bees, ants	had, I, can, see
27 - the letter o	o	on	
28 - the word is		bee, ant, bad, sad, cap, bat	is, good, a, has, see, the, can, bad, an, I, am
29 - the word on	on	zap, mat, sat, bee, ant	on, the, and, is, a, see, can, you, had, an
30 - the letter q	q	queen	I, am, a, an, at, can, see, the, you, and, in, had, is, on, good, bad
Reading Eggs Posters			
Reading Eggs Teaching Guide Book 2 Overview			
31 - the letter g	g	pig, bag	had, see, the, bad, on, is, good
32 - the letter l	l	lap, lad	
33 - the words he and she		cat, sat, tap, can, jam, van, man, Dan, zap, mat, fat, bee, see	he, she, on, had, the, can, see, is, you, and, in, a, I
34 - the letter k	k		
35 - the words as and has		cat, bat, mat, hat, can, map, rat, man, fan, ham	as, has, is, it, on, a, the, on
36 - the letter y	y	yoyo	had, has, can, is, she, he
37 - the words yes and you		hat, cat, ant, man, van, map, has, and, bat, Dan, can, fat, rat, bad, see, bee	yes, you, has, a, and, it, as, I, am, an, in, he, see, the, can
38 - the letter x	x	box, fox, wax, mix, six	yes, see
39 - the letter w	w	web, win, wig	
40 - Review	am, at, an, ap, ad	van, sad, dam, zap, hat, man, gap, ran, jam, bat, pad, ham, ram, cat, can, see, hid, in, tin, sits, pin, fin	he, she, as, has, yes, you, man, the, can, see, in, and, a
41 - the letter u	u	fun, sun, run	

Reading Eggs Teaching Guide Books 1 to 4 Overview Continued

Lesson	Phonic Letters and Sounds	Phonically Decodable Words	High Frequency Sight Words
42 - the alphabet	Alphabet	cat, mat, rat, ham, map, tap, hat, gap, zap, sat, bat, van, fan, can, man, ran, tan, pan, lap, cap, nap, jam, Sam, ant, fun, sun, fox, box, pin, fin, bee	words, it, the, see, you, yes
43 - the sound id	id	hid, lid, kid, Sid, did, bin, rid, hit, bat	has, a, the, can, see, I, am, yes, it, in, he
44 - the sounds ix and in	ix	six, fix, mix, tin, win, pin, fin, din, bin	in, him, I, can, see, you, yes, a
45 - the sound it	it	hit, sit, bit, fit, spin, lit, pit, wit	it, can, you, on, I, we, and
46 - the sound ig	ig	big, wig, dig, fig, gig, pig, rig	like, said, I, it, my, the, has
47 - the word this		wag, bin, kid, pig, big, wig, fig	this, is, yes, the, it, can, he
48 - the sound ip	ip	lip, zip, pip, rip, dip, hip, nip, sip, tip, wip	little, black, blue, big
49 - the sound il	ill	hill, will, sill, pill, bill, kill, till, mill, dill, fill, gill, jill	
50 - the sound ing	ing	king, ring, sing, wing	bird, two, cannot, has, the, can, this, and
51 - the word go		six	go, by, you, can, see, the
52 - the sound ot	ot	cot, dot, hot, pot, lot, got, jot, rot, not	look, got
53 - the sound og	og	dog, log, fog, cog, bog, hog, jog, rock, sock, shop	of, this, got, lots, the, had, to, go, at, and
54 - the sound op	op	cop, hop, mop, pop, top, shop, stop	play, got, can, the, we, all, in
55 - the sound o	o	lots, dog, hog, log, fog, jog, cog, bog, pop, mop, hop, top, sock, cot, put, dot, hot, not, nod	got, he, lots, of, the, on
56 - the word are		not	are, happy, said, not, this, you, yes, like, no, to
57 - the words his and her		dog	his, her, we, said, like, it, she, this, is, the, he, all
58 - the sound ock	od, ock, ox	fox, cod, rod, nod, god, pod, dock, lock, clock, boxes, sock, rock	
59 - the sound od, y at the end	ox, y at the end	puppy, muddy, bossy, messy, silly, sorry, pod, rod, cod, fox, box, rocks, socks, pot, cot, hot, dot, rot, got	very
60 - Review	ock, ot, og, od, op, ox	clock, dock, rock, sock, lock, pod, rod, cod, dog, cog, jog, hog, log, fog, dot, cot, hot, pot, rot, lot, top, mop, hop, pop, fox, box	
Reading Eggs Posters			
Reading Eggs Teaching Guide Book 3 Overview			
61 - the word me			me, be
62 - the sound up	ut, up	cup, pup, cut, up, but, gut, hut, jut, nut, put	three, green
63 - the sound ug	un, ug	bug, dug, hug, jug, mug, rug, tug, bun, sun, fun, gun, pun, run	
64 - the word to	uck	muck, duck, fluffy, luck, mud, bud	to
65 - the sound uck	uck	fluff, truck, puck, tuck, yuck, stuck	
66 - the word there		leaf, ant, green, duck, mud, sun	there, that, this, hello
67 - the word have		mug, log, cup, green, duck, bug, chin	have
68 - the word they		leg, dog, cat, sun, run	they
69 - the word do		jump, run	do, can, cannot
70 - Review	us	bus, bug, bun, cab, cup, cut, duck, hot, jog, muck, nun, not, pup, rug, run, slug, sun	
71 - the word come		band	come, my, here, goes, day, play
72 - the sound ed	ed, eg, ing	bed, red, leg, peg, beg, egg	baby, open, hello
73 - the sound et	ed, et	bed, fed, wed, red, led, ted, pet, net, jet, vet, wet, hen, ten, pen, leg, egg	
74 - the sound eg	en, et	pet, bet, get, jet, met, set, vet, wet, yet, den, pen, hen, ten, when, men, zen	where
75 - the word where		pen, ten, peg, men, hen, shop	where, when, down, up, go, now
76 - the sound en	eg	leg, beg, keg, peg, peck	
77 - the word who		peck, shell	who, lives, here, into
78 - the word what		wing, tail, log, bed, net, her	what
79 - the sound ell	ell	bell, tell, yell, fell, well, shell, sell, hell	who, what, where
80 - Review		egg, net, bed, red, jet, peg, ten, pen	seven

Lesson	Phonic Letters and Sounds	Phonically Decodable Words	High Frequency Sight Words
81 - the word with	short vowels	pen, pig, leg, log, mug, mop, hat, hug, bed, box	have, with, what, you
82 - the sound ie	ie, ile	pie, tie, lie, smile, crocodile	going, where, want
83 - the sound i-e	ie, ine, ike	lie, line, mine, like, hike	shoe, car, table
84 - the sound ine	ine, ide, ike	dine, pine, fine, spine, shrine	too, off, over, this
85 - the sound sh	sh	shell, shop, sheep, ship, shed	shop, bike
86 - the sound sh	sh	shelley, sheep, shop, shopping	buy, tried, these, new
87 - the sound ie	long i	kite, bite, bike, hike, hide, ride	white, nine, girl, boy
88 - the sound ch	ch	chat, chick, cheese, chin, chips, chest	says, ask, why
89 - the sound th	th	throw, thanks, thin, that, thud, thick, thorn, think	none, two, stayed, home
90 - the sound ch	ch	chimp, chicken, cheese, chilli	these, made, together
Reading Eggs Teaching Guide Book 4 Overview			
91 - the soft c sound	soft c	city, celery, cement, bicycle, park, shark, dark, bark	one, two, three, four, five
92 - the sound ice	ice	mice, rice, dice, slice, line, bike, nine, fine, lime, vine	fly, look, white, fine, nine
93 - the soft g sound	soft g	cage, page, sage, stage, rage	today, park, Saturday
94 - the sound ake	ake	cake, lake, rake, bake, take, snake, shake, make, wake	snake, giraffe, wheel, shark
95 - the sond a-e	long a, ane	cane, mane, lane, plane, cage, ape, game	flew, bowl, brother, everywhere, what, about, another
96 - the sound ace	ace	space, lace, face	clouds, sky, stars, above
97 - the vowels	vowels	life, space	hours, outside, white, purple, yellow, orange
98 - the vowel sounds	long vowel words	make, snake, five, ape	these, out, eight, blue
99 - the sound y	y on the end	itchy, hairy, floppy, rusty, party, creepy	sleep, party, work, easy, flew, plane, high
100 - Review		five, mice, cage	up, down, night, day, in, out, five, nine, eight
101 - the sound oo (short)	oo	cook, book, wool, foot, look, took	dressed, delicious, winner
102 - the sound oo (long)	oo	roof, zoo, noon, moon, cool, spoon, pool, hoop, wood, baboon, cockatoo, coop	moose, cocoon, kangaroo, raccoon, baboon
103 - the sound ole	ole	pole, sole, mole, hole, stole, woke, poke, joke, bone, stone, cone	wombat, ground, kangaroo, mole, phone, poke
104 - the sound o-e	long o, e sounds	rode, code, vote, rose, boat, coat, goat, float, tadpole, flagpole	tangled, seaweed, wavy, bubbly, foam
105 - blends	blends	frog, clam, slam, swam, grub, crab, plug, grab, slug, shell	phone
106 - more blends	blends	crab, clam, frog, fly, green, trunk, lunch, crash, tree	crash, butterfly, hungry
107 - the sound ea	ea	pea, seal, leaf, dream, peach, beach, beast, eat, peace	peace, sitting, scary
108 - the sound u-e	long u words	cube, flute, tune, duke, June, tube	worried, perfect, flute, choose, tongue,
109 - the sound er	er	helper, brother, sister, cleaner, badger, bigger, better, plumber, builder	garden, leaky
110 - adjectives	blends	strong, pretty, dry, crunchy, glossy, flower, ground, cloud, drank, crunchy, squishy	wept, weak, cloud, pretty, adjectives
111 - blends	blends	wanted, trip, crashed, stuck, three	happy, boat, leaf, clock
112 - syllables	syllables	exercise, somewhere, drink, growing, eaten	keeping, drinking, sunlight
113 - end blends	end blends	flamingo, rabbit, duckling, stamp, thump	stinky, wanted, running, wants, keeping
114 - the sound oa	oa	flowers, raincoat, house	picture
115 - the sound /er/	ir	sunlight, seedling, warm, leaf, fingernail	
116 - the sound igh	igh	moonlight, goodnight, sandpaper, icecube, caring	family, forest
117 - nouns	nouns	raincoat, coast, better, bathroom, friends	shirt, goat
118 - the sound or	or	boots, long pants, jumper, coat, cloudy	windy, snow, sunny, rainy, horse
119 - verbs	verbs	remember, imagine, insect, sideways, flap	whistle, squeal, swoop, scuttle, scared
120 - the sound ay	ay	their, apple, spelling, feet, crabs	library, cling, eight, walk

Lesson 1 the letter **m**

Learning objectives

Children will:

- identify the sound m.
- identify words that begin with m.
- recognise and write m and M.

Australian Curriculum Content Descriptions

Sound and letter knowledge

ACELA1439 identify and manipulate sounds (phonemes) in spoken words

ACELA1440 identify familiar and recurring letters and the use of upper and lower case in written texts

Creating texts

ACELY1653 follow clear demonstrations of how to construct each letter; learn to construct lower case letters

Expressing and developing ideas

ACELA1758 recognise the most common sound made by each letter of the alphabet, including consonants and short vowel sounds

Vocabulary words

moon, monkey, mice, mud, mop, men, mat, meat, moss, man, money, map, milk, mouse, mum, mug

ESL/ELL

The sounds /m/ and /n/ can be confusing as they sound and look similar, be sure to differentiate for students the difference between the two.

Extra assistance

Have them watch themselves in the mirror to make sure they are bringing both lips together when they make the sound. They can double check they are making the correct sound by placing two fingers on their neck to feel the gentle vibration as they voice /m/.

Classroom activities

Use a variety of materials such as playdough, paint, or sand to create the letter m.

Collage

Provide the children with a piece of paper that has a large m in the middle.

- trace over the m with a pencil
- find things starting with m in an old magazine, cut out and glue around the m on the paper to create a collage

Say it right! (Initial phoneme)

Fill a bag with objects and pictures of things. Pick something out of the bag (eg a ball) and say it incorrectly, using the wrong initial sound, eg tall. Children need to correctly repeat the word ball.

Reading Eggs Lesson sequence	**TEACH Content and skills**	**PRACTISE Children will:**	**APPLY**
Hear: *Animated Lesson*	Introduces the sound /m/ through words and the songs *Sounds like mmm!* and *Mmm, you're clever!*	identify and read /m/ sound in isolation and as an initial sound in CVC words.	**Worksheet 1** Phonemic awareness
Write: *Dot-to-Dot*	Reinforce correct letter formation of lower case m.	write the letter m.	**Worksheet 2** Handwriting
Find: *Letter Grid and Mark Your Letter*	Recognise m in different fonts in upper and lower case.	locate lower case m and upper case/capital M.	**Worksheet 3** Initial sounds
Vocabulary: *Letter Book & Label It*	Build vocabulary skills: Match pictures to spoken and written words.	understand key vocabulary and apply it in reading.	**Worksheet 4** Check
Read: *Book*	Read aloud book.	listen, follow the reading and read along.	**Reading Eggs Alphabet book** m

Related Reading Eggs Activities, Interactives, Songs and Books

Reading Eggs Playroom

Alphabet Activities: book and letter activities

Book shelf song books:

5 Little Monkeys

Old Macdonald had a Farm

Alphabet Song

Music Café

Sounds like mmm!

Mmm, you're clever!

Reading Eggs Puzzle Park

Alphabet Match

Reading Eggs Posters

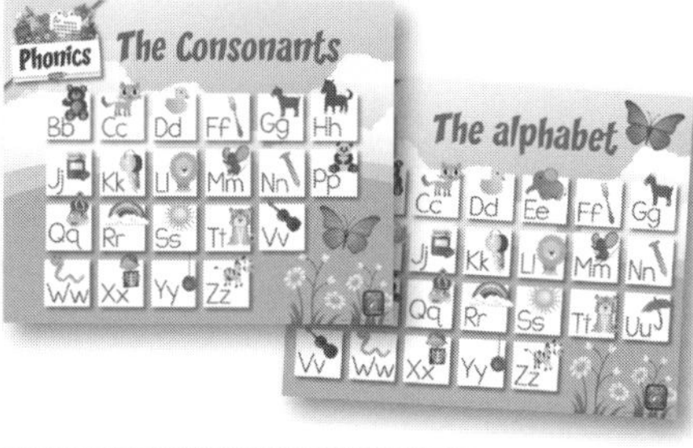

Teacher Toolkit

Targeting Handwriting Interactively

Alphabet Activities

Reading Eggs Apps

Eggy Alphabet

Reading Eggs Library Books

Alphabet Flashcards

Game 1 – focus on the m card.

Critter Card

Marshmallow mouse

Mm

Lesson 1 • Worksheet 1

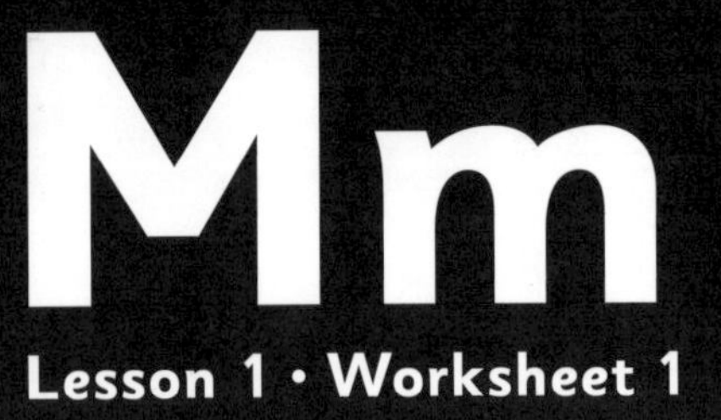

Name

Phonemic awareness

Circle the thing in each row that begins with **m**. Colour them.

m
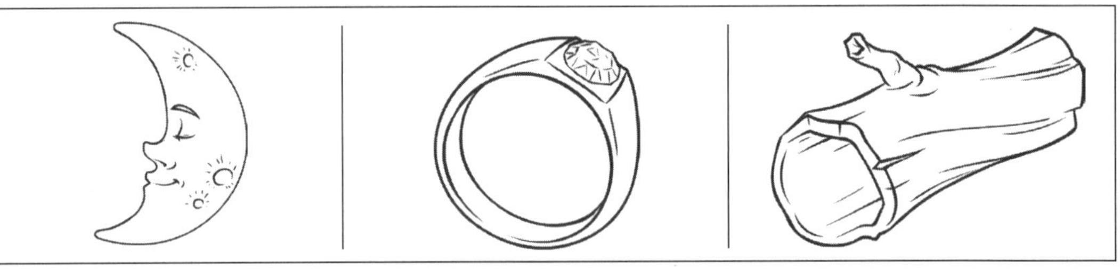

m
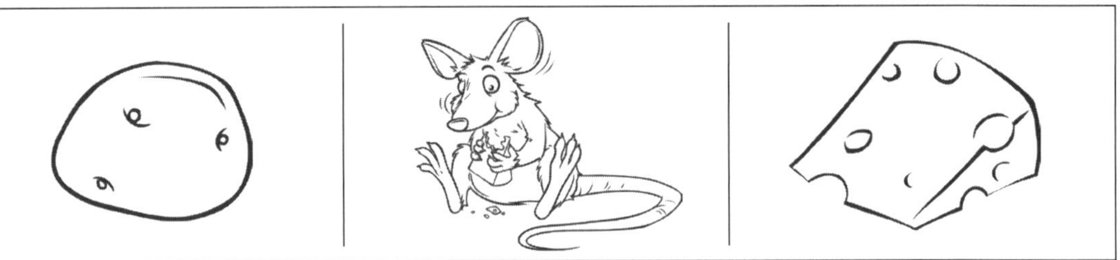

m
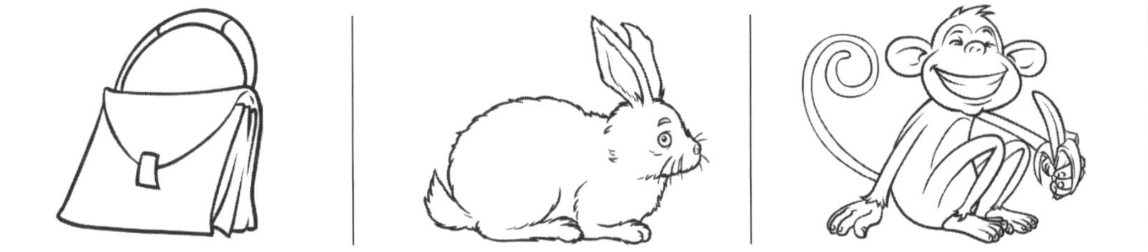

m
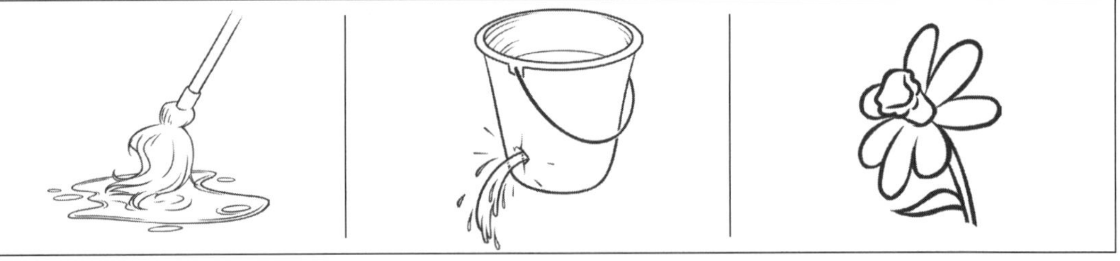

m
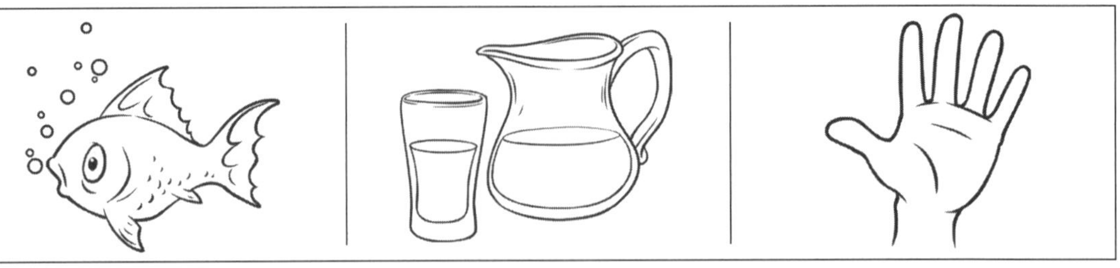

m
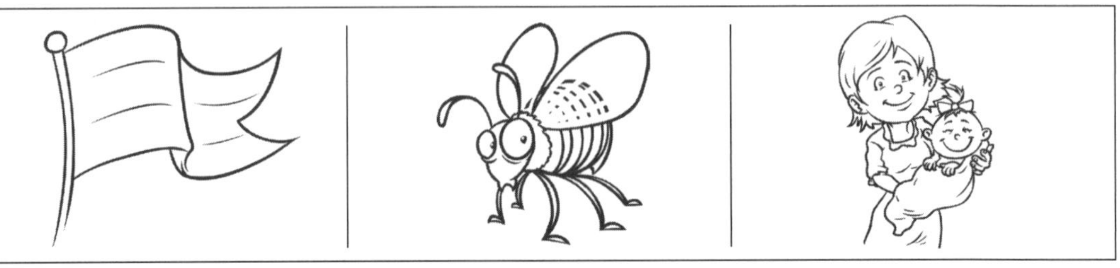

Name

Handwriting

1 Hop.

2 Trace and write.

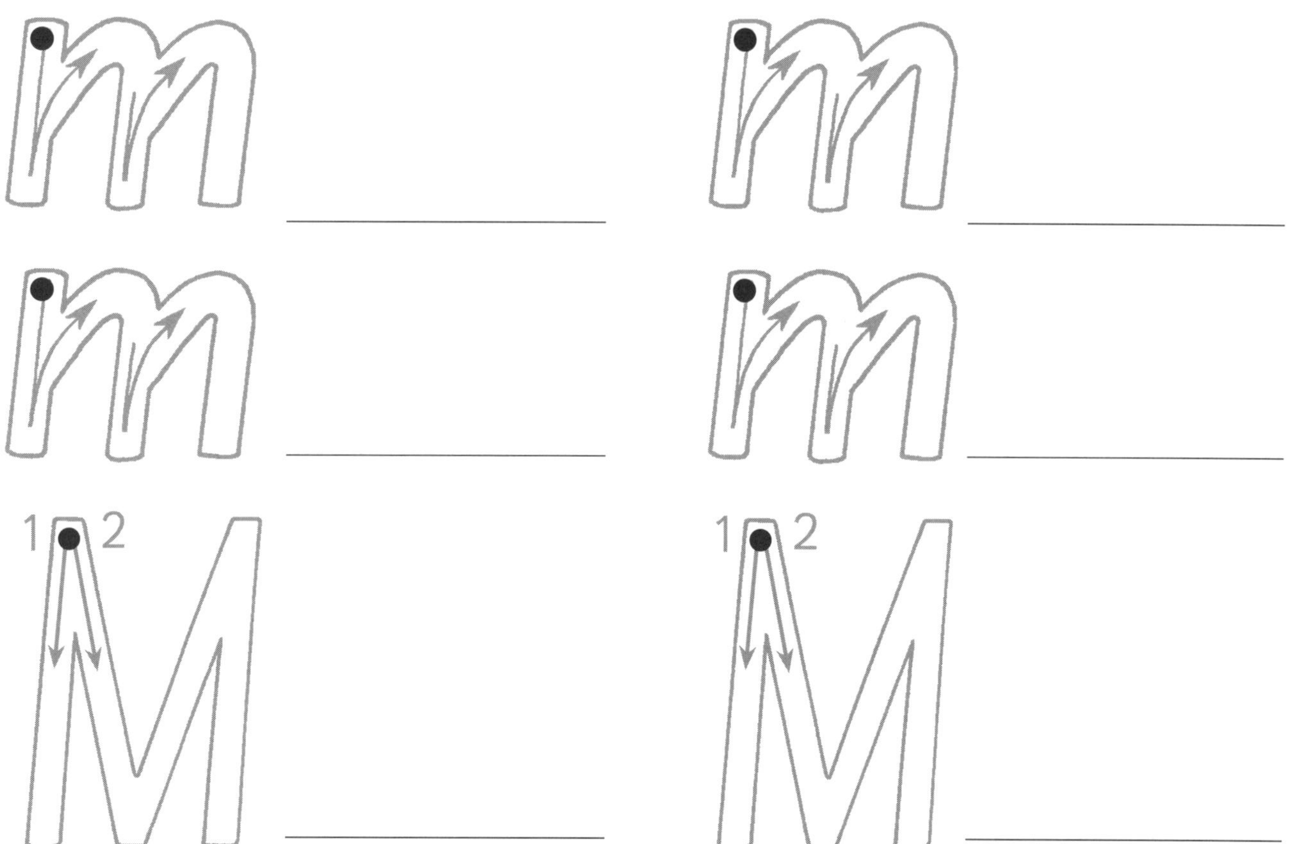

Find and tick your best letter.

Mm

Lesson 1 · Worksheet 3

Name

Initial sounds

Mutt the monster

1 Add **m**. Read the word.

m an

____ouse

____onkey

____oon

____ap

____ilk

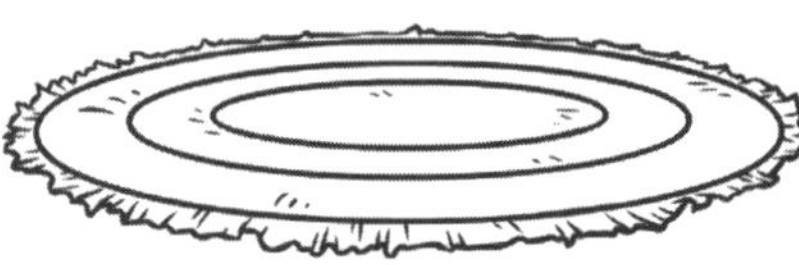

____at

____op

2 Draw a mask.

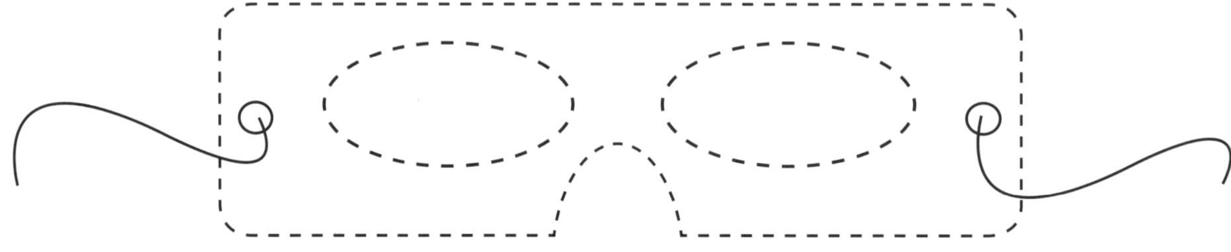

Name

Check

1 Colour things that begin with **m**.

2 Circle every **M**.

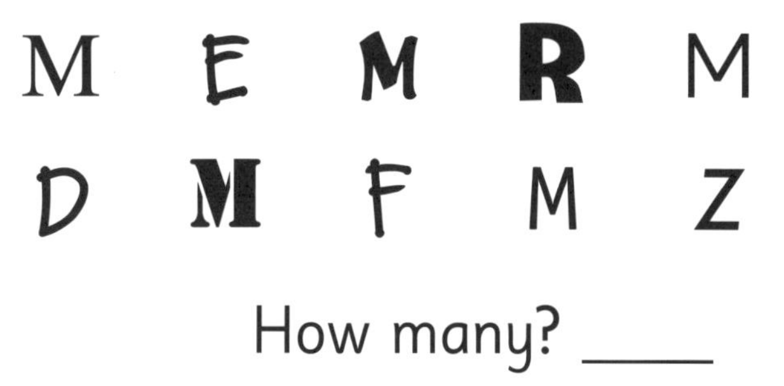

Circle every **m**.

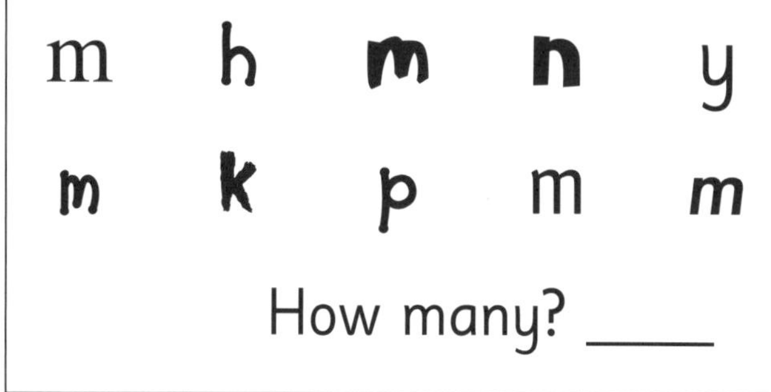

3 Write the letter **m**.

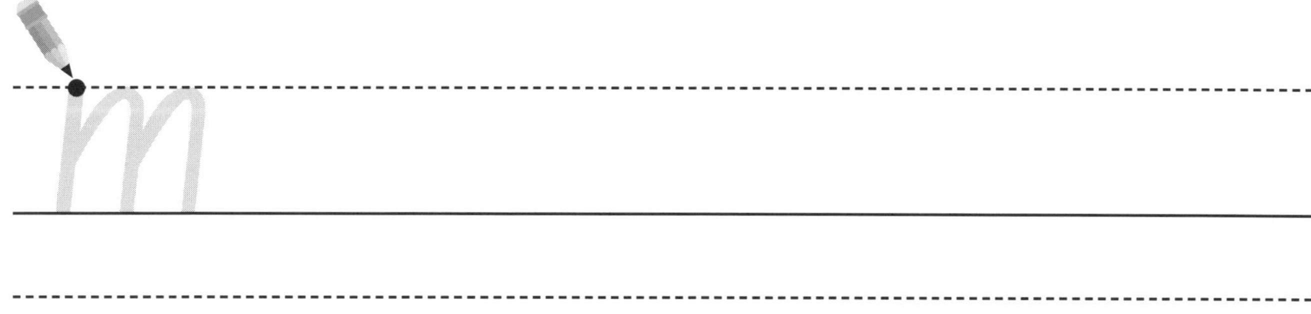

Lesson 2 the letter **s**

Learning objectives

Children will:

- identify the sound s.
- identify words that begin with s.
- recognise and write s and S.

Australian Curriculum Content Descriptions

Sound and letter knowledge

ACELA1439 identify and manipulate sounds (phonemes) in spoken words

ACELA1440 identify familiar and recurring letters and the use of upper and lower case in written texts

Creating texts

ACELY1653 follow clear demonstrations of how to construct each letter, learn to construct lower case letters

Expressing and developing ideas

ACELA1758 recognise the most common sound made by each letter of the alphabet, including consonants and short vowel sounds

Vocabulary words

sock, seven, sat, sing, soap, see, six, seed, sandwich, spaghetti, spoon, stand, stamp, snail, sun, strawberry, snake, sleep, slip, ship, saw, said

ESL/ELL

In Spanish, s is always preceded or followed by a vowel, so some students may put an /e/ sound at the front of words starting with an s blend, eg stomp may become es-tomp. They will need to practise correct pronunciation of English s blend words.

Extra assistance

The sounds for s and z can be confusing as they sound similar as well as looking very similar. Give students opportunities to differentiate between the two aurally.

Classroom activities

Decorate the Letters

Provide the students with a piece of paper that has many different forms of the letter s on it – some dotted, some in bubble writing, some solid letters, a couple of capitals.

- trace over the dotted letters with different coloured pencils, textas or crayons
- glue collage materials such as paper bits, leaves or wool to the solid letters
- colour in the bubble letters with dots, stripes or shapes

Which Hat?

Place two hats on the floor with the labels m and s. Discuss the sounds. Have a pile of objects or pictures of objects that start with m and s. Each student chooses one and works out which hat it must go in. Discuss their choice with the class.

Reading Eggs Lesson sequence	**TEACH Content and skills**	**PRACTISE Children will:**	**APPLY**
Hear: *Animated Lesson*	Introduce the sound /s/ through words and the song *Sam's Scare.*	identify and read /s/ sound in isolation and as an initial sound in words.	**Worksheet 1** Phonemic awareness
Write: *Dot-to-Dot*	Reinforce correct letter formation of lower case s.	write the letter s.	**Worksheet 2** Handwriting
Find: *Letter Grid, Birds and Mark Your Letter*	Recognise s in different fonts in both upper and lower case.	locate lower case s and upper case/capital S.	**Worksheet 3** Initial sounds
Vocabulary: *Letter Book and Label It*	Build vocabulary skills: Match pictures to spoken and written words.	understand key vocabulary and apply it in reading.	**Worksheet 4** Check
Read: *Book*	Read aloud book.	listen, follow the reading and read along.	**Reading Eggs Alphabet book** s

Related Reading Eggs Activities, Interactives, Songs and Books

Reading Eggs Playroom

Alphabet Activities

Book Shelf Song

Books:

Alphabet Song

Incy Wincy Spider

Puzzle Table:

Swap Parts and Shape puzzle

Music Café

Sam's Scare

Reading Eggs Puzzle Park

Alphabet Match

Reading Eggs Posters

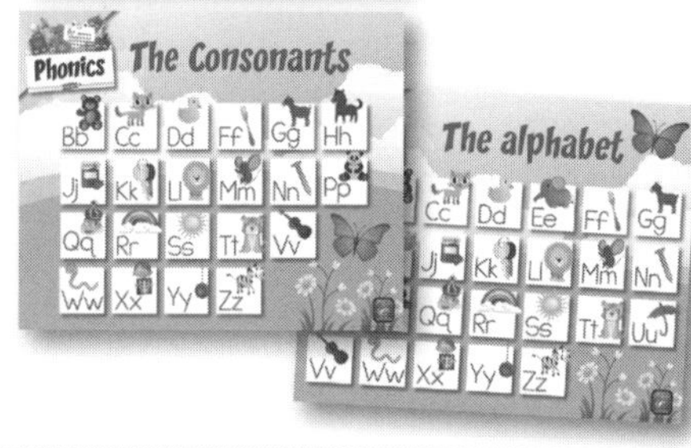

Teacher Toolkit

Targeting Handwriting Interactively

Alphabet Activities

Reading Eggs Apps

Eggy Alphabet

Reading Eggs Library Books

Alphabet Flashcards

Game 3 – Sound hunt using the card for s.

Critter Card

Sunny snail

Ss

Lesson 2 • Worksheet 1

Name

Phonemic awareness

Circle the thing in each row that begins with **s**. Colour them.

Name

Handwriting

Ss

Lesson 2 • Worksheet 2

1 Follow Sunny snail's trails.

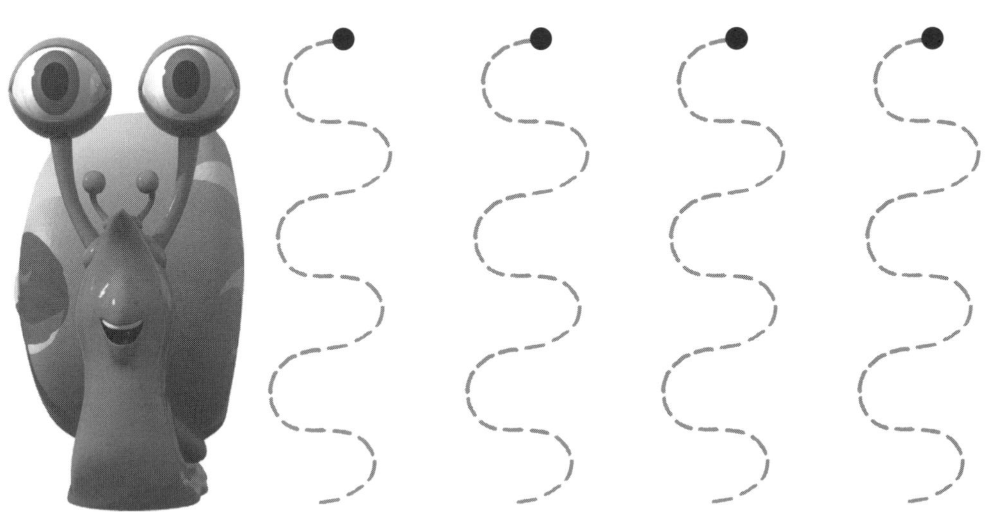

2 Trace and write.

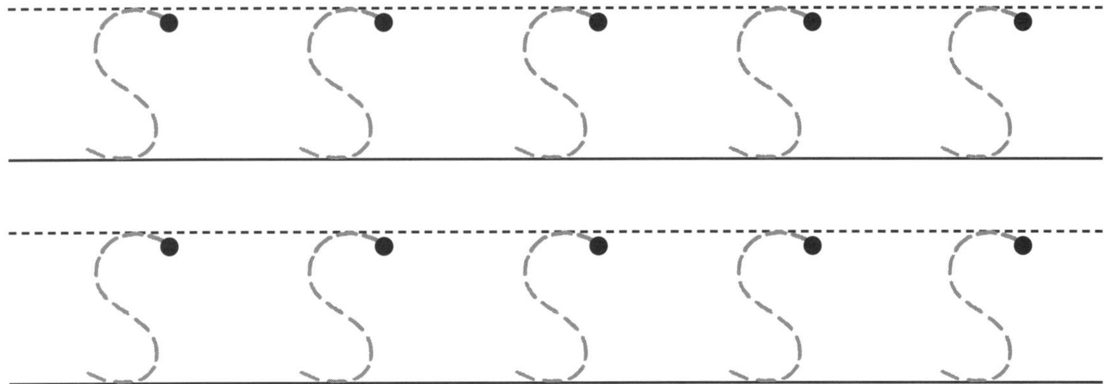

Circle your best letter.

Ss

Lesson 2 · Worksheet 3

Name

Initial sounds

Hello I'm Sam!

1 Add **s**. Read the word.

__s__un

_____ock

_____ix

_____andwich

_____nake

_____nail

_____tar

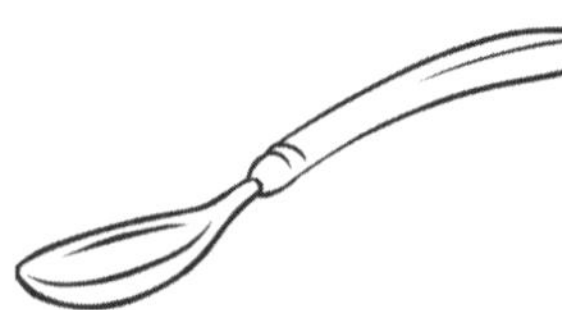

_____poon

2 Draw six socks.

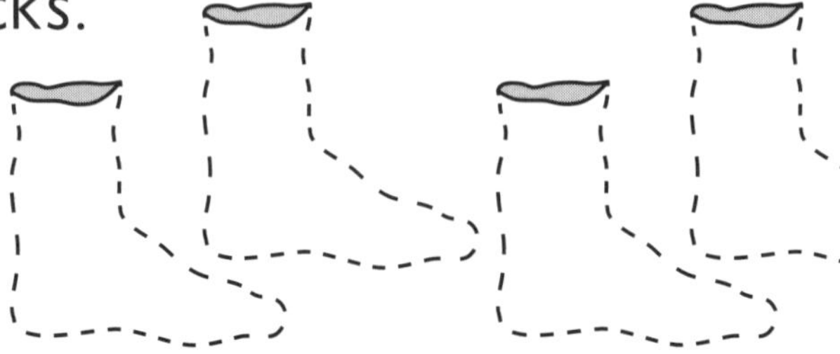

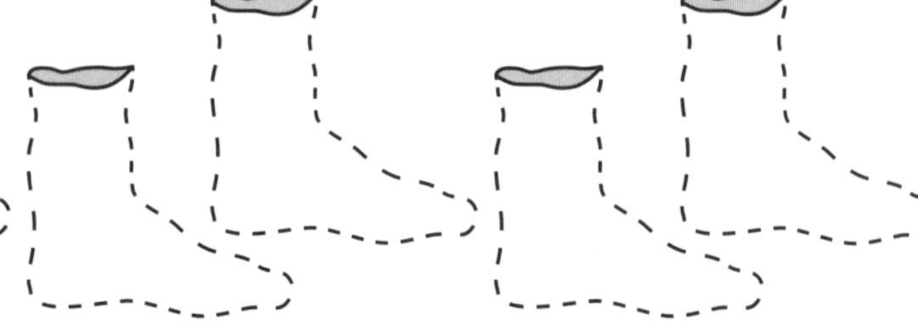

Name

Check

Ss

Lesson 2 • Worksheet 4

1 Colour things that begin with **s**.

2 Circle every **S**.

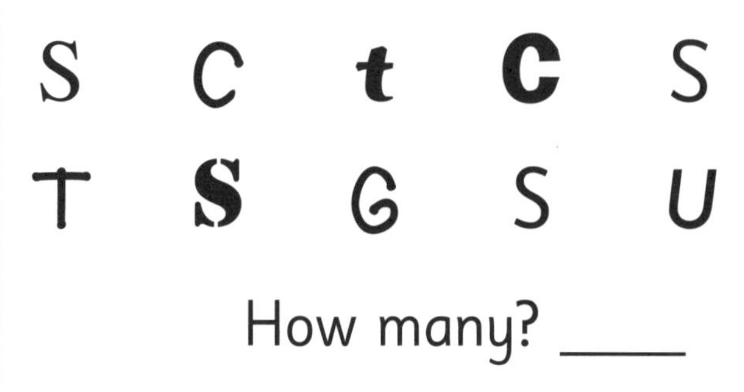

Circle every **s**.

s s d c s
a r b s y

How many? ____

3 Write the letter **s**.

Lesson 3 words I and am, and the letter i

Learning objectives

Children will:

- identify the words I and am.
- use the rime am to build words.
- recognise and write i and I.
- read and write the words I and am.

Australian Curriculum Content Descriptions

Sound and letter knowledge

ACELA1439 identify and manipulate sounds (phonemes) in spoken words

ACELA1440 identify familiar and recurring letters and the use of upper and lower case in written texts

Creating texts

ACELY1653 follow clear demonstrations of how to construct each letter, learn to construct lower case letters

Expressing and developing ideas

ACELA1758 recognise the most common sound made by each letter of the alphabet, including consonants and short vowel sounds

Sight words

I, am

Word family

lamb, ham, ram, dam, jam, pram, stamp, lamp, clam

Vocabulary words

ice-cream, igloo, ice, insects, ink, ill, itch, internet

ESL/ELL

Students whose native language is not English may pronounce the sound /i/ as /ee/. Give students opportunities to practise correct pronunciation with matching pairs of words eg sit and seat, bit and beat, mitt and meet.

Extra assistance

Students who use a language other than English at home may have learnt a different set of graphemes before coming to school. If the Roman alphabet is new to them, the idea of lower case and upper case or capital letters may be new to them too. Be sure to stress the differences between them.

Reading Eggs Lesson sequence	TEACH Content and skills	PRACTISE Children will:	APPLY
Hear: *Animated Lesson*	Introduce the words I and am through words and the songs *I can fly!* and *I am, I am, I am…*	identify and read the words I and am in isolation and in a sentence.	**Worksheet 1** Phonemic awareness
Write: *Dot-to-Dot*	Reinforce correct letter formation of upper case I.	write the letter I.	**Worksheet 2** Handwriting
Find: *Letter Grid and Leaping Penguins*	Recognise i in upper and lower case. Recognise a word.	locate lower case i and upper case I. Find the word Sam in a group.	**Worksheet 3** Initial sounds
Vocabulary: *Label It and Blend a Word*	Build vocabulary skills: Match pictures to words. Blend and recognise words.	recognise words with the rime am. Blend sounds to read words.	**Worksheet 4** Check
Read: *Book*	Read aloud book.	listen, follow the reading and read along.	**Reading Eggs Alphabet book** i

Classroom activities

Sentence Shuffle

Write an enlarged version of the sentence I am Sam and read it with the children. Reproduce each word on smaller pieces of card so students can make the sentence themselves and read it.

Make your own sentences

Students use their own names to complete the I am sentence. Then they create other endings to the I am sentence:

I am Alex. I am five. I am tall.

Related Reading Eggs Activities, Interactives, Songs and Books

Reading Eggs Playroom

Alphabet Activities

Book Shelf Song

Books:

Alphabet Song

Incy Wincy Spider

Play Kitchen:

Ice-cream

Music Café

I can fly!

I am, I am, I am…

Reading Eggs Puzzle Park

Alphabet Match

Reading Eggs Posters

Teacher Toolkit

Targeting Handwriting Interactively

Alphabet Activities

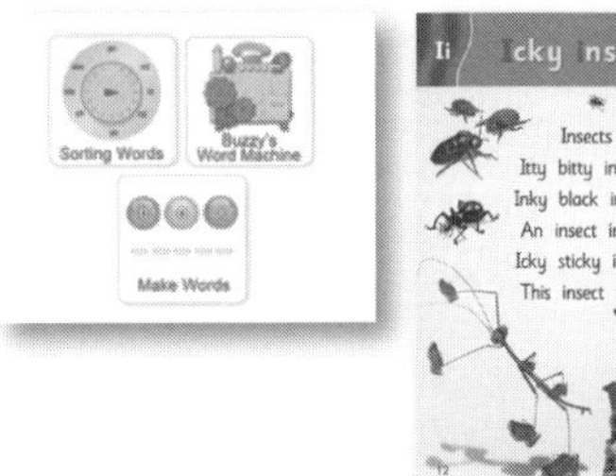

Reading Eggs Apps

Eggy Alphabet

Eggy Sight words

Reading Eggs Library Books

Alphabet Flashcards

Game 7 – Making Words ending with am.

Critter Card

Pramlamb

Lesson 3 • Worksheet 1

Name

Phonemic awareness

Circle the thing in each row that begins with **i**. Colour them.

i	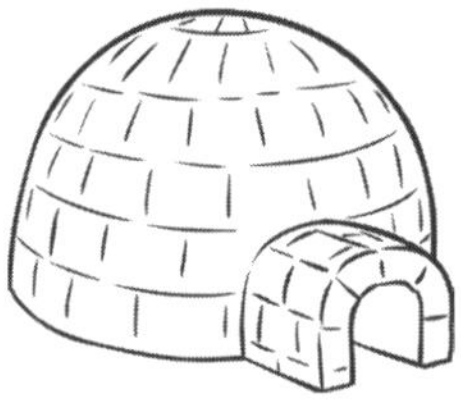	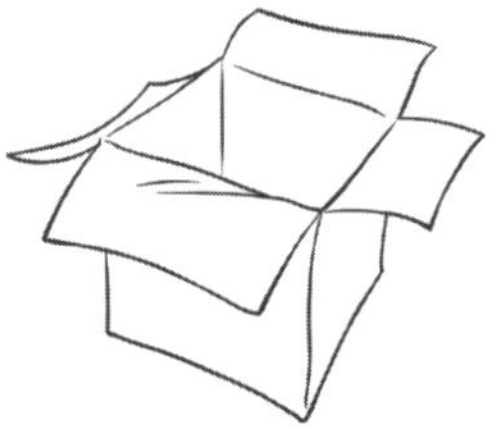	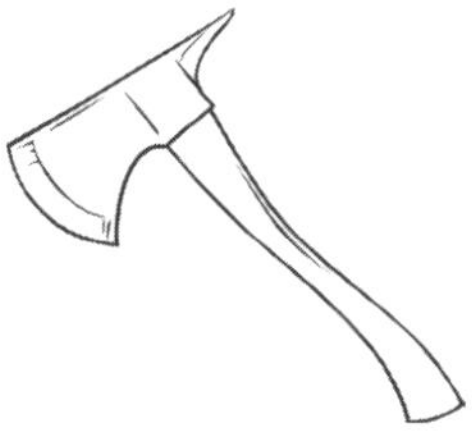
i	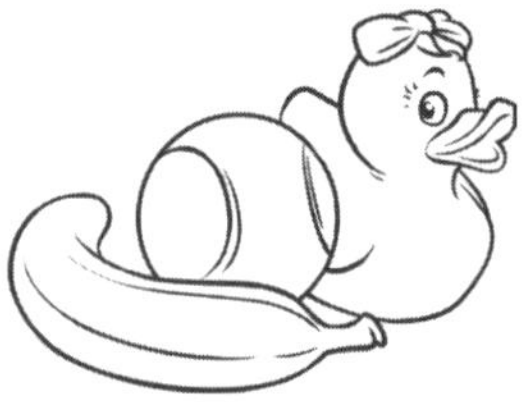	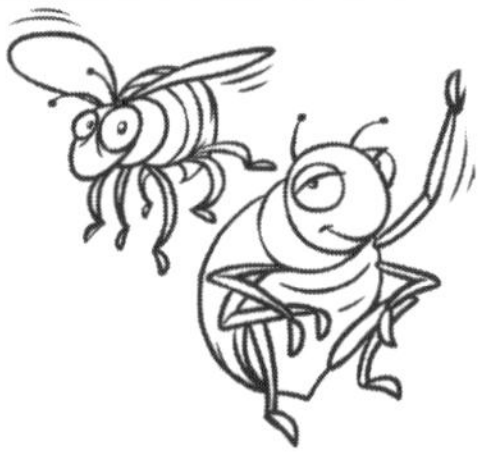	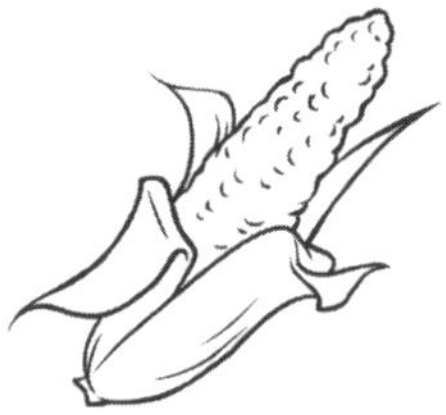
i	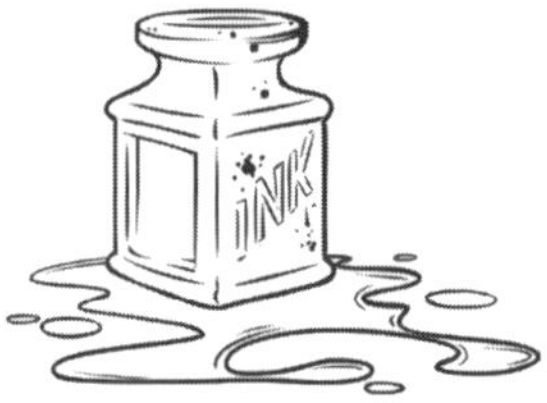	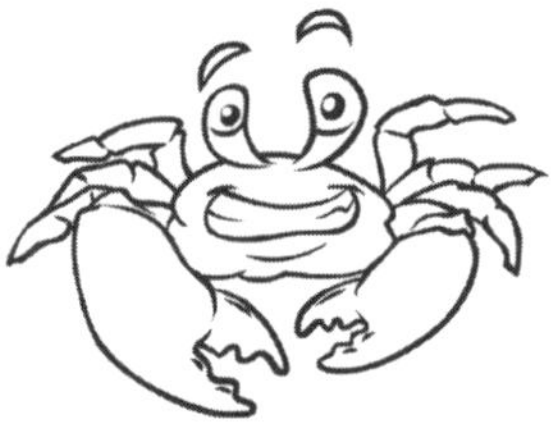	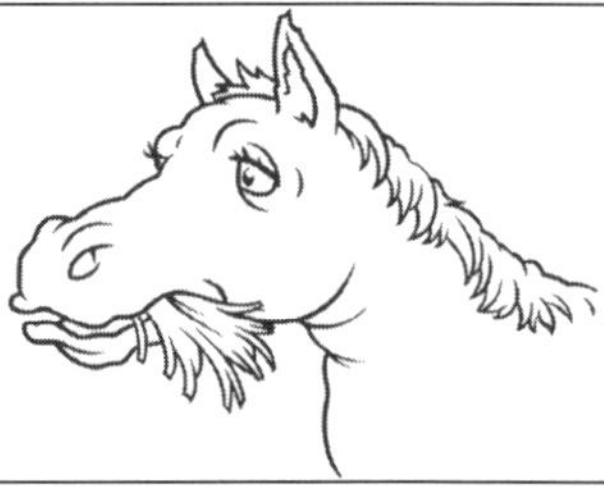
i	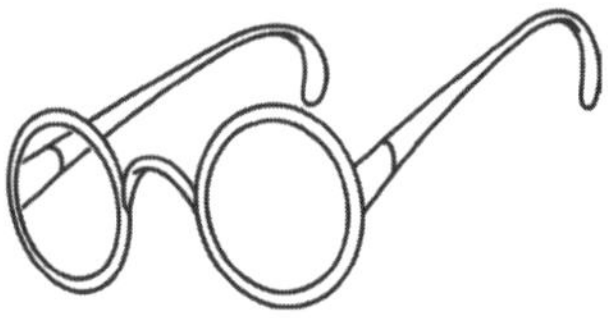	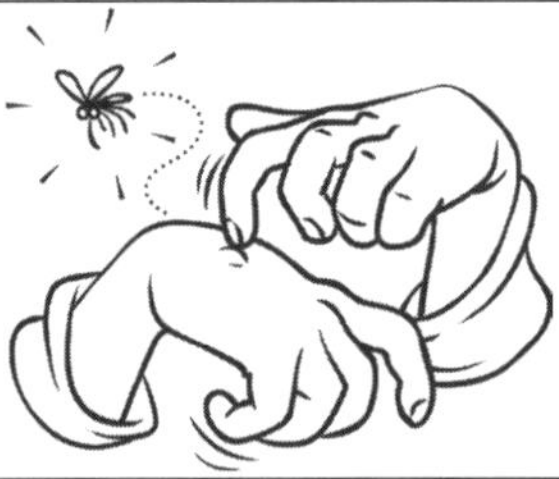	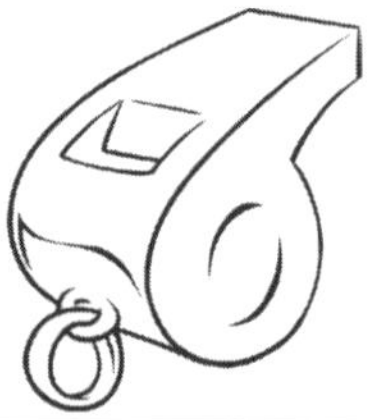
i	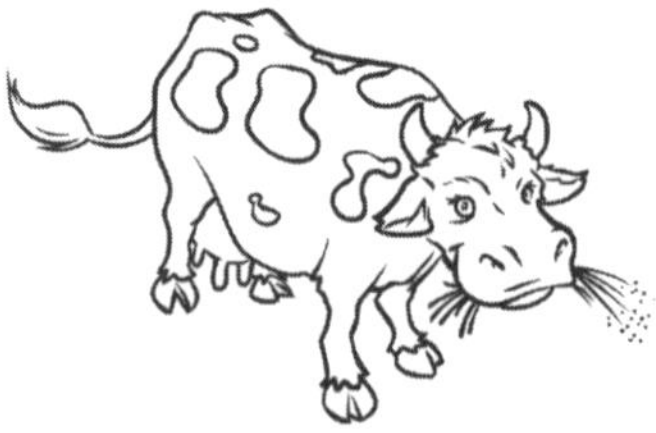	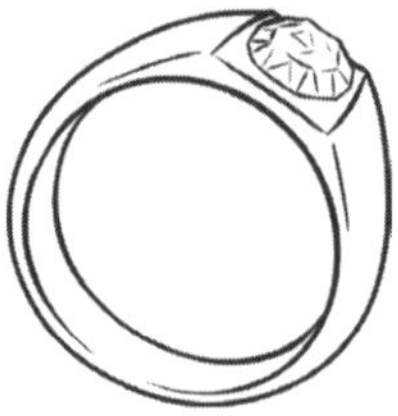	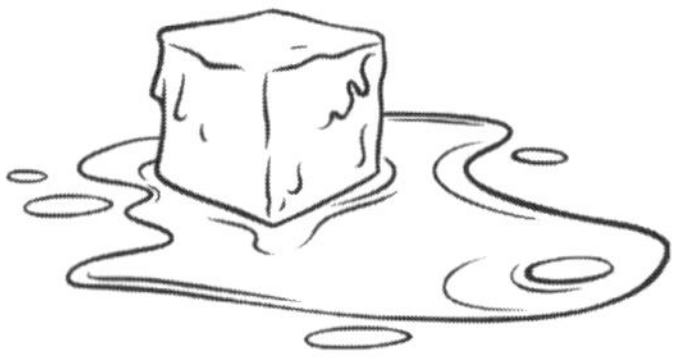
i			
i			

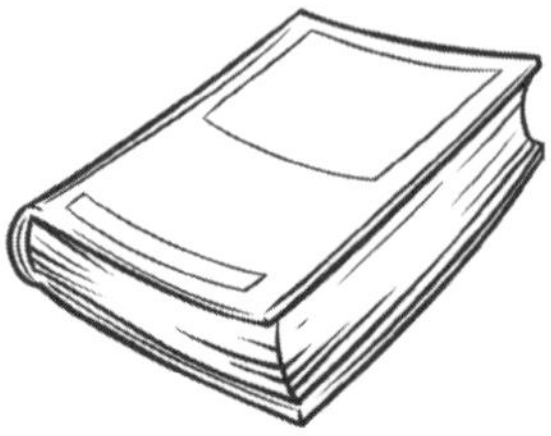

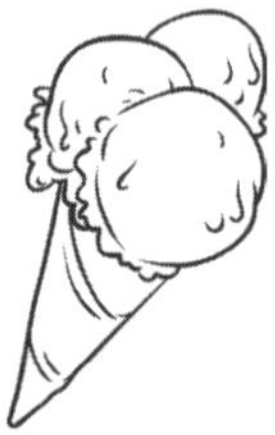

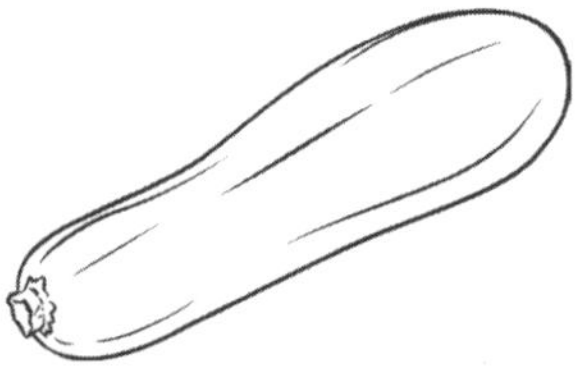

Name

Handwriting

Lesson 3 • Worksheet 2

1 Trace and write.

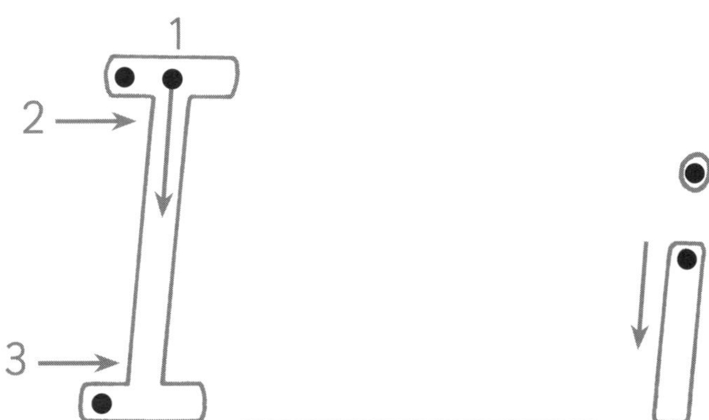

2 Circle every **I**.

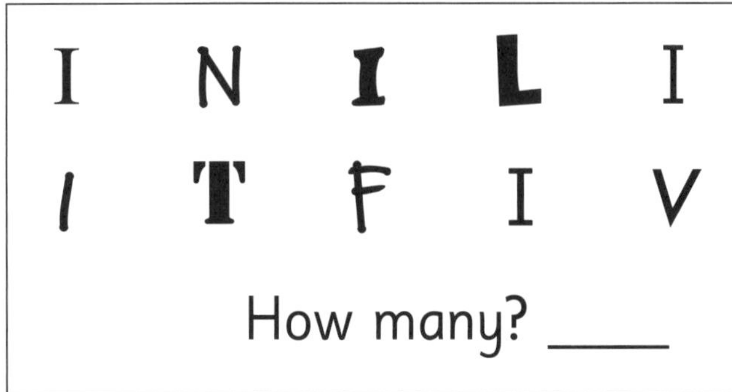

How many? ____

Circle every **i**.

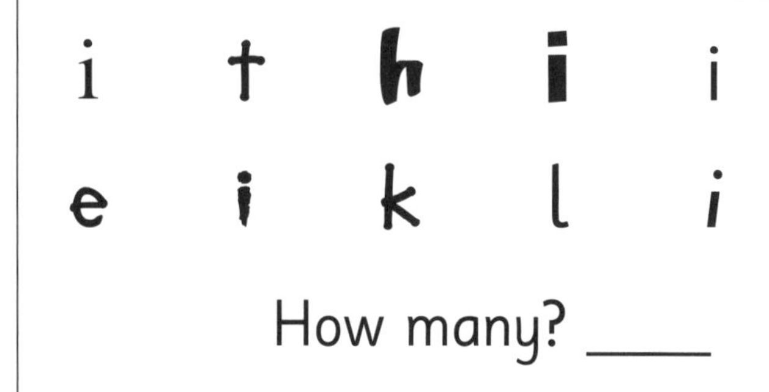

How many? ____

3 Trace.

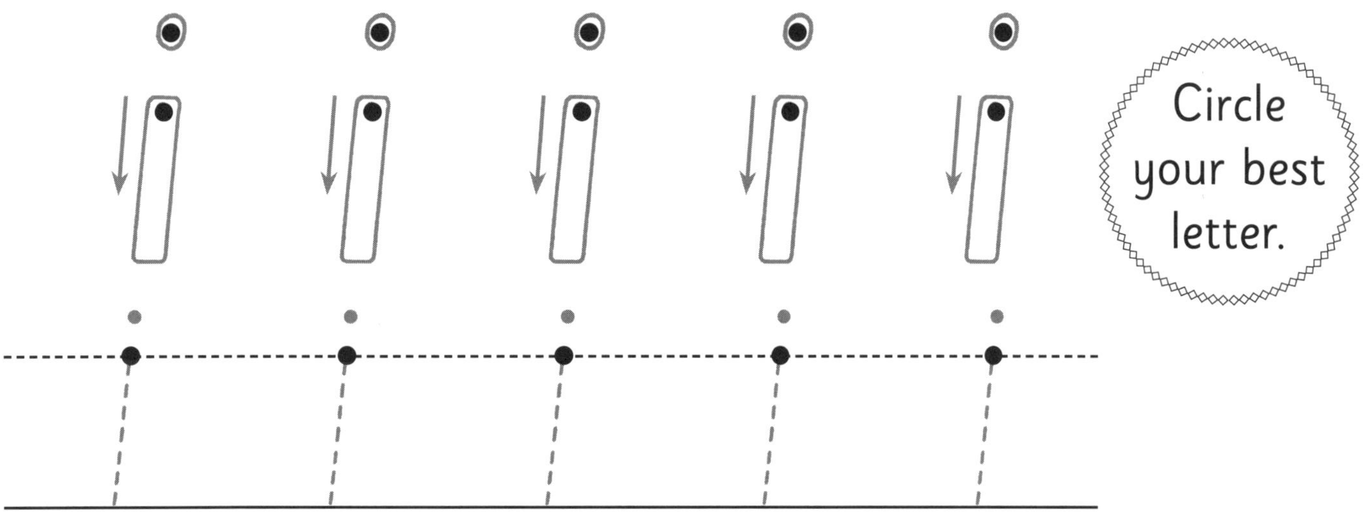

Circle your best letter.

Lesson 2 · Worksheet 3

Name

Initial sounds

1 Add **i**. Read the word.

i____nk

____nsects

____tch

____nternet

____ce

____ce-cream

2 Draw more insects on the icy igloo.

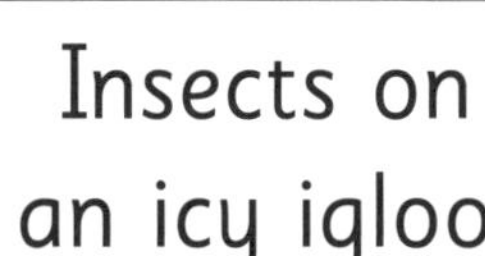

Name

Check

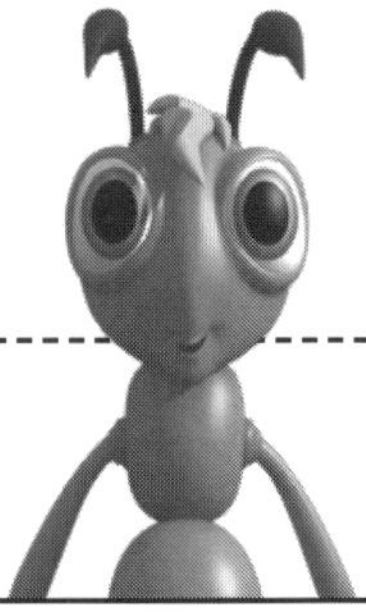

I am Sam.

What is your name?

I am

How old are you?

I am 4 5 6

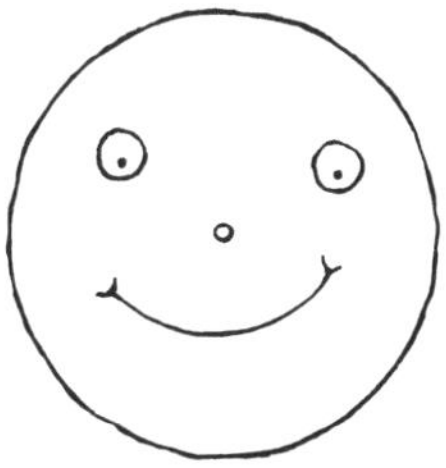

I am happy.

Lesson 4 the letter **t**

Learning objectives

Children will:

- identify the sound t.
- identify words that begin with t.
- recognise the letters t and T.

Australian Curriculum Content Descriptions

Sound and letter knowledge

ACELA1439 identify and manipulate sounds (phonemes) in spoken words

ACELA1440 identify familiar and recurring letters and the use of upper and lower case in written texts

Expressing and developing ideas

ACELA1758 recognise the most common sound made by each letter of the alphabet, including consonants and short vowel sounds

Vocabulary words

tent, toe, turtle, table, teeth, triangle, train, tractor, tap, tomato, tooth, teepee, three, tv, ticket, toy, top, tiger, tie, ten, truck, telephone

ESL/ELL

Many Russian, Spanish or French speakers pronounce their ts softly, unlike the hard English /t/ sound. Give these students opportunities to practise the /t/ sound with their tongue tapping their top teeth in a short burst of sound.

Extra assistance

A fun way to practise a sound repetitively is with tongue twisters. You should say it first, then ask the student to repeat it after you. Break the sentence into sections of 3 to 5 words if that is easier to start with. For the sound /t/ try these ones:

Mr. Tongue Twister tried to train his tongue to twist and turn to learn the letter "T".

Two tiny tigers take two taxis to town.

Classroom activities

Which Hat?

Place three hats on the floor with the labels m, s and t. Discuss the sounds. Have a pile of objects or pictures of objects that start with m, s and t. Each student chooses one and works out which hat it must go in. Discuss their choice with the class.

Bingo!

Give students a laminated board with 10 squares on it. Ask them to write a letter in each square from the list m, s, i, t (use whiteboard markers). Hold up pictures of items starting with m, s, i, t and say the name of the item in the picture. Students put a cross on that initial letter on their board. First one to 10 calls out 'bingo' and wins!

Reading Eggs Lesson sequence	TEACH Content and skills	PRACTISE Children will:	APPLY
Hear: *Animated Lesson*	Introduce the sound /t/ through words and the song *To the Top.*	identify and read /t/ sound in isolation and as a sound in words.	**Worksheet 1** Phonemic awareness
Find: *Letter Grid, Birds and Trains*	Recognise t in both upper and lower case.	locate lower case t and capital T.	**Worksheet 2** Handwriting
Match: *In the Box*	Match pictures to spoken and written words.	match pictures to their initial letter.	**Worksheet 3** Initial sounds
Vocabulary: *Label It and Letter Book*	Build vocabulary skills: Match pictures to spoken and written words.	understand key vocabulary and apply it in reading.	**Worksheet 4** Check
Read: *Book*	Read aloud book.	listen, follow the reading and read along.	**Reading Eggs Alphabet book** t

Related Reading Eggs Activities, Interactives, Songs and Books

Reading Eggs Playroom

Alphabet Activities

Book Shelf song books:
Alphabet Song,
Twinkle Twinkle Little Star,
I'm a Little Teapot

Animal Corner:
Tails

Music Café

To the Top

Reading Eggs Puzzle Park

Alphabet Match

Reading Eggs Posters

Teacher Toolkit

Targeting Handwriting Interactively

Alphabet Activities

Aa Bb Cc Dd Ee Ff
Gg Hh Ii Jj Kk Ll
Mm Nn Oo Pp Qq Rr
Ss Tt Uu Vv Ww Xx
Yy Zz

Reading Eggs Apps

Eggy Alphabet

Reading Eggs Library Books

Alphabet Flashcards

Game 1 – Letter shape using the cards for m, s, i and t.

Critter Card

Tiger turtle

Tt

Lesson 4 • Worksheet 1

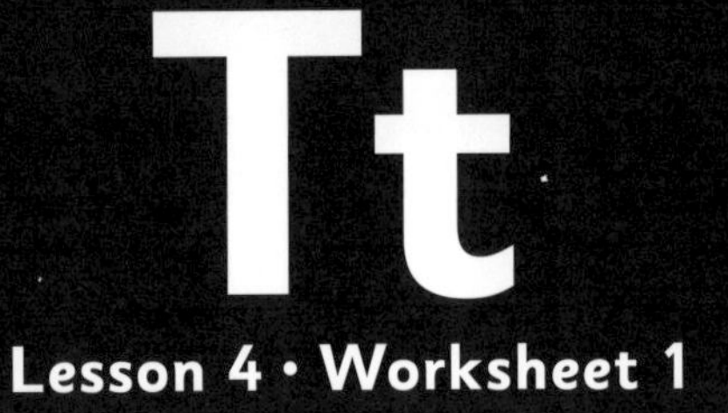

Name

Phonemic awareness

Circle the thing in each row that begins with **t**. Colour them.

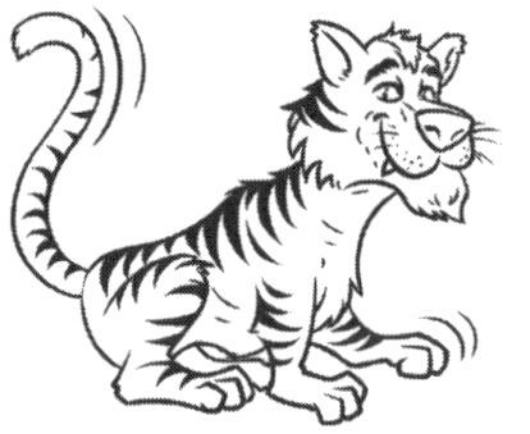 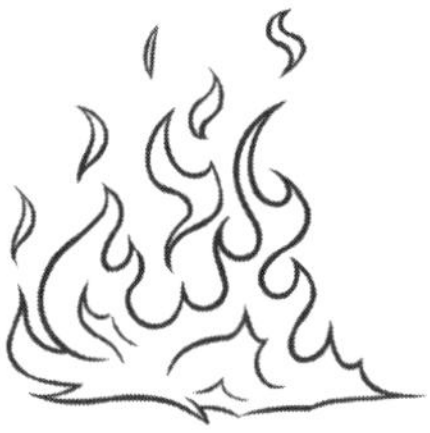 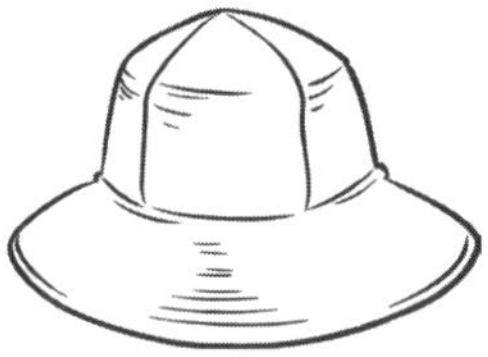

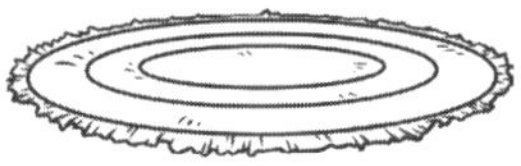 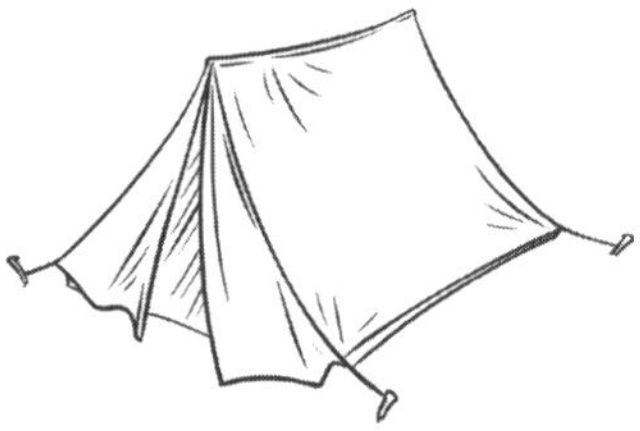 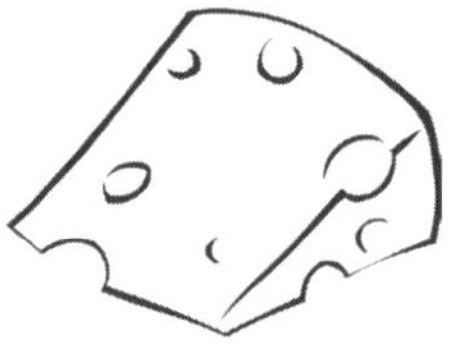

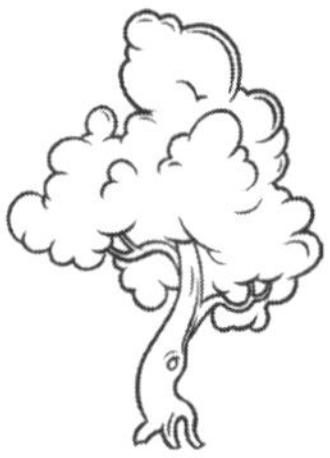 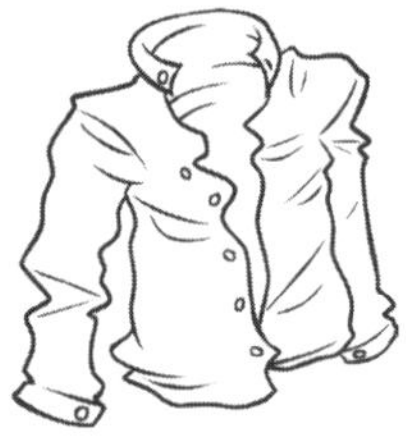 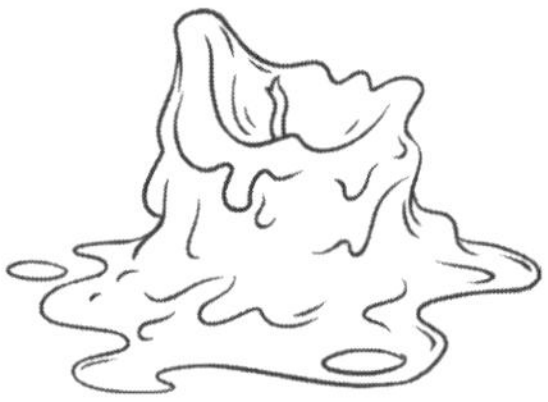

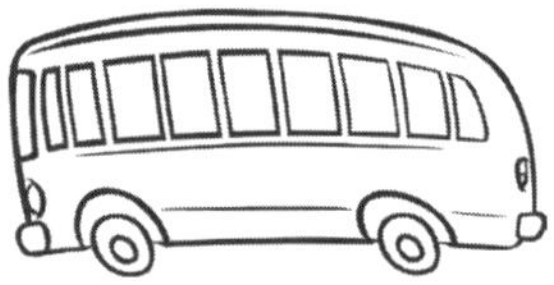 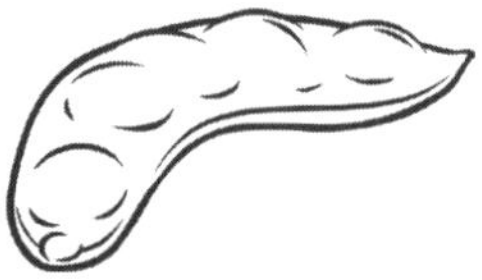 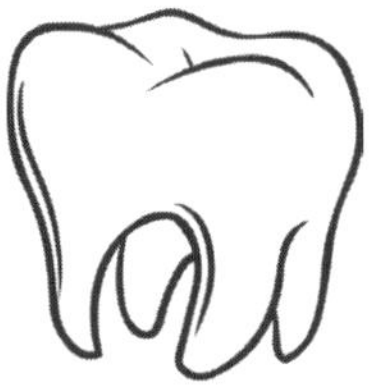

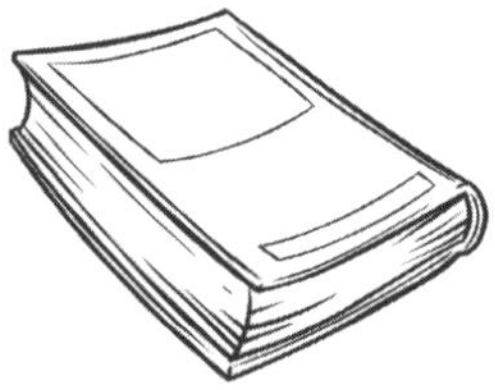 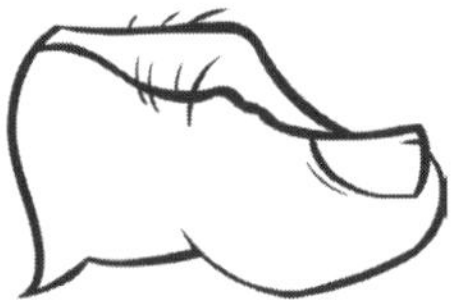 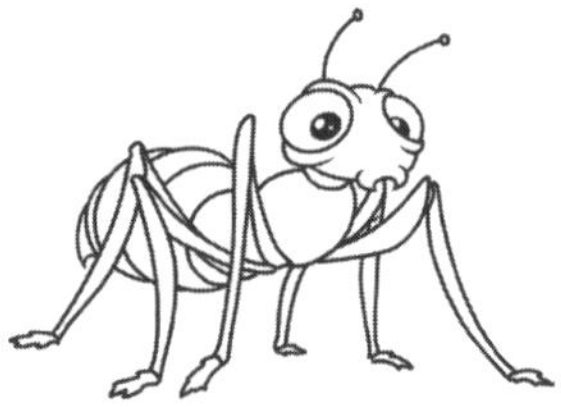

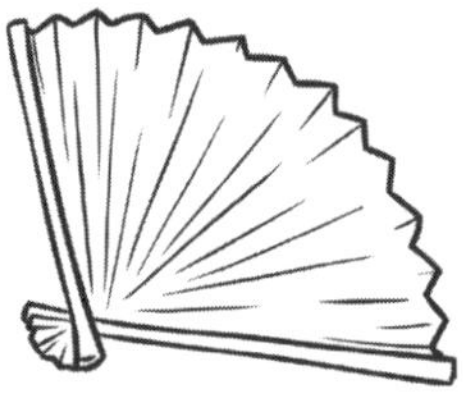 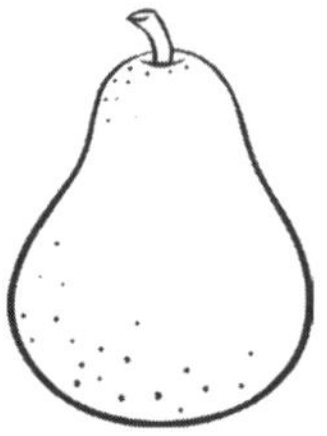 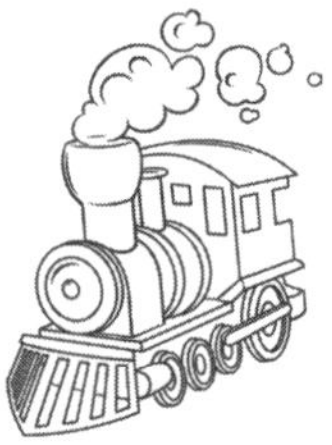

Name

Handwriting

Tt

Lesson 4 • Worksheet 2

1 Finish Tiger turtle's trees.

Tiger turtle is terrific!

2 Trace.

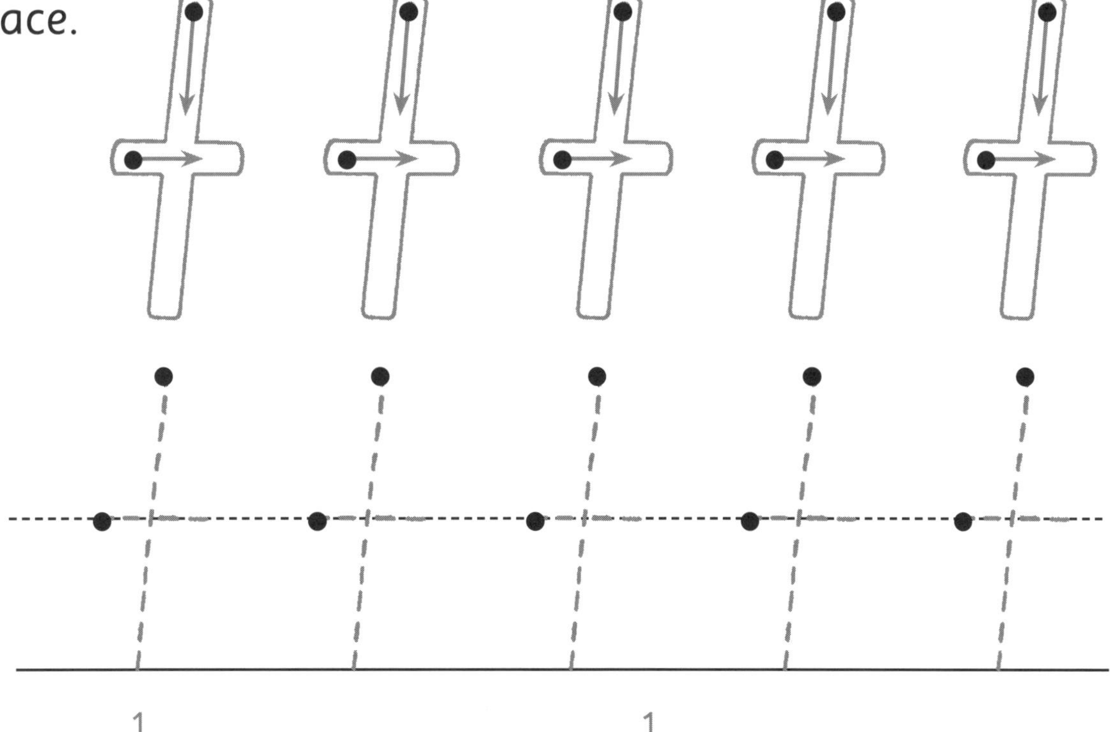

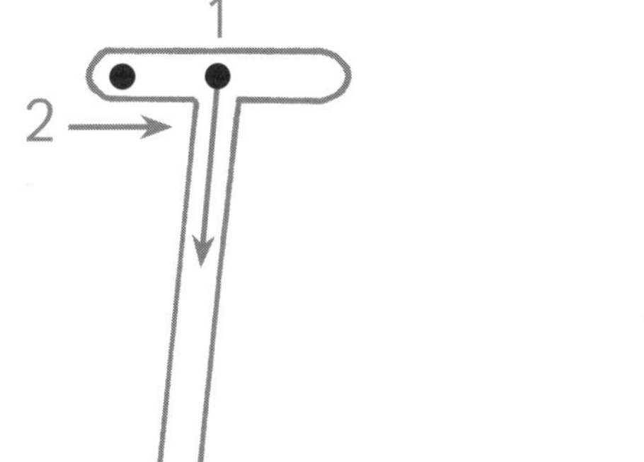

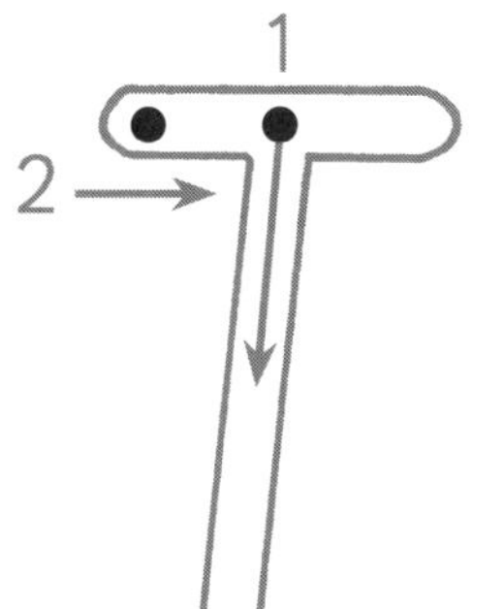

Circle your best letter.

Name

Initial sounds

Ten tiny toes

1 Add **t**. Read the word.

 ____iger	 ____urtle
 ____ent	 ____ree
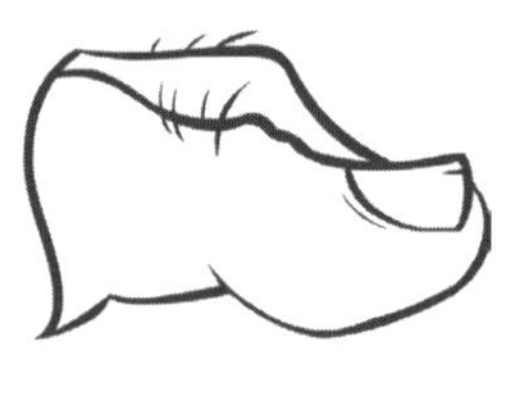 ____oes	 ____eddy
 ____op	 ____ap

2 Draw some teeth.

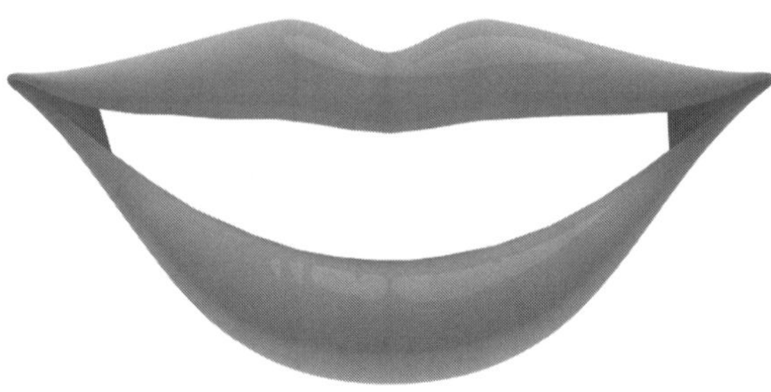

Name

Check

1 Trace the letter. Join to a picture that begins with that sound.

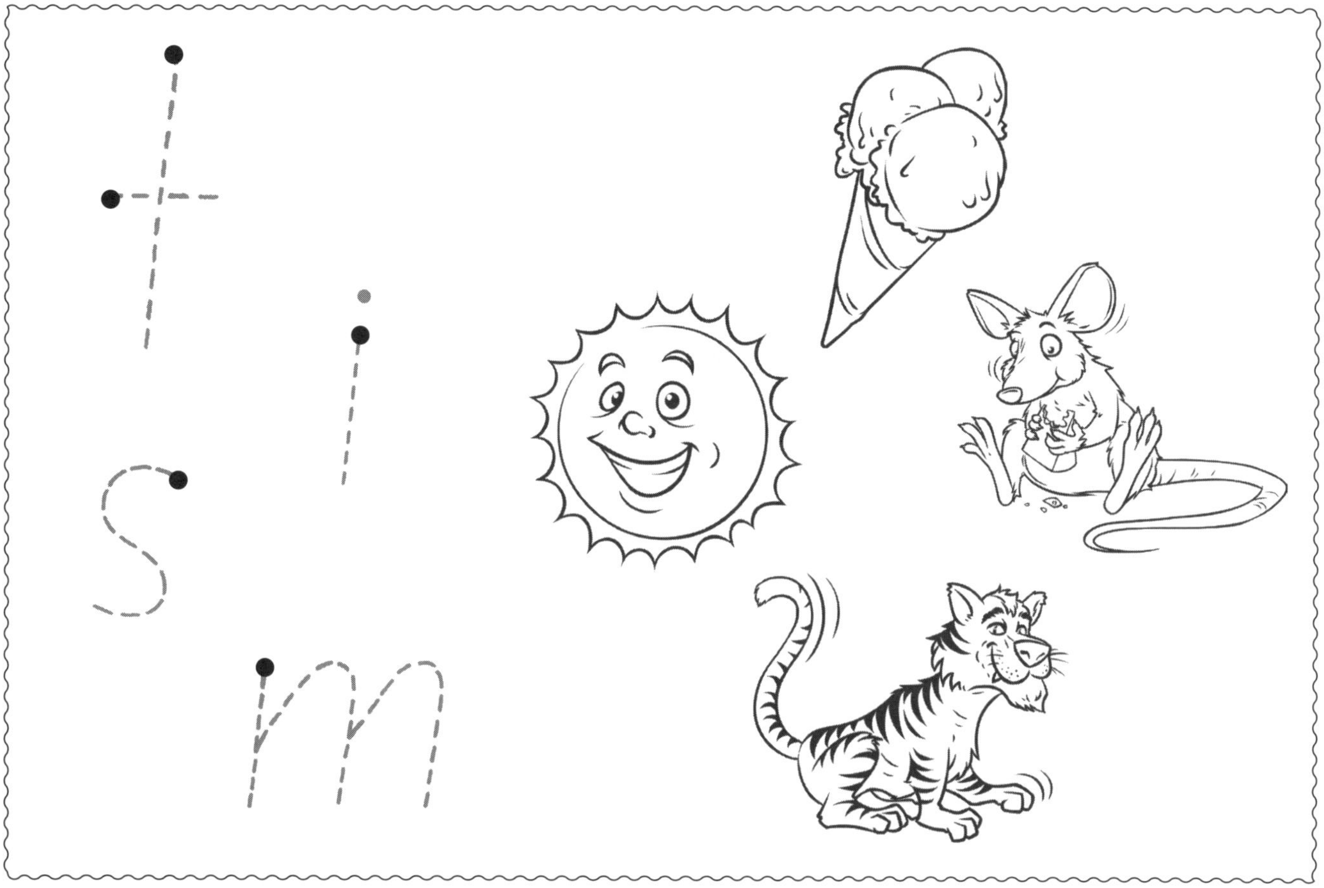

t i s m

2 Circle the beginning sound. Write the letter.

Lesson 5 the word and sound **at**

Learning objectives

Children will:

- identify the sound a.
- recognise the rime at and the word at.
- identify words that contain the rime at.

Australian Curriculum Content Descriptions

Sound and letter knowledge

ACELA1439 identify and manipulate sounds (phonemes) in spoken words

Expressing and developing ideas

ACELA1758 recognise the most common sound made by each letter of the alphabet, including consonants and short vowel sounds; write consonant-vowel-consonant words by writing letters to represent the sounds in the spoken words

Sight words

at, a, I, am

Word family

bat, cat, fat, pat, rat, sat, mat, hat

Vocabulary words

apple, ant, alien, axe, ambulance, ankle, arrow, astronaut

ESL/ELL

Students who speak Spanish, Tagalog or Russian at home may mispronounce /a/ as /ar/ as in last. Give them opportunities to practise their pronunciation with matching pairs of words, like tap and tarp, fat and father, cap and car.

Extra assistance

When making word family lists, teach students to run through the alphabet and try each letter as a starting sound, looking for the "real" words. For example:

at bat cat ~~dat~~ –> this is not a real word

Classroom activities

How does it end?

Give the students a letter each (b, c, f, h, j, m, p, r or s), either written on a card or a magnetic letter. Write the sounds at and am on the top of the board. Each student comes to the board and writes the words they can make using their initial letter and one or both endings. Discuss their words together.

Letter Pictures

Provide the students with a piece of paper that has a large a in the middle:

- trace over the a with a pencil
- draw things that start with a around the letter a and colour them in

Reading Eggs Lesson sequence	TEACH Content and skills	PRACTISE Children will:	APPLY
Hear: *Animated Lesson*	Introduce the rime at through words and the song *What you lookin' at?*	identify and read the rime at in isolation and in words.	**Worksheet 1** Word family
Find: *Catch the Fish and Honey Bees*	Recognise a word using the rime at and the word I.	find the words mat and I in a group of words.	**Worksheet 2** Sight words
Match: *Label It and Tiles*	Match pictures to words. Identify letters to make a word.	read key vocabulary and match letters to make words.	**Worksheet 3** Phonics
Vocabulary: *Blend a Word and Make a Sentence*	Build vocabulary skills: Blend sounds into words. Recognise correct word order for a sentence.	blend sounds to read and recognise words. Choose the correct words to make a sentence.	**Worksheet 4** Read and write
Read: *Book*	Read aloud book.	listen, follow the reading and read along.	**Reading Eggs Alphabet book** a

Related Reading Eggs Activities, Interactives, Songs and Books

Reading Eggs Playroom

Alphabet Activities

Book Shelf Song Books:
The Ants Go Marching,
Alphabet Song

Animal Corner:
Animal games

Music Café

What you lookin' at?

Reading Eggs Puzzle Park

Alphabet Match

Reading Eggs Posters

Teacher Toolkit

Targeting Handwriting Interactively

Alphabet Activities

Reading Eggs Library Books

Alphabet Flashcards

Game 4 – Make the critters using m, s, i, t, a.

Reading Eggs Apps

Eggy Alphabet

Eggy Phonics 1

Critter Card

Ding bat

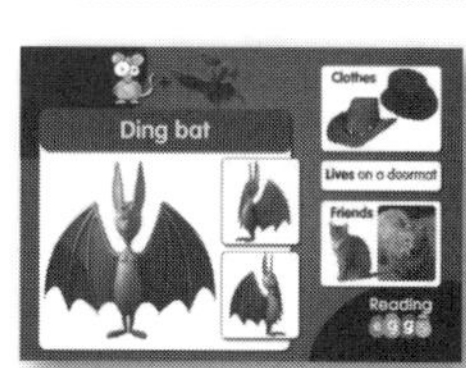

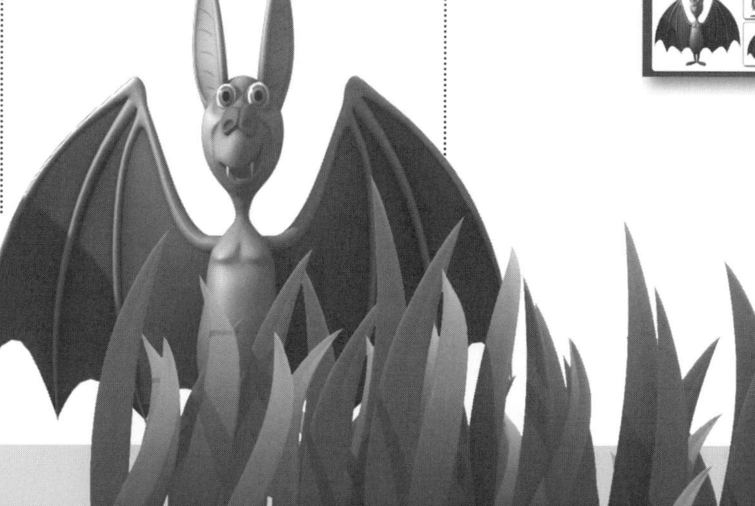

Name

Word families

1 Match to a picture.

2 Write **at** words. Complete the matching picture.

Name

Sight words

1 Trace and write.

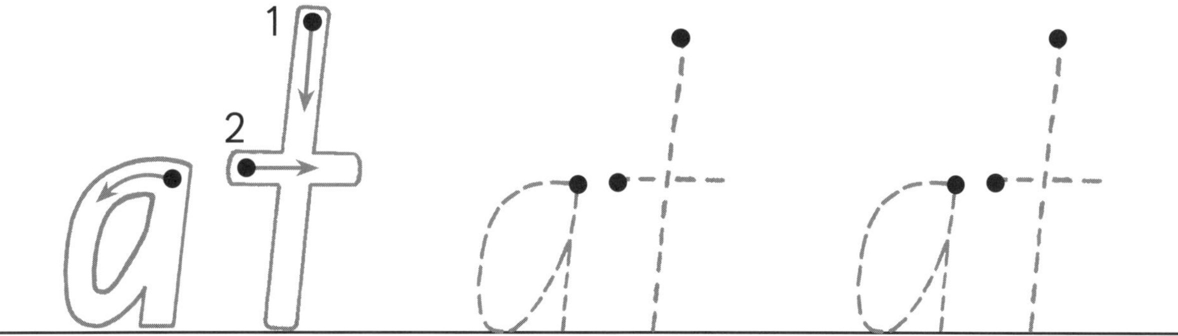

2 Read. Tick where you are.

I am at home. 

I am at school. 

3 Match the words to a picture.

I sat

mat

Lesson 5 · Worksheet 3

Name

Phonics

1 Label each picture. Write the word.

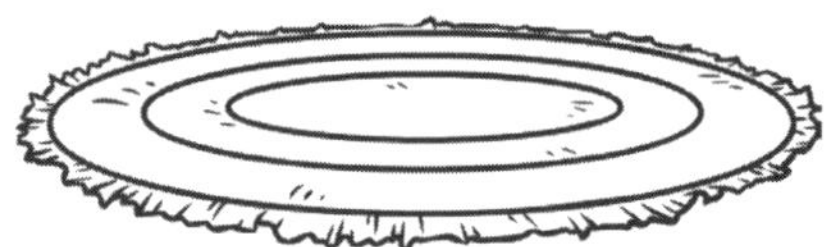

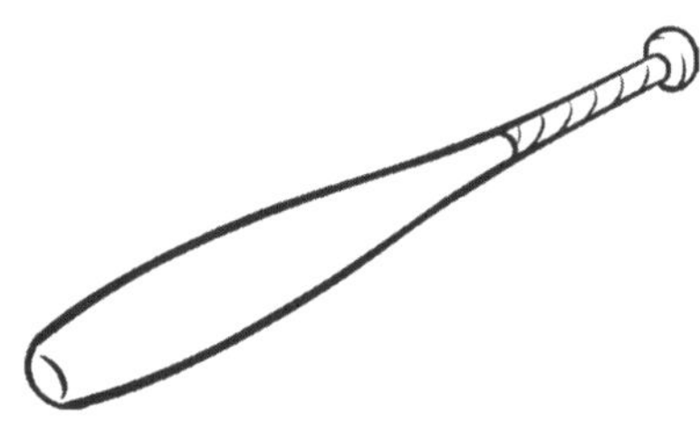

2 Draw a **fat cat**.

Name

Read and write

1 Complete each sentence with a word from the box.

Sam fat

I am ____________

I am ____________

rat hat

I am a ____________

I am a ____________

Lesson 6 the letter **b**

Learning objectives

Children will:

- identify the sound b.
- identify words that begin with b.
- recognise and write b and B.

Australian Curriculum Content Descriptions

Sound and letter knowledge

ACELA1439 identify and manipulate sounds (phonemes) in spoken words

ACELA1440 identify familiar and recurring letters and the use of upper and lower case in written texts

Creating texts

ACELY1653 follow clear demonstrations of how to construct each letter, learn to construct lower case letters

Expressing and developing ideas

ACELA1758 recognise the most common sound made by each letter of the alphabet, including consonants and short vowel sounds

Vocabulary words

bread, bag, balloon, bell, book, bone, bath, baby, bear, bee, bank, ball, bat, boat

ESL/ELL

Some students may mix up the sounds /b/, /p/ and /d/. Teach them to pronounce these letters correctly by mimicking you using sets of rhyming words like ban, pan, dan and bin, pin, din or bay, pay, day. Be sure to reinforce the initial sound.

Extra assistance

To differentiate /p/ and /d/, show students how the lips come together to make /p/ and stay open to make /d/. In /d/ the tongue starts behind the top teeth and pulls down, while in /p/ the tongue doesn't really move.

Classroom activities

Buzzy Bee

Sit in a circle. Everyone says, *'Buzzy Bee, Buzzy Bee, what have you got in your hive for me? Something beginning with b!'* Then students take turns around the circle naming something that begins with the sound /b/.

Decorate the Letters

Provide the students with a piece of paper that has many different forms of the letter b on it – some dotted, some in bubble writing, some solid letters, a couple of capitals.

- trace over the dotted letters with different coloured pencils, textas or crayons
- glue collage materials such as paper bits, leaves or wool to the solid letters
- colour in the bubble letters with dots, stripes or shapes

Reading Eggs Lesson sequence	TEACH Content and skills	PRACTISE Children will:	APPLY
Hear: *Animated Lesson*	Introduce the sound /b/ through words and the song *Being on a Boat.*	identify the letter b in isolation and in words, and as an initial sound.	**Worksheet 1** Phonemic awareness
Write: *Dot-to-Dot*	Reinforce correct letter formation of lower case b.	write the letter b.	**Worksheet 2** Handwriting
Find: *Letter Grid, Trains and Birds*	Recognise b in different fonts in both upper and lower case.	locate lower case b and upper case/capital B.	**Worksheet 3** Initial sounds
Vocabulary: *Letter Book and Label It*	Build vocabulary skills: Match pictures to spoken and written words.	understand key vocabulary and apply it in reading.	**Worksheet 4** Check
Read: *Book*	Read aloud book.	listen, follow the reading and read along.	**Reading Eggs Alphabet book** b

Related Reading Eggs Activities, Interactives, Songs and Books

Reading Eggs Playroom

Alphabet Activities

Book Shelf Song

Books:
Baa Baa Black Sheep, Alphabet Song

Play Mat:
Teddy Bear Bounce, Ball Bounce

Music Café

Being on a Boat

Reading Eggs Puzzle Park

Alphabet Match

Reading Eggs Posters

Teacher Toolkit

Targeting Handwriting Interactively

Alphabet Activities

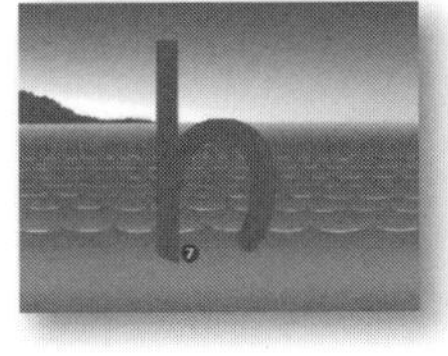

Reading Eggs Apps

Eggy Alphabet

Reading Eggs Library Books

Alphabet Flashcards

Game 2 – Sound puzzles using known letters.

Critter Card

Bee bee bear

Lesson 6 • Worksheet 1

Name

Phonemic awareness

1 Colour the bubbles that begin with **b**.

2 Match each letter to a picture.

Name

Handwriting

Bb

Lesson 6 • Worksheet 2

1 Draw a ball next to each bat.

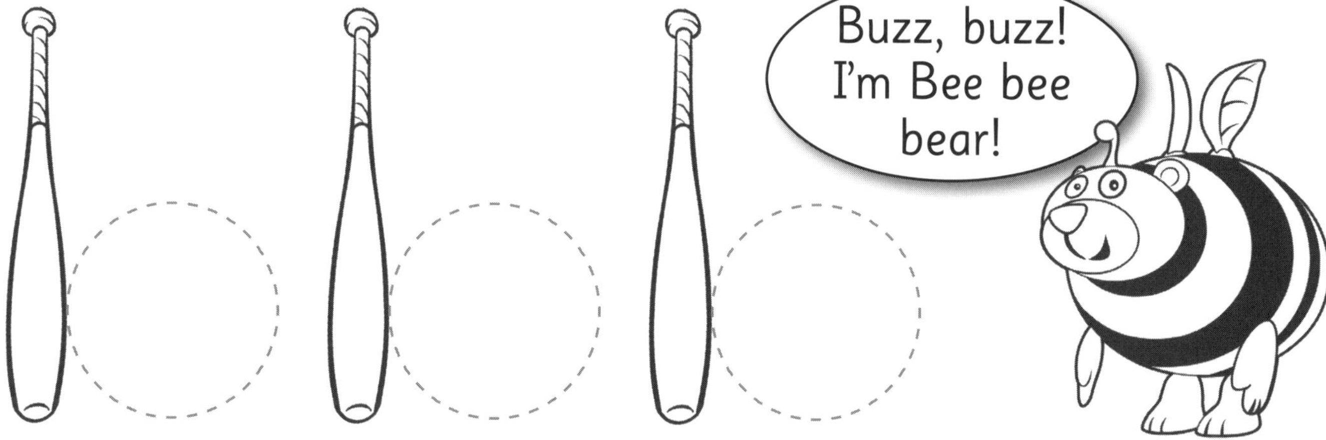

2 Trace and write.

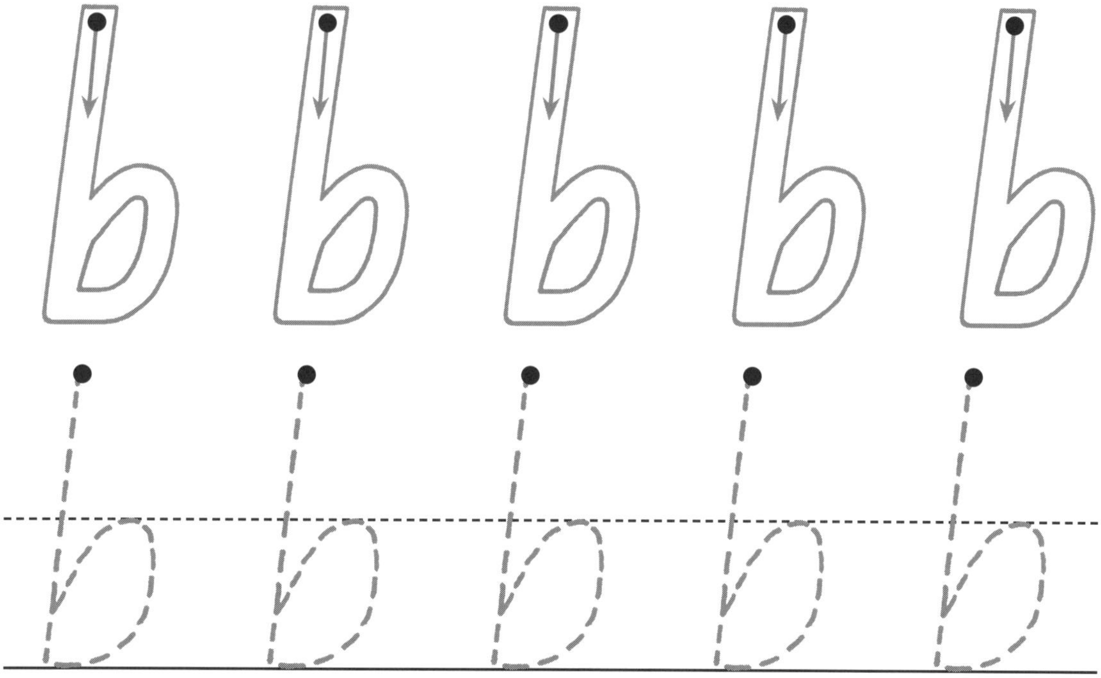

b b b b b

b b b b b

1 2 B ______ 1 2 B ______

Circle your best letter.

Bb

Lesson 6 · Worksheet 3

Name

Initial sounds

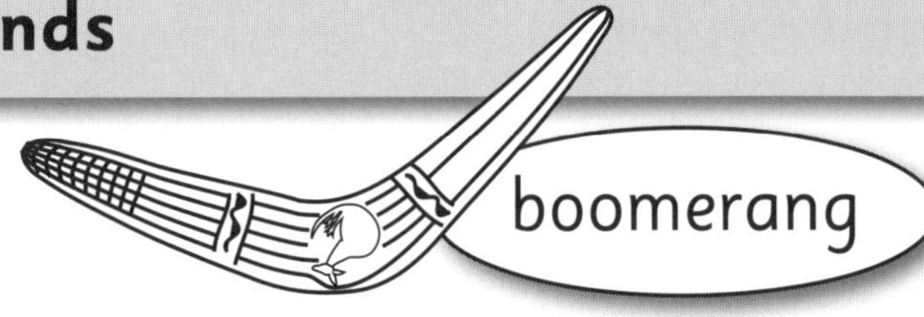

1 Add **b**. Read the word.

b ee	___ear
___all	___ook
___ag	___ath
___ell	___alloon

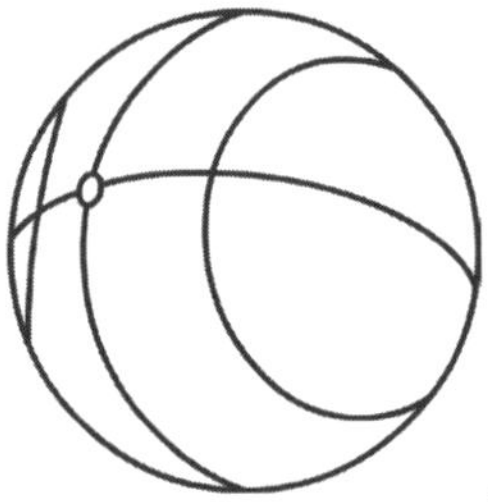

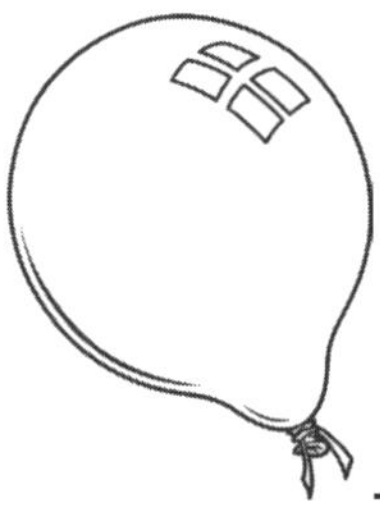

2 Draw the bug's legs.

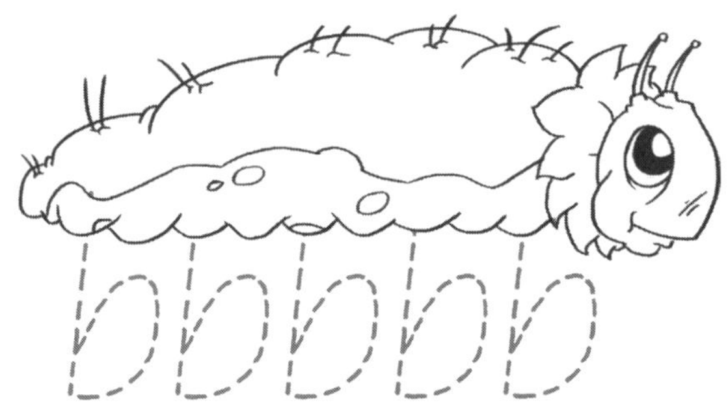

Name

Check

Bb

Lesson 6 • Worksheet 4

1 Trace the letter. Join to a picture that begins with that sound.

t m s b a

2 Circle the beginning sound. Write the letter.

s i t

t b m

Lesson 7 the letter c

Learning objectives

Children will:

- identify the sound /k/ for c.
- identify words that contain c.
- recognise and write c and C.

Australian Curriculum Content Descriptions

Sound and letter knowledge

ACELA1439 identify and manipulate sounds (phonemes) in spoken words

ACELA1440 identify familiar and recurring letters and the use of upper and lower case in written texts

Creating texts

ACELY1653 follow clear demonstrations of how to construct each letter, learn to construct lower case letters

Expressing and developing ideas

ACELA1758 recognise the most common sound made by each letter of the alphabet, including consonants and short vowel sounds

Vocabulary words

coat, clam, cap, can, cow, cup, car, crab, camel, cry, cupboard, camera, carrot, corn, can, cart, coin, cat, cold, carp, cat, cake

ESL/ELL

Students whose language background is Asian may have trouble distinguishing the hard c /k/ sound from the /g/ sound. Give them oral practise with pairs of words such as coat and goat, coal and goal, clam and glam.

Extra assistance

Some students will try to use the /s/ sound for all c's. Give them some tongue twisters to practise and embed the /k/ sound for c:

The coloured cat can crawl carefully under the cot.
Clever crabs clamp onto the clingy clams.

Classroom activities

Collage

Provide students with a piece of paper that has a large c in the middle.

- trace over the c with a pencil
- find things starting with c in an old magazine, cut out and glue around the c on the paper to create a collage

Find the Letter

Give each student 3 cards with the letters c, t and m. Say a word and ask students to listen to the initial sound. They should hold up the card which makes that initial sound. Use clear, recognisable words such as:

tap	cat	moon
toy	monkey	carrot

Reading Eggs Lesson sequence	TEACH Content and skills	PRACTISE Children will:	APPLY
Hear: *Animated Lesson*	Introduce the sound /k/ for c through words and the song *Sam's Search for c.*	identify and read c in isolation and as an initial sound in words.	**Worksheet 1** Phonemic awareness
Write: *Dot-to-Dot*	Reinforce correct letter formation of lower case c.	write the letter c.	**Worksheet 2** Handwriting
Find: *Letter Grid and Birds*	Recognise c in different fonts in both upper and lower case.	locate lower case c and upper case/capital C.	**Worksheet 3** Initial sounds
Vocabulary: *Letter Book, Label It and Blend a Word*	Build vocabulary skills: Match pictures to words. Blend and recognise words.	blend sounds to read and recognise words.	**Worksheet 4** Check
Read: *Book*	Read aloud book.	listen, follow the reading and read along.	**Reading Eggs Alphabet book** c

Related Reading Eggs Activities, Interactives, Songs and Books

Reading Eggs Playroom

Alphabet Activities

Book Shelf Song

Books:
Hickory Dickory Dock,
Alphabet Song

Paint Easel:
Colour in the Crocodile

Music Café

Sam's Search for c

Reading Eggs Puzzle Park

Alphabet Match

Reading Eggs Posters

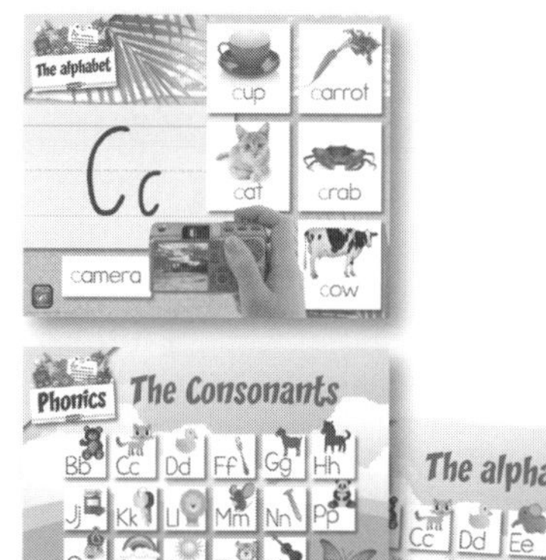

Teacher Toolkit

Targeting Handwriting Interactively

Alphabet Activities

Reading Eggs Apps

Eggy Alphabet

Reading Eggs Library Books

Alphabet Flashcards

Game 1 – Letter shape using known letters.

Critter Card

Catty cake

Name

Phonemic awareness

1 Colour the pictures that begin with **c**.

2 Match each letter to a picture.

Name

Handwriting

Cc

Lesson 7 • Worksheet 2

1 Complete the cats.

Catty cake is cute!

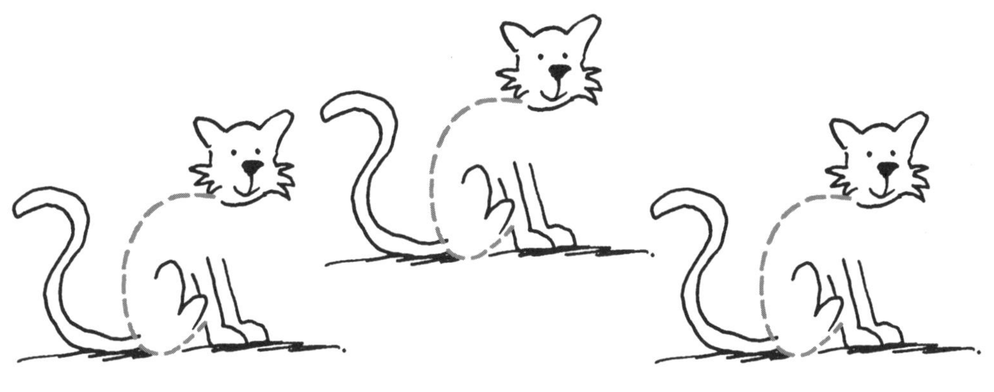

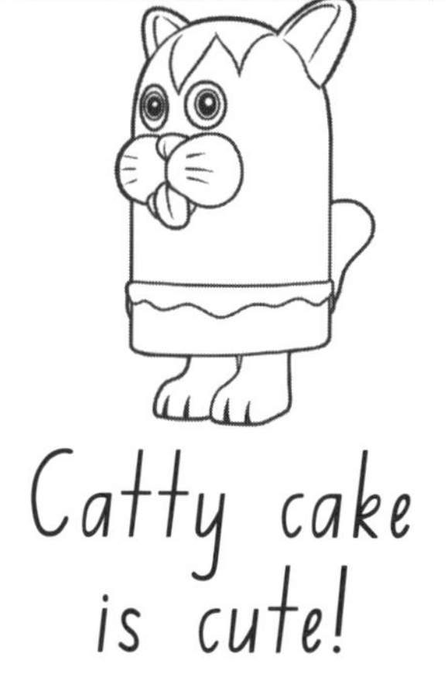

2 Trace and write.

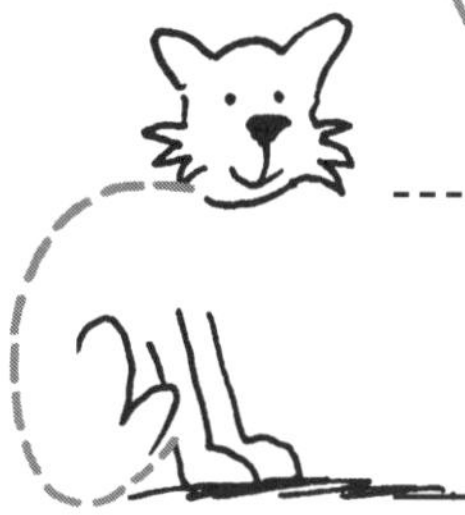

Circle your best letter.

Cc

Lesson 7 · Worksheet 3

Name

Initial sounds

1 Add **c**. Read the word.

c at

____amel

____oat

____arrot

____up

____ow

____ake

____orn

2 Draw curly curls.

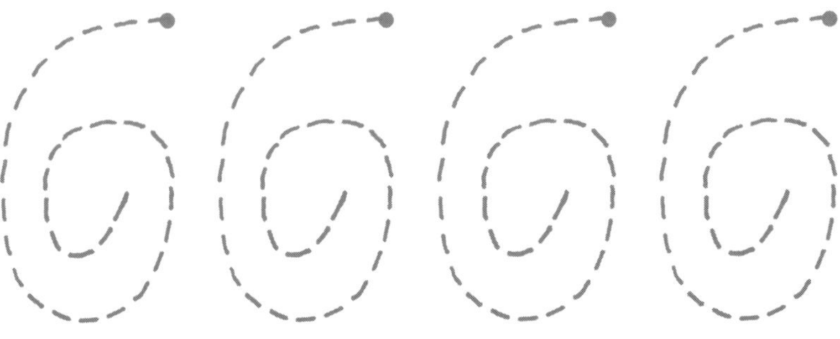

Name

Check

Cc

Lesson 7 · Worksheet 4

1 Circle the beginning sound.

b m c

m c b

t a i

c b a

a c b

i m t

c t b

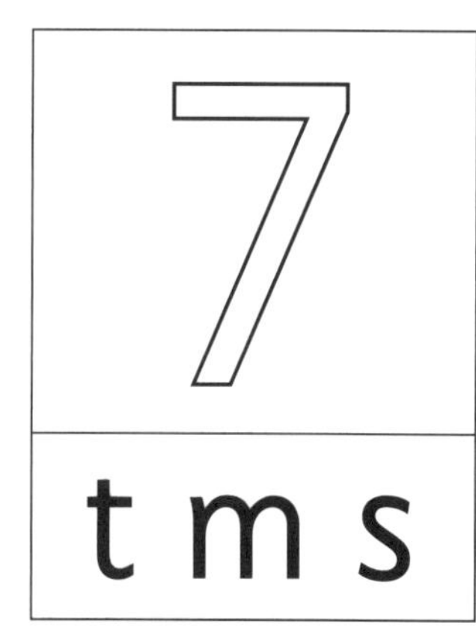

t m s

i t b

m b a

t i a

a b c

2 Write the word **cat**.

Lesson 8 the letter **f**

Learning objectives

Children will:

- identify the sound f.
- recognise and write f and F.
- blend onsets and the rime at to make words.

Australian Curriculum Content Descriptions

Sound and letter knowledge

ACELA1439 identify and manipulate sounds (phonemes) in spoken words

ACELA1440 identify familiar and recurring letters and the use of upper and lower case in written texts

Creating texts

ACELY1653 follow clear demonstrations of how to construct each letter, learn to construct lower case letters

Expressing and developing ideas

ACELA1758 recognise the most common sound made by each letter of the alphabet, including consonants and short vowel sounds; write consonant-vowel-consonant words by writing letters to represent the sounds in the spoken words

Word families

cat, bat, fat, mat, sat

Vocabulary words

fish, fly, foot, feather, frog, flower, fire, fox, football, fin, fan, flag

ESL/ELL

Many students may find it hard to differentiate between the sounds /f/ and /v/. For both sounds the top teeth rest on the bottom lip for a continuous blow. Practise hearing and pronouncing the difference with sentences like:

The fan is in the van.
The vast fairy is very fast.

Extra assistance

Blending different onsets with a rime to make new words can cater for visual learners by using animal bodies for rimes and a variety of animal heads for the onsets. Students can have fun making crazy creatures while learning to blend and recognise words they know, reinforcing the idea of the onset and the rime.

Reading Eggs Lesson sequence	TEACH Content and skills	PRACTISE Children will:	APPLY
Hear: *Animated Lesson*	Introduce the sound /f/ through words and the song *Floating Flobbies*. Blend words using the rime at and the song *At Sea*.	identify and read /f/ sound in isolation and as an initial sound in words. Blend sounds to read words.	**Worksheet 1** Phonemic awareness
Write: *Dot-to-Dot*	Reinforce correct letter formation of lower case f.	write the letter f.	**Worksheet 2** Handwriting
Find: *Letter Grid, Trains and In the Box*	Recognise both upper and lower case f. Identify the initial sound of a word.	locate lower and upper case f. Match pictures to their initial letter.	**Worksheet 3** Initial sounds
Vocabulary: *Letter Book, Word Windows and Tiles*	Build vocabulary skills: Match pictures to words. Blend and recognise words.	blend sounds to read words, match to a picture and make the word.	**Worksheet 4** Vocabulary
Read: *Book*	Read aloud book.	listen, follow the reading and read along.	**Reading Eggs Alphabet book** f

Classroom activities

Brainstorm

Brainstorm a list of words that end with the at sound. Start with single letter onsets, going through the letters they know first. Then ask if anyone knows of any other beginnings such as th and fl.

Throw it Away!

Sit in a circle with a box in the middle. Students each hold two items or pictures or words on cards. The teacher says a word. If the child has an object starting with the same first letter they throw it into the box. Discuss the objects in each round.

Related Reading Eggs Activities, Interactives, Songs and Books

Reading Eggs Playroom

Alphabet Activities

Book Shelf Song

Books:
1-2-3-4-5,
Alphabet Song

Dress Up Corner:
Fairy and Fireman

Music Café

Floating Flobbies

At Sea

Reading Eggs Puzzle Park

Alphabet Match

Reading Eggs Posters

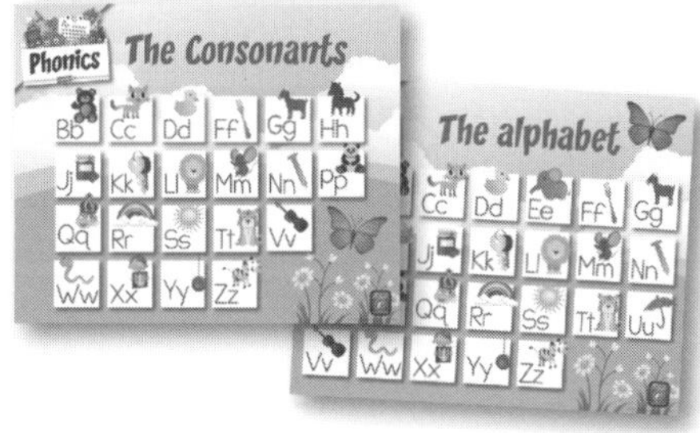

Teacher Toolkit

Targeting Handwriting Interactively

Alphabet Activities

Reading Eggs Apps

Eggy Alphabet

Reading Eggs Library Books

Alphabet Flashcards

Game 6 – Critter concentration with known letters.

Critter Card

Frogfish

Ff

Lesson 8 • Worksheet 1

Name

Phonemic awareness

1 Colour the pictures that begin with **f**.

2 Match each letter to a picture.

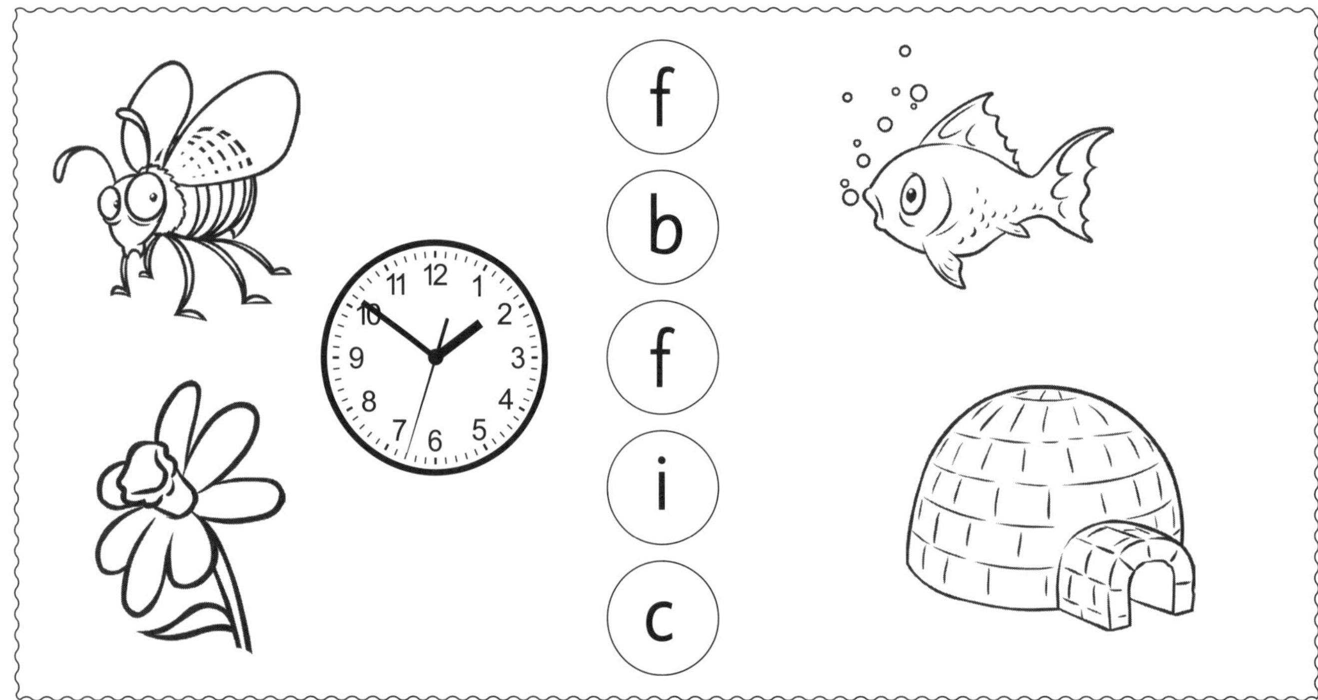

Name

Handwriting

Ff

Lesson 8 · Worksheet 2

1 Finish the flowers.

Hi, I'm Frogfish I have fins.

2 Trace and write.

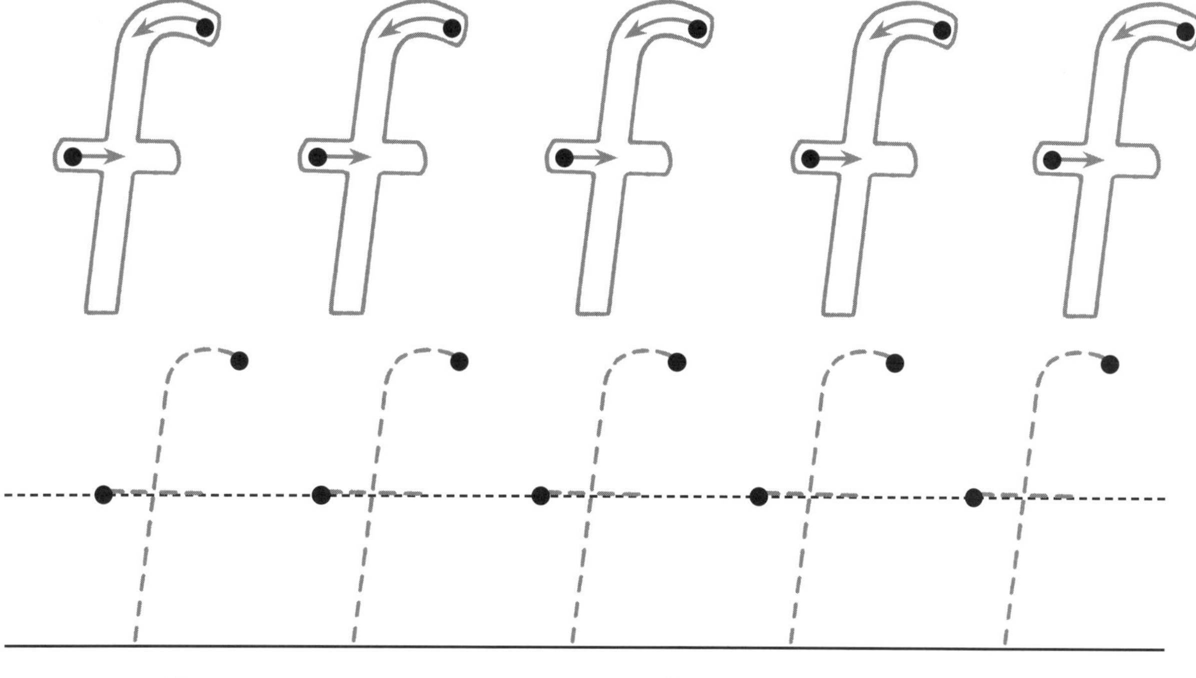

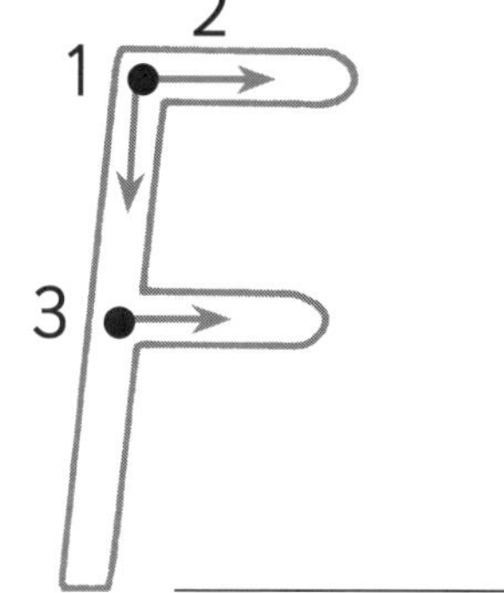

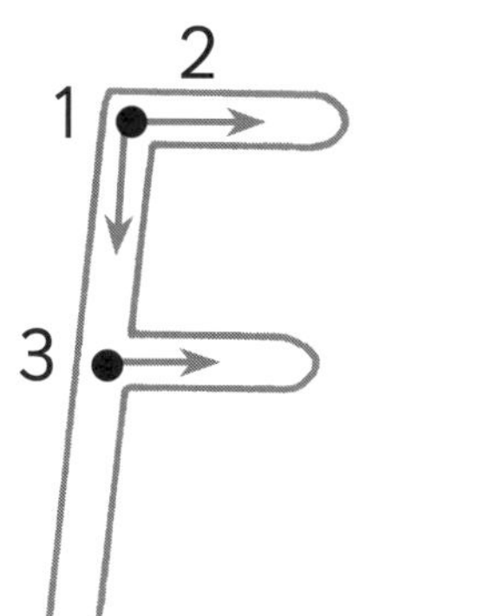

Circle your best letter.

Ff

Lesson 8 • Worksheet 3

Name

Initial sounds

1 Add **f**. Read the word.

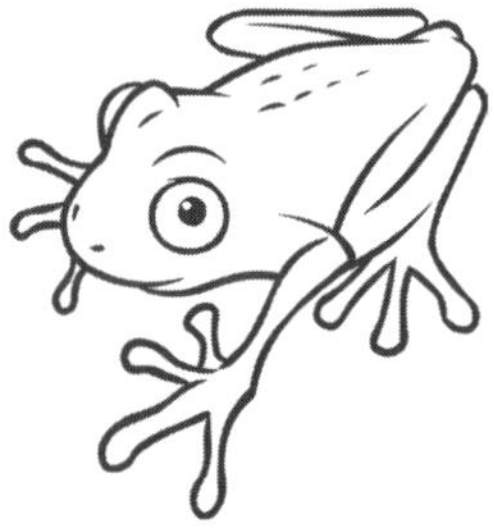

f rog	____ish
____oot	____ly
____lag	5 ____ive
____inger	____ootball

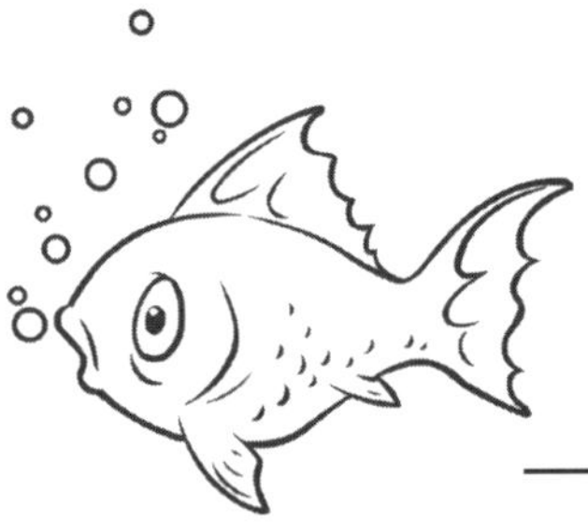

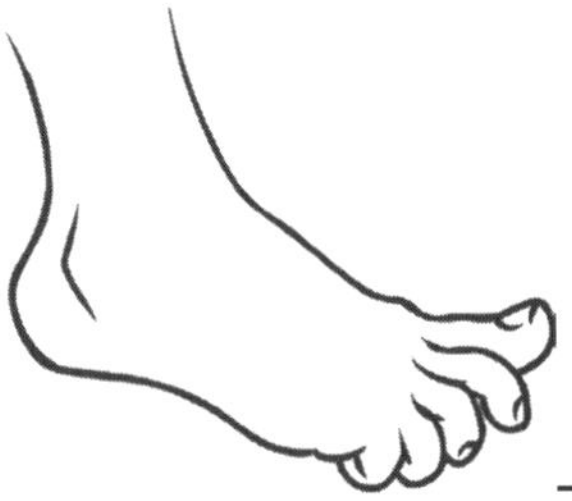

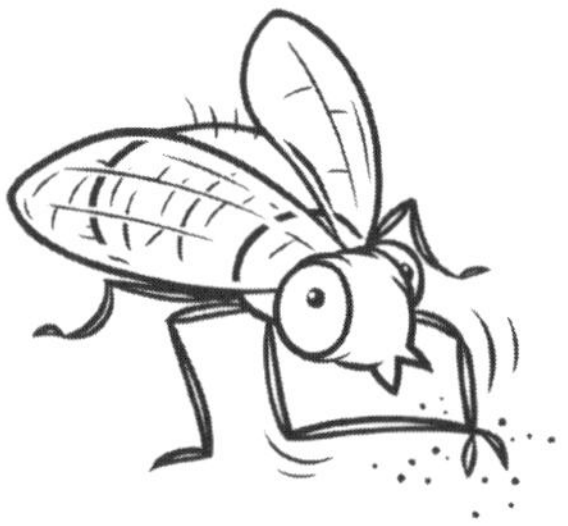

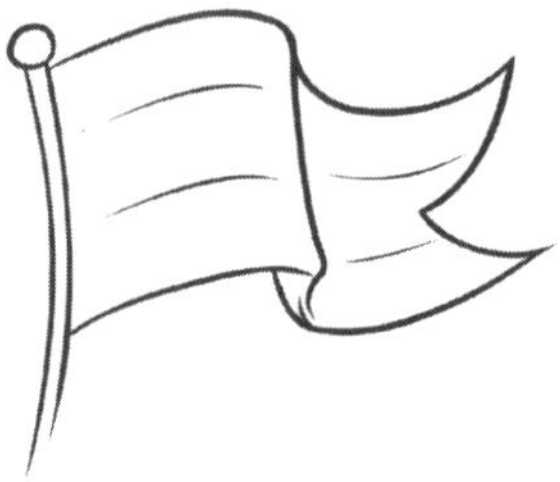

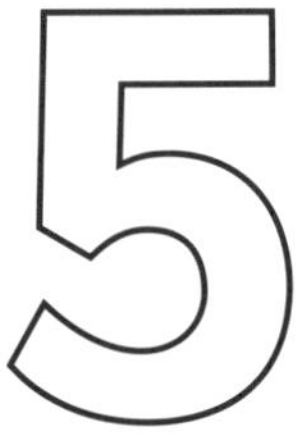

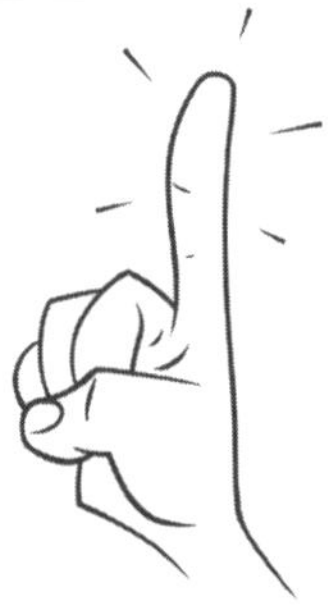

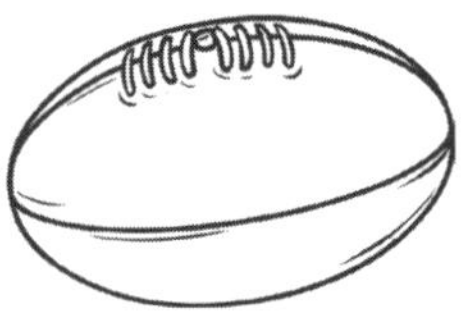

2 Draw funny faces on the fish.

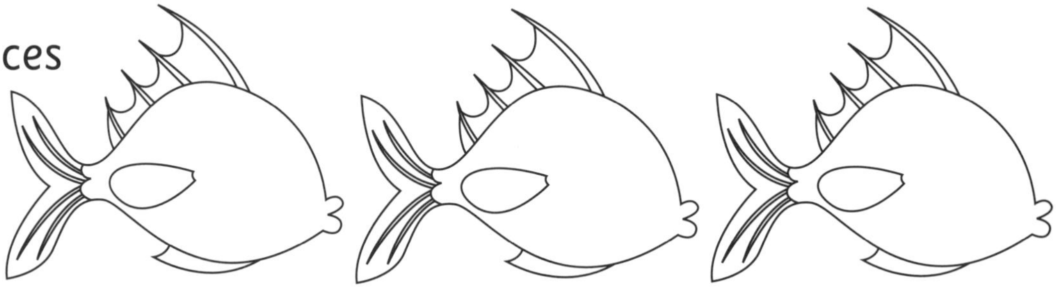

Name

Vocabulary

Ff

Lesson 8 • Worksheet 4

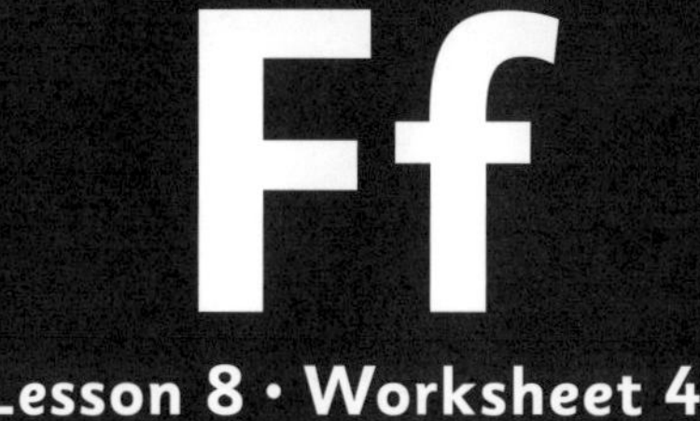

1 Read the word. Colour the picture that matches.

cat	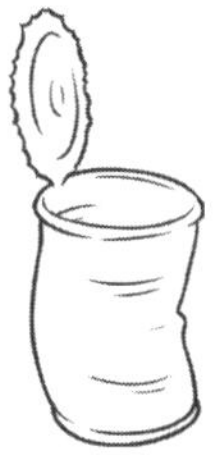	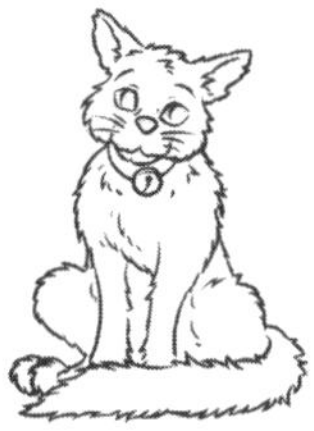	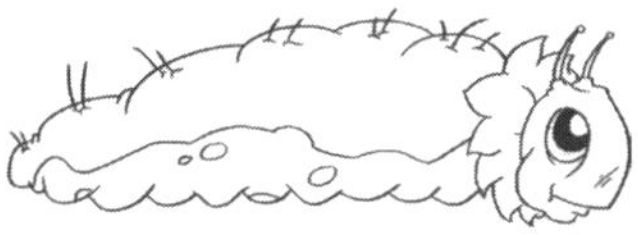
bat	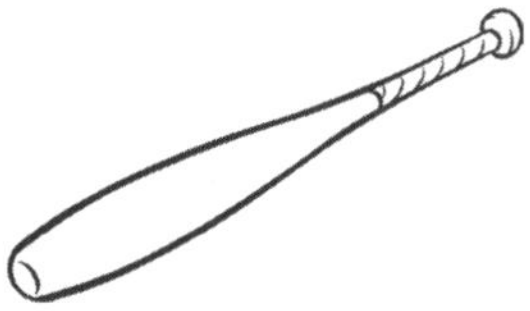	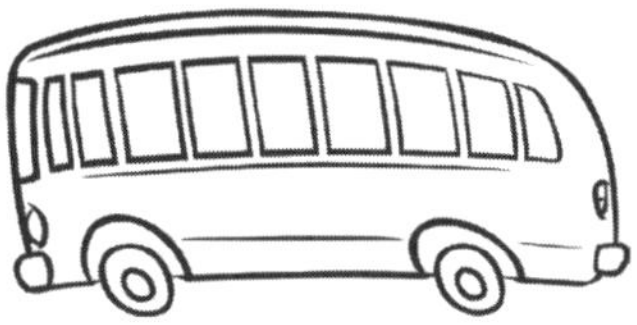	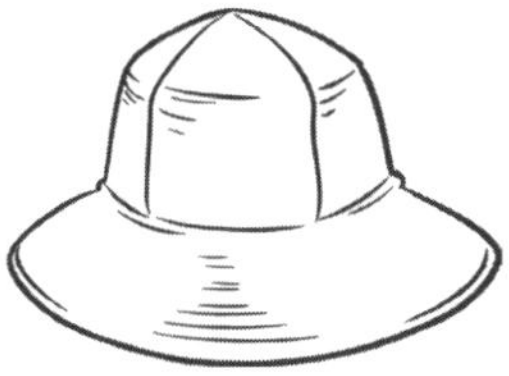
mat	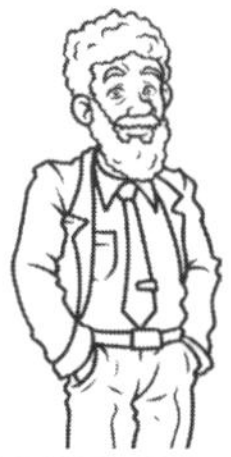	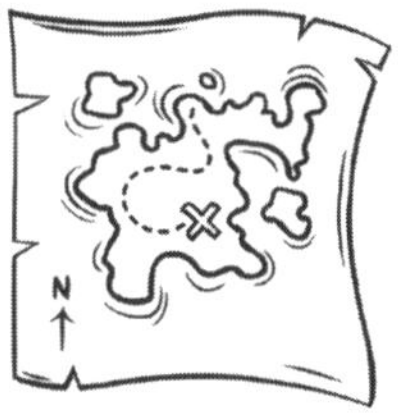	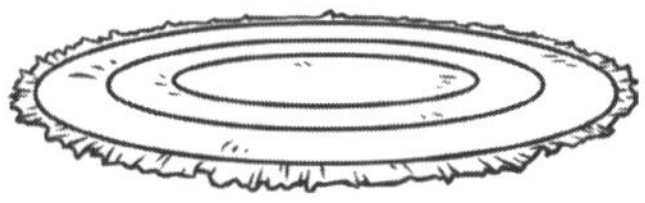
fat	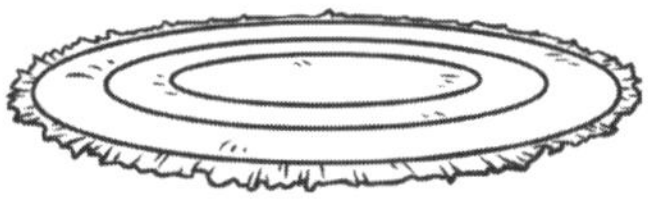	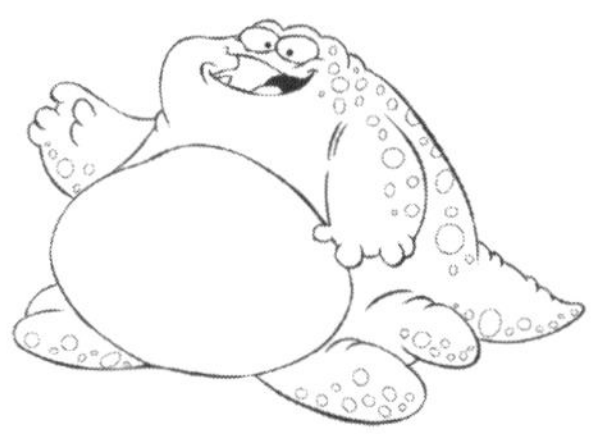	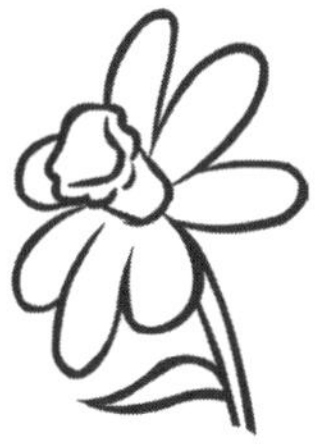

2 Draw a **fat frog**.

Lesson 9 the word **a**, the letter **a**

Learning objectives

Children will:

- recognise and write the letter a.
- read the words a, I and am in sentences.
- read and identify words using the rime at.

Australian Curriculum Content Descriptions

Sound and letter knowledge

ACELA1439 identify and manipulate sounds (phonemes) in spoken words

ACELA1440 identify familiar and recurring letters and the use of upper and lower case in written texts

Creating texts

ACELY1653 follow clear demonstrations of how to construct each letter, learn to construct lower case letters

Expressing and developing ideas

ACELA1758 recognise the most common sound made by each letter of the alphabet, including consonants and short vowel sounds; write consonant-vowel-consonant words by writing letters to represent the sounds in the spoken words

Sight words

a, I, am

Word families

am, Sam, cat, bat, fat, mat

Vocabulary words

apple, astronaut, ankle, ambulance, ant, alien, arrow

ESL/ELL

Other languages often do not distinguish between long and short vowel sounds. Students may mix them up when reading aloud and speaking. Find games for them to play where correct pronunciation and identification of sounds is important, like Bingo with word pairs such as fan and farm, cat and cart, and so on.

Extra assistance

As students learn more letters, be sure to give them lots of opportunities to revise the letters they have already learnt. A lot of games traditionally played with a pack of cards or with numbers can be played using letter cards with both the lower and upper case letters on them: Bingo, Snap, Go Fish and Concentration or Memory for example.

Reading Eggs Lesson sequence	TEACH Content and skills	PRACTISE Children will:	APPLY
Hear: *Animated Lesson*	Introduce the word a and revise the words I and am.	identify and read the words a and I in isolation and in sentences.	**Worksheet 1** Sight words
Write: *Dot-to-Dot*	Reinforce correct letter formation of lower case a.	write the letter a.	**Worksheet 2** Handwriting
Find: *Label It, Jumping Astronauts and Missing Sound*	Match pictures to words. Identify the correct onset letter to complete the word.	find the correct word in a group. Choose the correct letter to match the word to the picture.	**Worksheet 3** Phonemic awareness
Vocabulary: *Blend a Word and Wheel of Words*	Build vocabulary skills: Match pictures to words. Blend and recognise words.	blend sounds to read words and recognise them in a group.	**Worksheet 4** Read and write
Read: *Book*	Read aloud book.	listen, follow the reading and read along.	**Reading Eggs Story Book** I am

Classroom activities

Mind the Gap!

Write this sentence on the board: I am a ___.

Ask students to read this sentence by themselves, write it down and fill in the gap with a word of their own. Discuss their individual sentences as a group.

All Change!

Students sit in a circle with an object or picture in their hands that starts with a, b, c, f, i, m, s or t (make sure at least two students have each letter). The teacher calls out a word starting with one of those letters and the students whose objects start with that letter have to jump up and swap places.

Related Reading Eggs Activities, Interactives, Songs and Books

Reading Eggs Playroom

Alphabet Activities: book and letter activities

Book Shelf Song Books: Dingle Dangle Scarecrow, I'm a Little Teapot

Dress Up Corner: I am a …

Music Café

I am, I am, I am …

What you lookin' at?

Reading Eggs Puzzle Park

Alphabet Match

Reading Eggs Posters

Teacher Toolkit

Targeting Handwriting Interactively

Alphabet Activities

Reading Eggs Library Books

Alphabet Flashcards

Game 7 – Making words ending with at.

Critter Card

Appley ant

Reading Eggs Apps

Eggy Alphabet

Eggy Sight words

I am a

Lesson 9 • Worksheet 1

Name

Sight words

1 Write each word.

I am a

I am a

2 Complete each sentence with one of the words.

I am ________ cat.

I ________ a bat.

________ am a fat cat.

I ________ Sam.

Name

Handwriting

Aa

Lesson 9 • Worksheet 2

1 Trace and write.

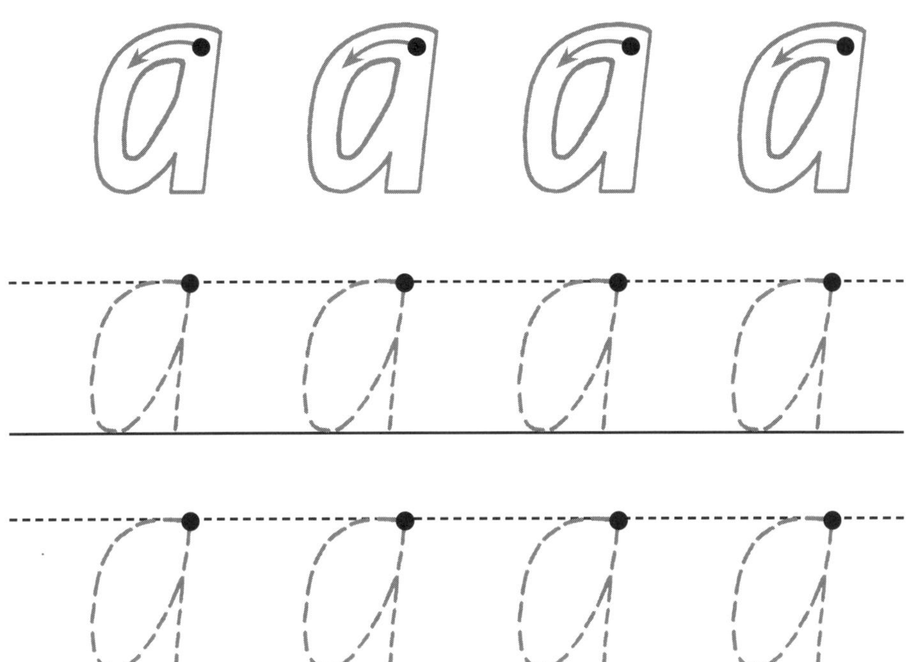

2 Circle every **A**.

A B A E S
T A N A A

How many? ____

Circle every **a**.

a c n a g
c a o a a

How many? ____

3 Trace and write.

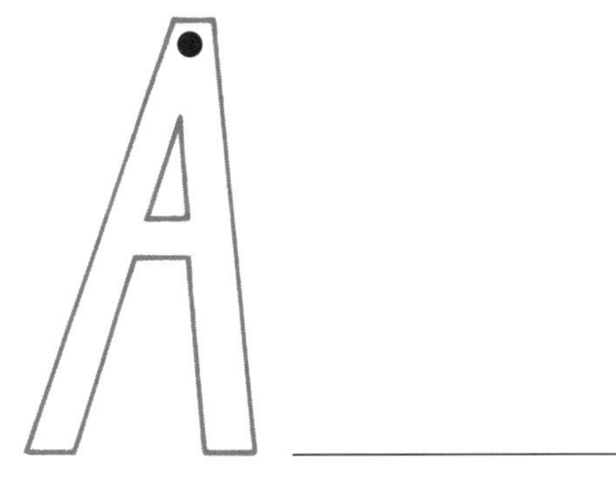

Circle your best letter.

Aa

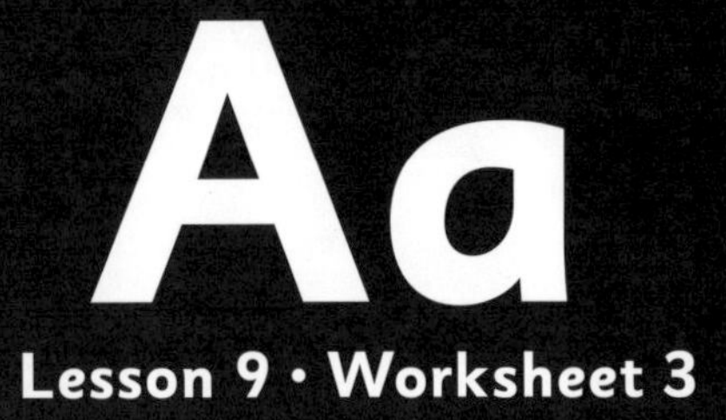

Lesson 9 • Worksheet 3

Name

Phonemic awareness

Circle the thing in each row that begins with **a**. Colour them.

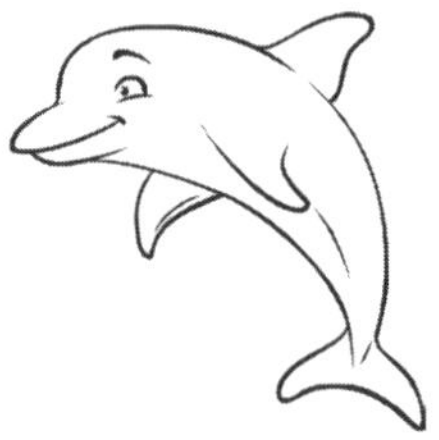

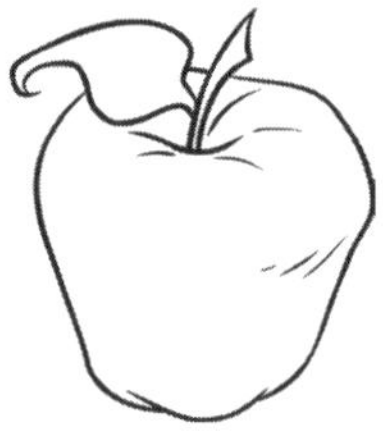

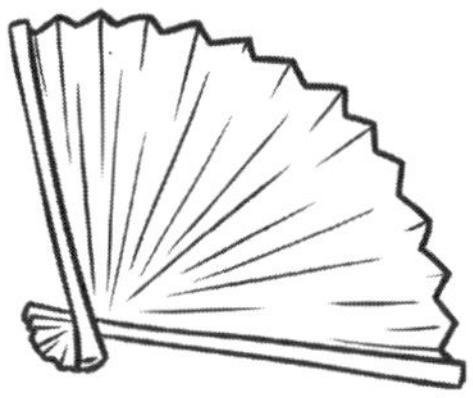

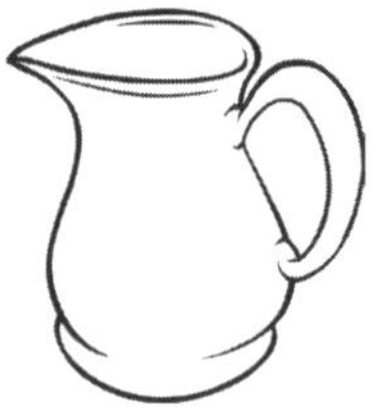

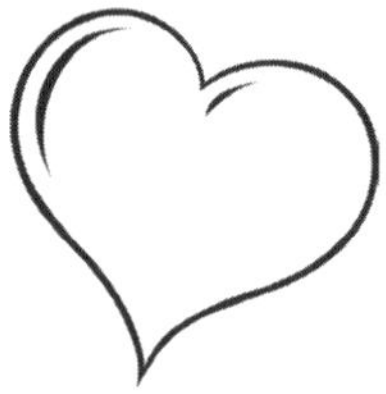

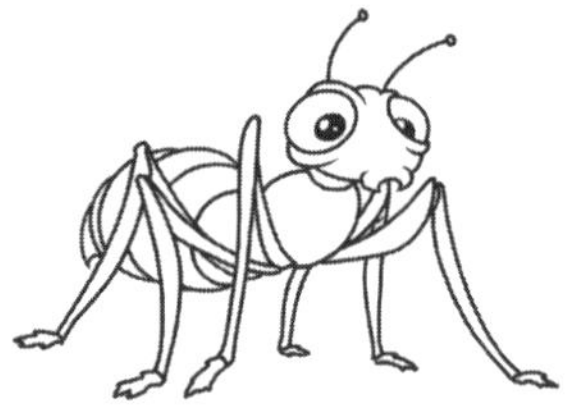

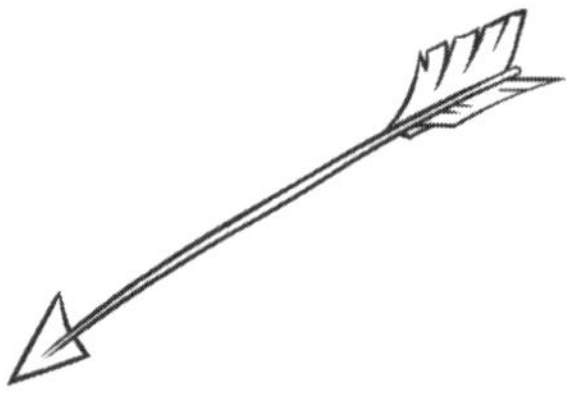

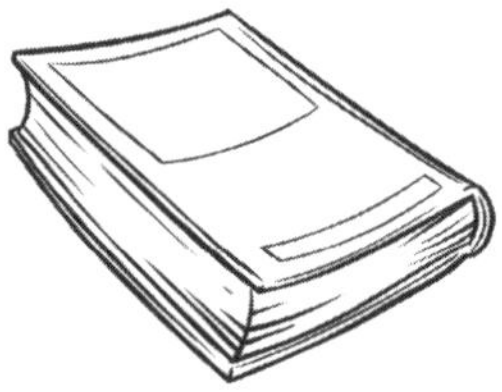

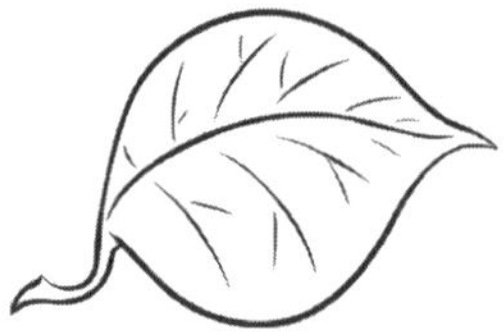

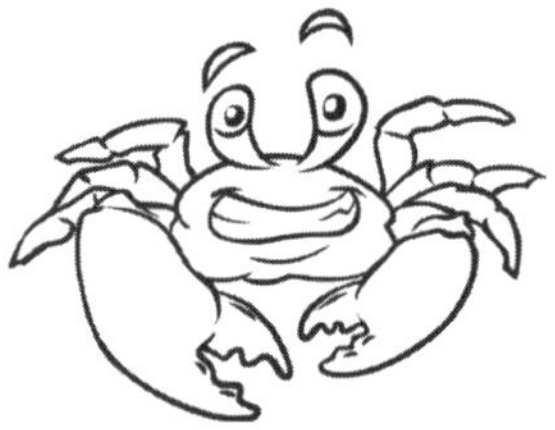

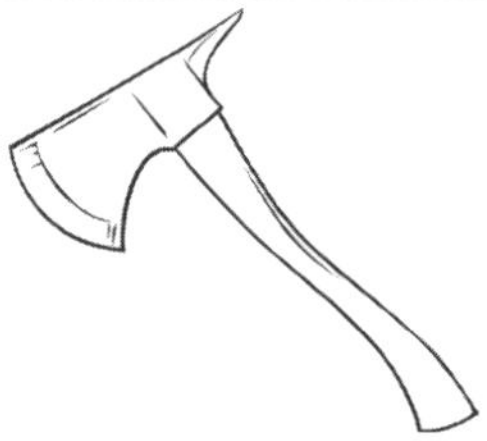

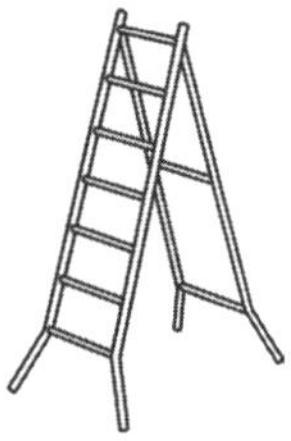

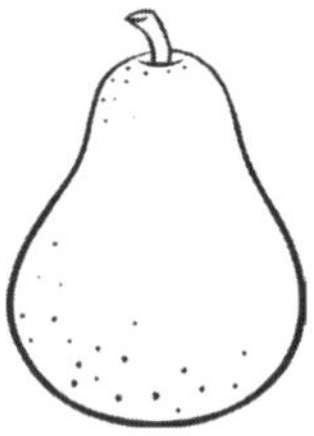

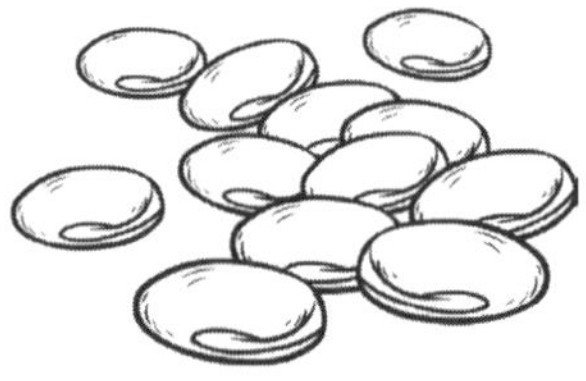

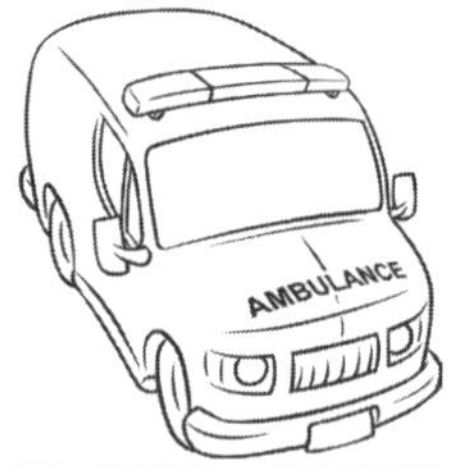

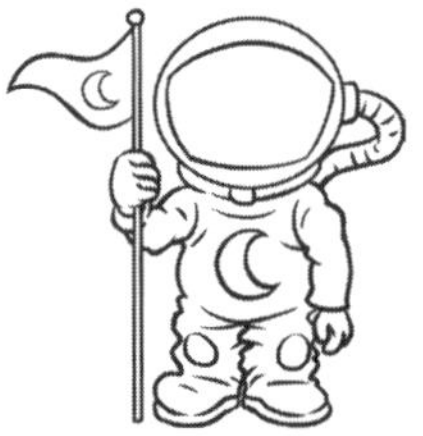

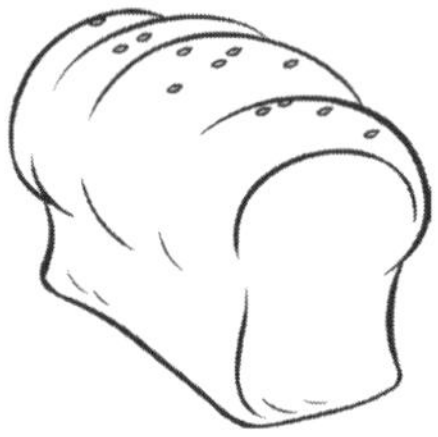

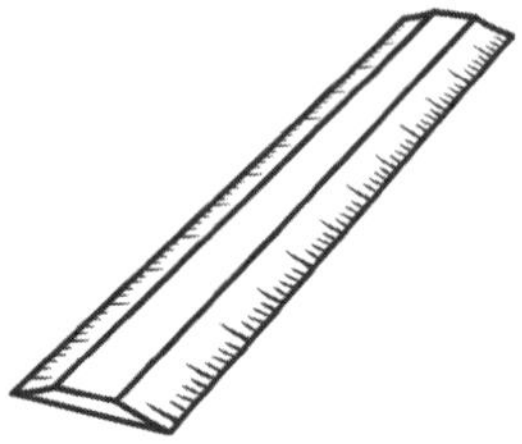

Name

Read and write

I am a

Lesson 9 · Worksheet 4

1 Complete each sentence with a word from the box.

cat bat Sam

I am a

________________.

I am a

________________.

I am

________________.

I am a fat

________________.

Lesson 10 Review

Learning objectives

Children will:

- review the sounds a, b, c, f, i, m, s and t.
- revise the rimes at and am.
- review the words I, am, a.

Australian Curriculum Content Descriptions

Sound and letter knowledge

ACELA1439 identify and manipulate sounds (phonemes) in spoken words

ACELA1440 identify familiar and recurring letters and the use of upper and lower case in written texts

Expressing and developing ideas

ACELA1435 learn that word order in sentences is important for meaning

ACELA1758 recognise the most common sound made by each letter of the alphabet, including consonants and short vowel sounds; write consonant-vowel-consonant words by writing letters to represent the sounds in the spoken words

Sight words

a, am, at, I

Word families

at, bat, cat, fat, mat, sat

ESL/ELL

Students learning a second language need to practise, practise, practise! Choral responses, where groups of students recite the same word, phrase, sentence or sound, are an effective tool to build familiarity with new sounds and vocabulary.

Extra assistance

Once students are learning to sound out simple consonant-vowel-consonant words like dog and cat, the idea of a head, body and tail can be used. For visual learners this could be done using cut-outs of animal heads, bodies and tails either with letters printed on them or blank to have letters written on them. For kinaesthetic learners it could involve nodding, wriggling and stamping as they sound the word out.

Classroom activities

Flashcard Snap

Have at least 2 sets of flashcards for the letters a, b, c, f, i, m, s and t. Shuffle and deal between 2 players. Keep cards face down. Players take turns to put a card from their pile onto a central pile, sounding out the letter they turn over. If the 2 cards on top are the same, the players shout SNAP! The first to do so takes the central pile. Play continues until one player runs out of cards.

Reading Eggs Lesson sequence	TEACH Content and skills	PRACTISE Children will:	APPLY
Hear: *Animated Lesson*	Revise the words I and am, and the sounds a, b, c, f, m, s, t and at through identification and the song *I feel great!*	identify and read the words I and am, and the sounds a, b, c, f, m, s, t and at in isolation.	**Worksheet 1** Initial sounds
Write: *Make a Sentence*	Recognise correct word order for sentences.	choose the correct words to make sentences.	**Worksheet 2** Handwriting
Find: *Rhyming Squares, Frog Hops and Letter Lights*	Identify rhyming words. Recognise the word am. Recognise matching upper and lower case letters.	find images of rhyming words. Find the given word in a group. Match lower and upper case letters.	**Worksheet 3** Final sounds
Vocabulary: *Blend a Word, Fishing Boats and Tiles*	Build vocabulary skills: Blend and recognise words. Match words to pictures.	blend sounds to read and make words. Understand key vocabulary and apply it.	**Worksheet 4** Vocabulary
Read: *Book*	Read aloud book.	listen, follow the reading and read along.	**Reading Eggs Story book** A cat sat

Classroom activities

Bingo!

Give students a laminated board with 10 squares on it. Ask them to write a letter in each square from the list a, b, c, f, i, m, s and t (use whiteboard markers). Hold up pictures of items starting with those letters and say the name of the item in the picture. Students put a cross on that initial letter on their board. First one to 10 calls out 'bingo' and wins!

Related Reading Eggs Activities, Interactives, Songs and Books

Reading Eggs Playroom

Alphabet Activities

Book Shelf Song

Books:

Look for rhyming words in the songs

Play Mat:

Letter blocks

Music Café

Running Revision

Reading Eggs Puzzle Park

Alphabet Match

Reading Eggs Posters

Teacher Toolkit

Targeting Handwriting Interactively

Alphabet Activities

Reading Eggs Apps

Eggy Alphabet

Eggy Sight words

Reading Eggs Library Books

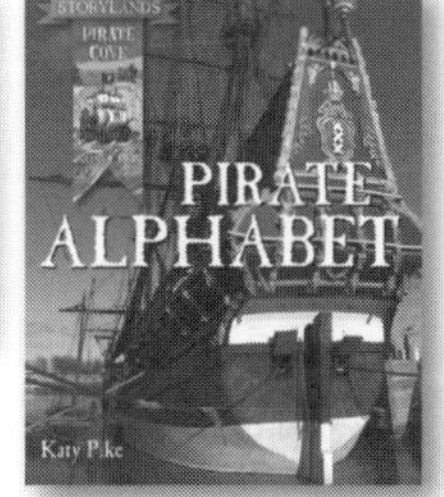

Alphabet Flashcards

Game 5 – From a to z using known letters.

Critter Card

Sam the ant

Review

Lesson 10 • Worksheet 1

Name

Initial sounds

1 Match each picture to its beginning sound.

2 What sound does the word begin with? Write the letter.

Name

Handwriting

Review

Lesson 10 · Worksheet 2

1 Trace and colour.

a

b

c

f

i

m

s

t

2 Label each picture. Write the word.

b ____________

____

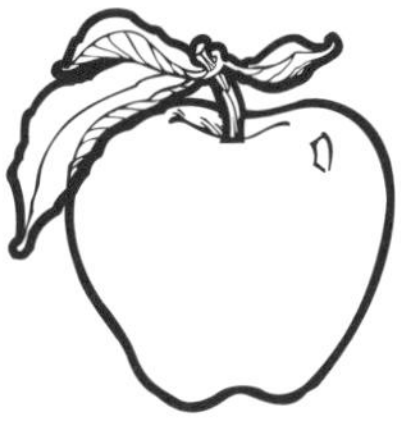

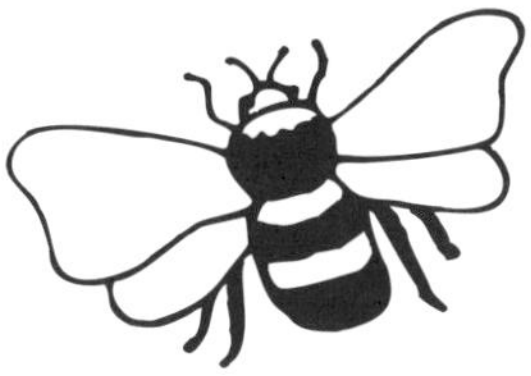

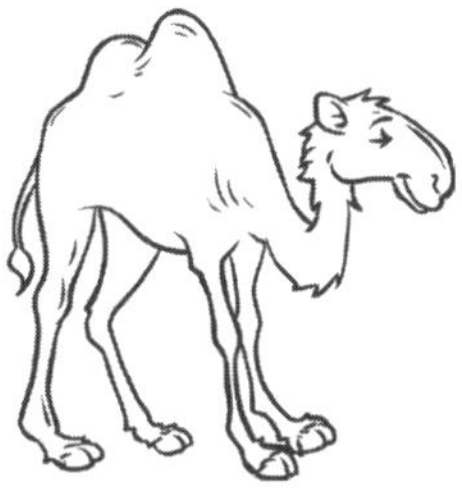

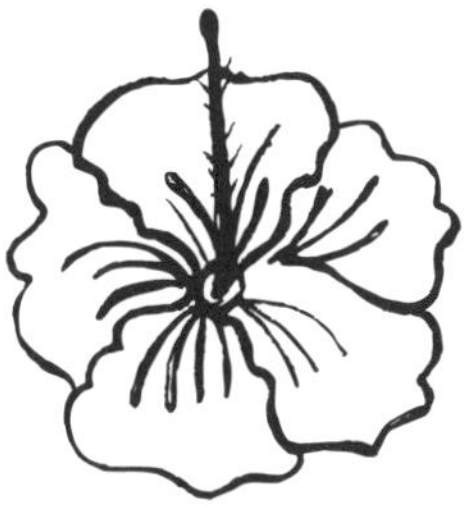

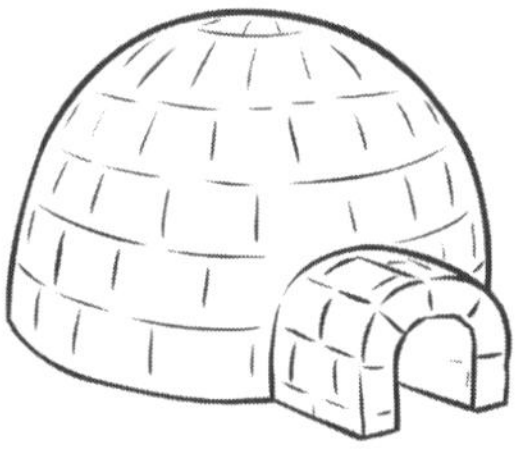

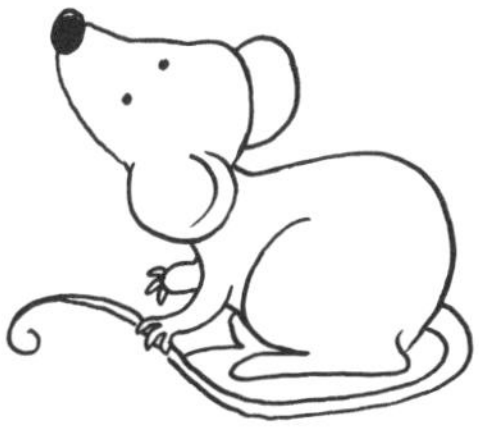

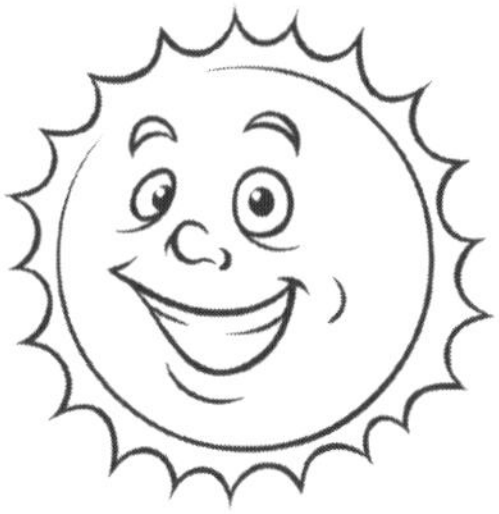

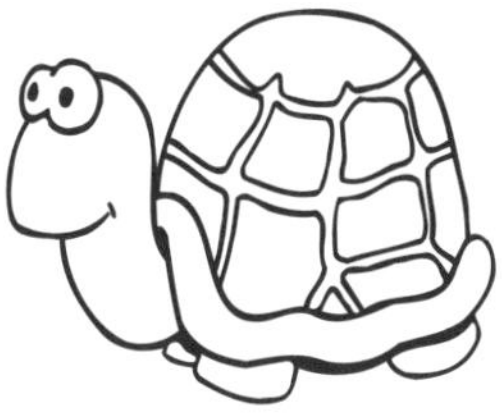

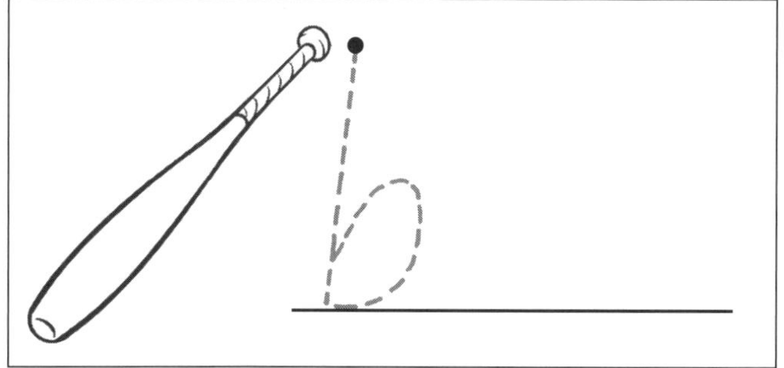

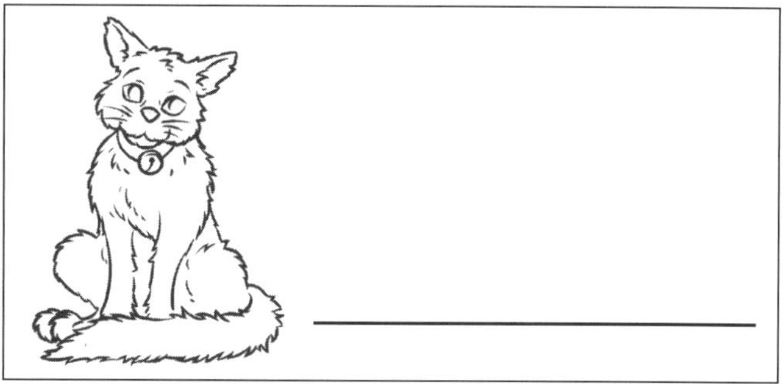

Review

Lesson 10 • Worksheet 3

Name

Final sounds

1 What sound do you hear at the end of the word?

s t	t s	m t	m s

s t	t s	m t	m t

2 Complete the word.

ca____

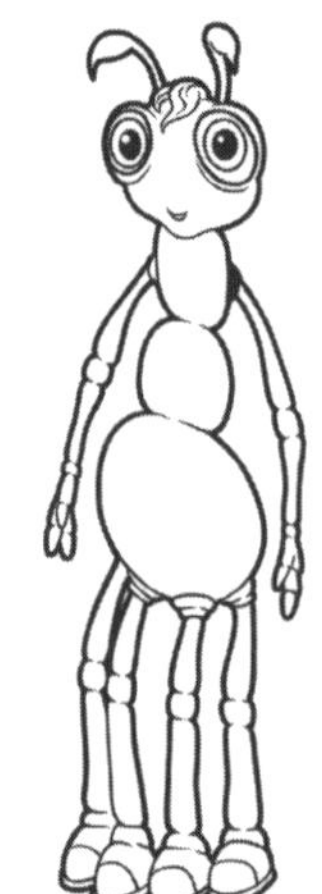

I am Sa____ .

Name

Vocabulary

Review

Lesson 10 • Worksheet 4

1 Join each letter to the word machine.
Write each word you make.

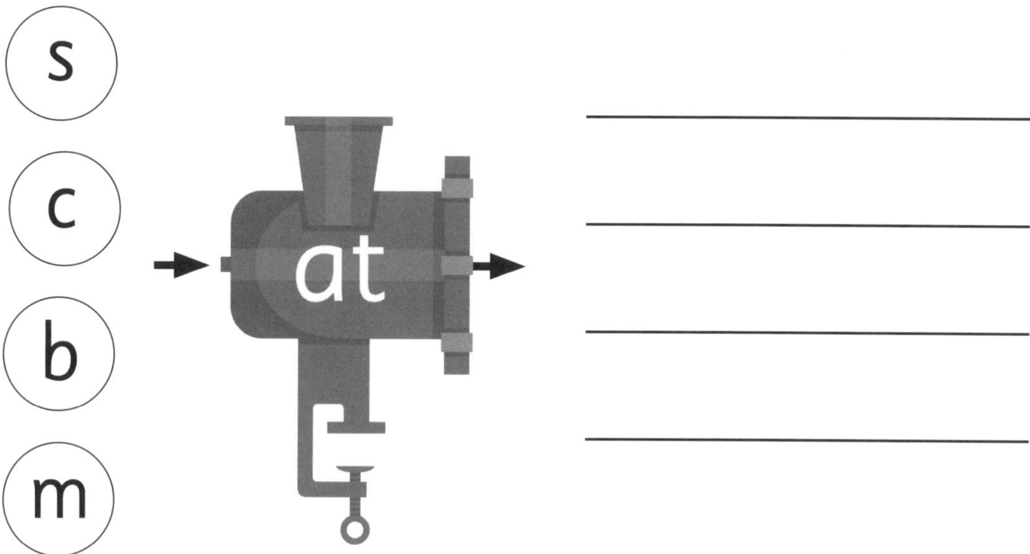

2 Colour the pictures that rhyme.

Lesson 11 the letter n

Learning objectives

Children will:

- identify the sound n.
- identify words that contain n.
- recognise and write n and N.

Australian Curriculum Content Descriptions

Sound and letter knowledge

ACELA1439 identify and manipulate sounds (phonemes) in spoken words

ACELA1440 identify familiar and recurring letters and the use of upper and lower case in written texts

Creating texts

ACELY1653 follow clear demonstrations of how to construct each letter, learn to construct lower case letters

Expressing and developing ideas

ACELA1758 recognise the most common sound made by each letter of the alphabet, including consonants and short vowel sounds

Sight words

I

Word families

cat, sat, bat

Vocabulary words

nurse, nail, nose, nest, needle, nut, net, nine, neck, nap

ESL/ELL

Some students may mix up the sounds /n/ and /l/. Give them oral and aural practise differentiating the sounds using pairs of words such as net and let, nit and lit, night and light.

Extra assistance

If students are having trouble with the sounds /m/ and /n/, have them practise letter formation with their mouths. For /m/ the lips are together, tongue flat. For /n/ the tongue tip is behind the top teeth and the lips are a little open.

Classroom activities

Find the Start

Give students a list of words with the first letter missing. Ask them to figure out which letter could be the starter for all the given words, for example:

_ut _est _et _eck

Discuss the answers as a class. Was there more than 1 possible answer?

Find the Letter

Give each student 3 cards with the letters n, t and m. Say a word and ask students to listen to the initial sound. They should hold up the card which makes that initial sound. Use clear, recognisable words such as:

tap	nap	moon
toy	neck	monkey

Reading Eggs Lesson sequence	TEACH Content and skills	PRACTISE Children will:	APPLY
Hear: *Animated Lesson*	Introduce the sound /n/ through words and the song *Knowing nnn.*	identify and read /n/ sound in isolation and in words.	**Worksheet 1** Phonemic awareness
Write: *Dot-to-Dot*	Reinforce correct letter formation of lower case n.	write the letter n.	**Worksheet 2** Handwriting
Find: *Letter Grid, Birds, Leaping Penguins and Trains*	Recognise upper and lower case letters. Recognise I.	locate lower case and upper case letters. Find the word I.	**Worksheet 3** Vocabulary
Vocabulary: *Letter Book, Word Windows and Missing Sound*	Build vocabulary skills: Blend and recognise words. Match pictures to words.	blend sounds to read words and recognise them.	**Worksheet 4** Check
Read: *Book*	Read aloud book.	listen, follow the reading and read along.	**Reading Eggs Alphabet book** n

Related Reading Eggs Activities, Interactives, Songs and Books

Reading Eggs Playroom

Alphabet Activities
Book Shelf Song
Books:
Alphabet Song,
Little Peter Rabbit

Music Café

Knowing nnn

Reading Eggs Puzzle Park

Alphabet Match

Reading Eggs Posters

Reading Eggs Library Books

My Program Books

Alphabet Flashcards

Game 2 – Sound puzzles using n and 4 known letters.

Teacher Toolkit

Targeting Handwriting Interactively

Alphabet Activities

Reading Eggs Apps

Eggy Alphabet

Critter Card

Nutty newt

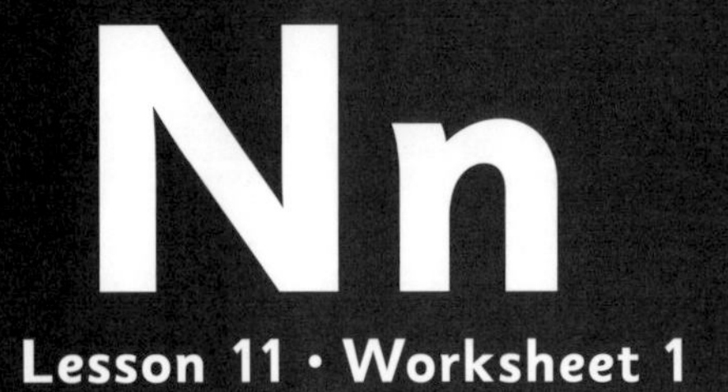

Name

Phonemic awareness

1 Colour the pictures that begin with **n**.

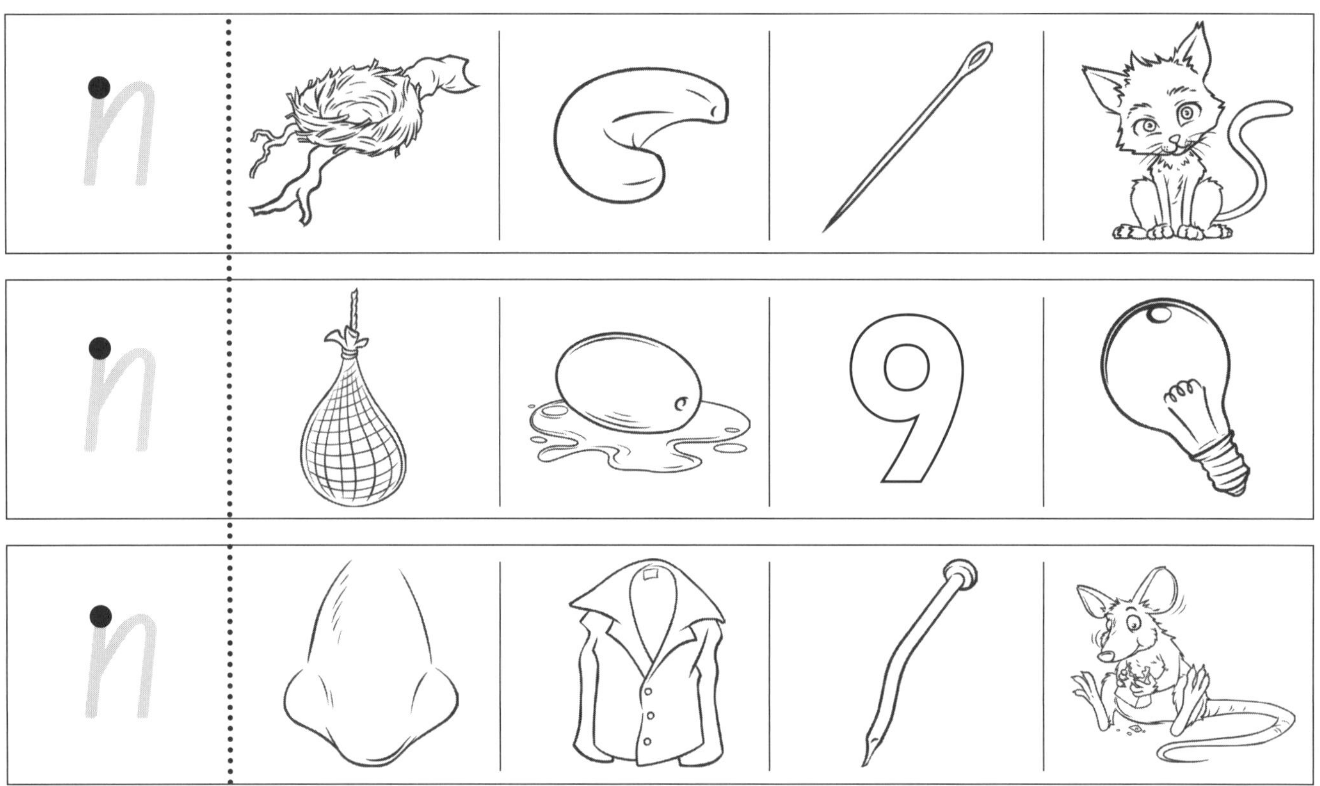

2 Match each letter to a picture.

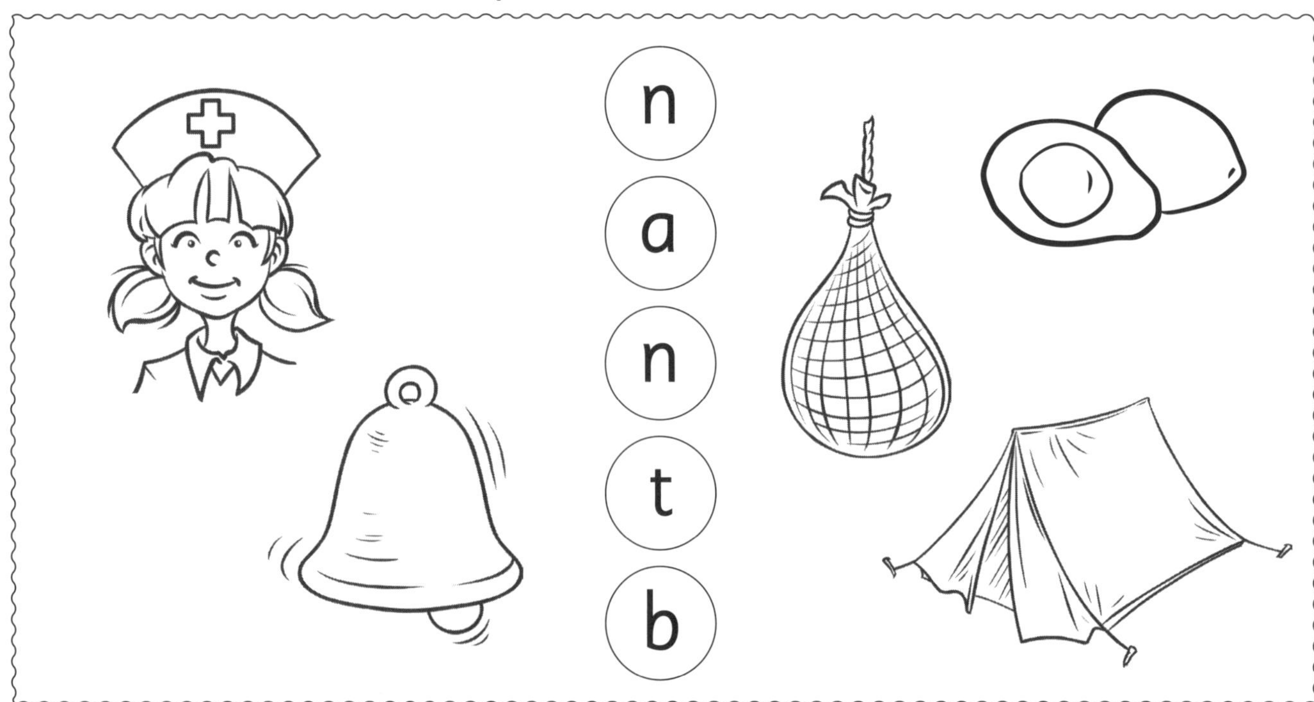

Name

Handwriting

Nn

Lesson 11 • Worksheet 2

1 Hop across to Nutty newt.

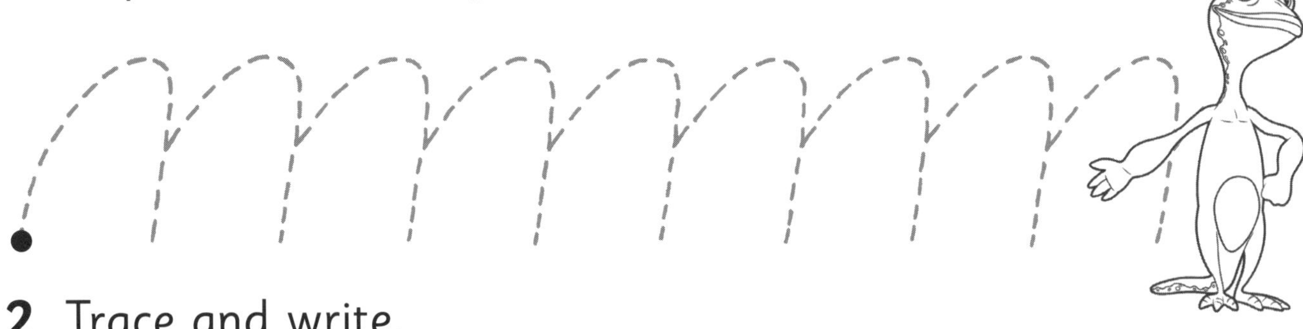

2 Trace and write.

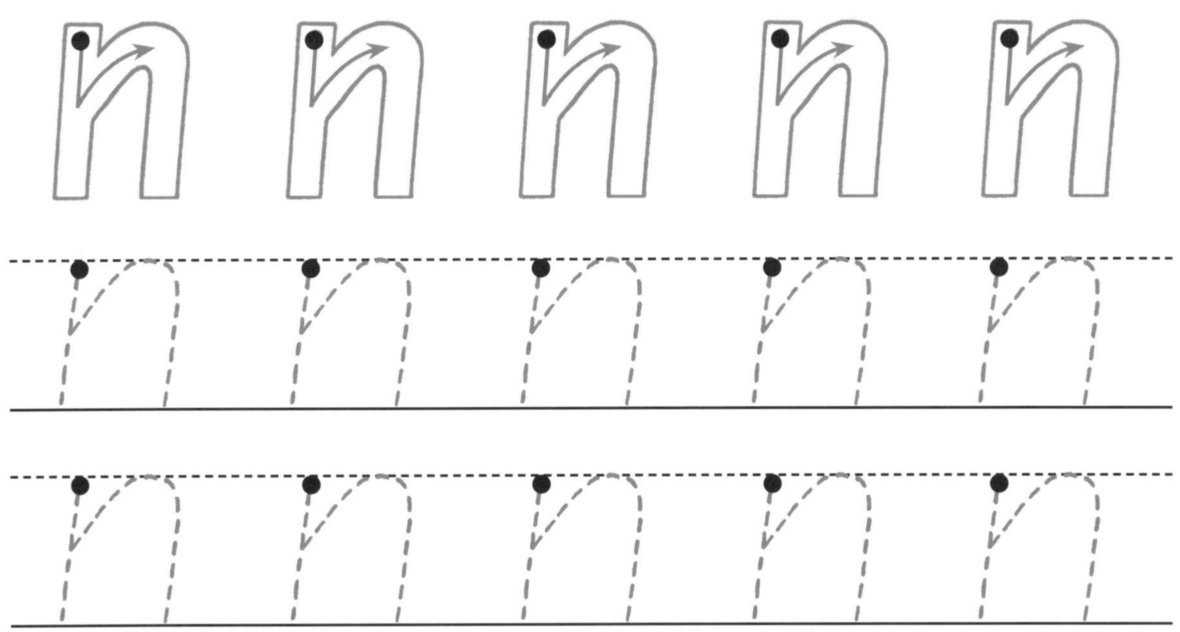

3 Trace over the horse's door.

4 Trace and write.

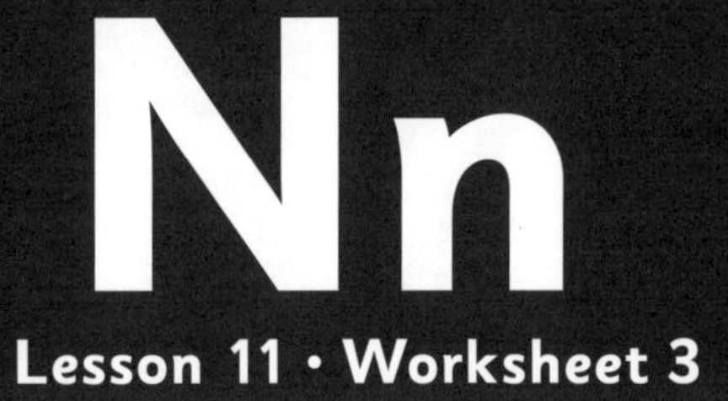

Name

Vocabulary

1 Finish the sentences.

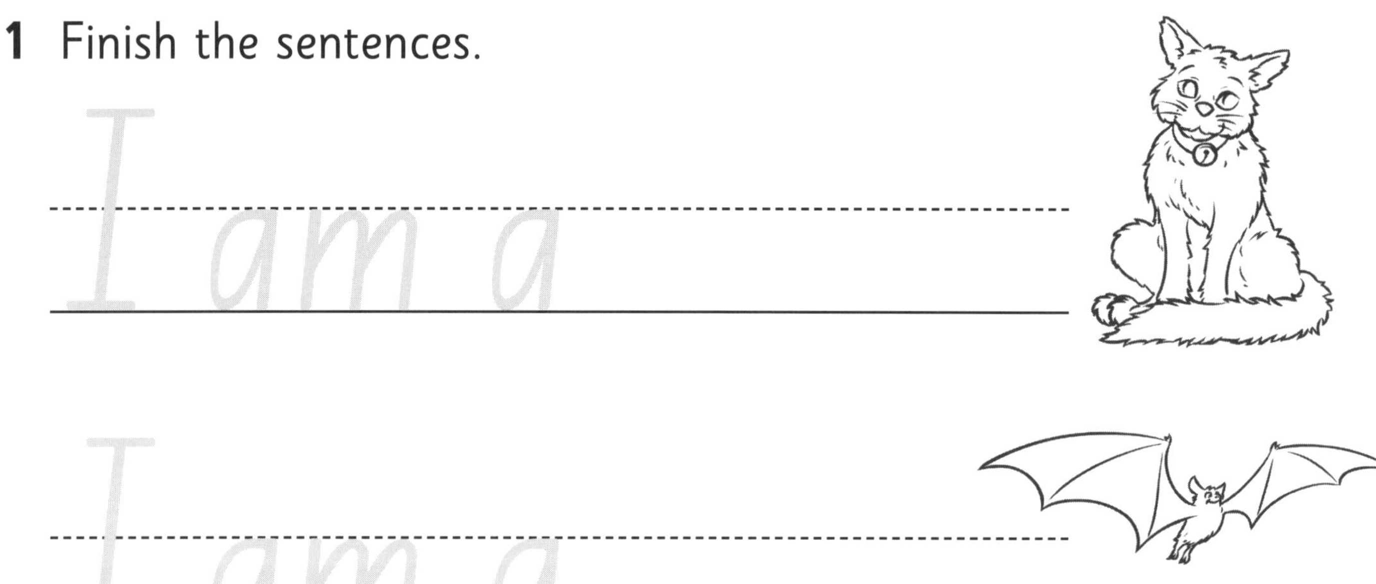

I am a

I am a

2 Draw nine nuts.

Name

Check

Nn

Lesson 11 • Worksheet 4

1 Add **n**. Read the word.

 _n_ut	 ____est
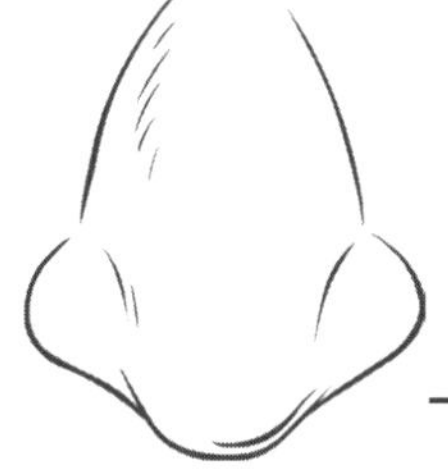 ____ose	 ____eck
 ____ail	 ____et
 ____ine	 ____urse

2 Circle every **N**.

N	N	N	Z	T
H	M	J	N	N

How many? ____

Circle every **n**.

n	n	h	n	n
a	n	m	o	r

How many? ____

Lesson 12 the letter p

Learning objectives

Children will:

- identify the sound p.
- identify words that contain p.
- recognise and write p and P.

Australian Curriculum Content Descriptions

Sound and letter knowledge

ACELA1439 identify and manipulate sounds (phonemes) in spoken words

ACELA1440 identify familiar and recurring letters and the use of upper and lower case in written texts

Creating texts

ACELY1653 follow clear demonstrations of how to construct each letter, learn to construct lower case letters

Expressing and developing ideas

ACELA1758 recognise the most common sound made by each letter of the alphabet, including consonants and short vowel sounds

Sight words

am

Vocabulary words

pencil, peach, peanut, potato, pig, pie, pear, peas, pan, plate, pen, pot, pat, panda

ESL/ELL

Some students may have trouble with the sounds /p/, /b/ and /d/. Let them practise the sounds using sets of words like pan, dan, ban, or pig, big, dig. Be sure to reinforce the initial sound.

Extra assistance

The sound /p/ is a great one for tongue twisters as so many words start with p. Teach the children the classic: *Peter Piper picked a peck of pickled peppers.*

Then ask students to make up their own /p/ tongue twisters and practise them in class.

Classroom activities

Buzzy Bee

Sit in a circle. Everyone says, *'Buzzy Bee, Buzzy Bee, what have you got in your hive for me? Something beginning with p!'* Then students take turns around the circle naming something that begins with the sound /p/. Can repeat with b, c, t.

Flashcard Snap

Have at least 2 sets of flashcards for the letters a, b, c, f, m, p, s and t. Shuffle and deal between 2 players. Keep cards face down. Players take turns to put a card from their pile onto a central pile, sounding out the letter they turn over. If the 2 cards on top are the same, the players shout SNAP! The first to do so takes the central pile. Play continues until one player runs out of cards.

Reading Eggs Lesson sequence	**TEACH Content and skills**	**PRACTISE Children will:**	**APPLY**
Hear: *Animated Lesson*	Introduce the sound /p/ through words and the song *Where is p?*	identify and read /p/ sound in isolation and in words.	**Worksheet 1** Phonemic awareness
Write: *Dot-to-Dot*	Reinforce correct letter formation of lower case p.	write the letter p.	**Worksheet 2** Handwriting
Find: *Letter Grid, Letter Lights and Birds*	Recognise p in both upper and lower case.	locate lower case p and upper case P.	**Worksheet 3** Initial and end sounds
Vocabulary: *Letter Book, Kick a Goal and In the Box*	Build vocabulary skills: Match pictures to words. Recognise the word am.	understand key vocabulary and apply it. Match pictures to their initial letter.	**Worksheet 4** Check
Read: *Book*	Read aloud book.	listen, follow the reading and read along.	**Reading Eggs Alphabet book** p

Related Reading Eggs Activities, Interactives, Songs and Books

Reading Eggs Playroom

Alphabet Activities

Book Shelf Song

Books:
Miss Polly,
Alphabet Song

Puzzle Table

Play Kitchen:
Pizza

Music Café

Where is p?

Reading Eggs Puzzle Park

Alphabet Match

Reading Eggs Posters

Reading Eggs Library Books

My Program Books

Alphabet Flashcards

Game 3 – Sound hunt with the letter p.

Teacher Toolkit

Targeting Handwriting Interactively

Alphabet Activities

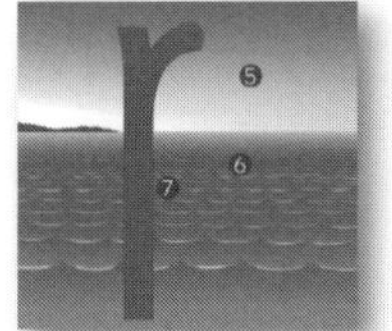

Reading Eggs Apps

Eggy Alphabet

Critter Card

Pinkipoo

Pp

Lesson 12 • Worksheet 1

Name

Phonemic awareness

1 Colour the pictures that start with **p**.

2 Match each letter to a picture.

Name

Handwriting

Pp

Lesson 12 • Worksheet 2

1 Trace and write.

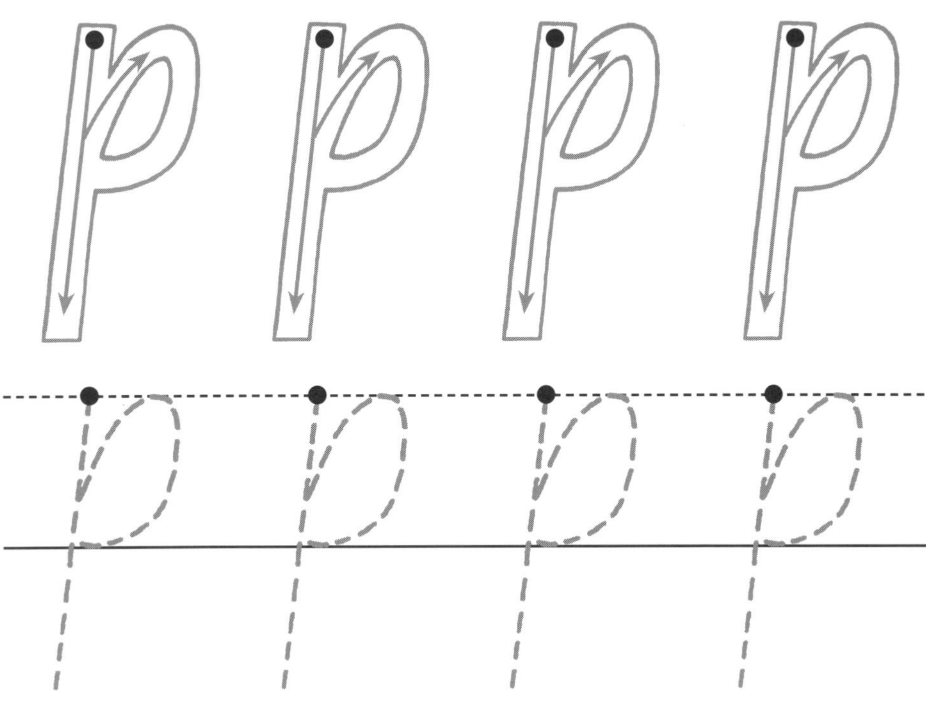

Peek a boo!
I'm Pinkipoo.

2 Complete each pair of scissors.

3 Trace and write.

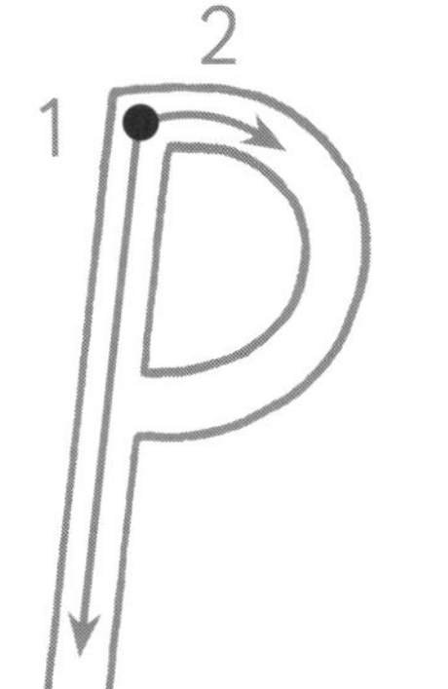

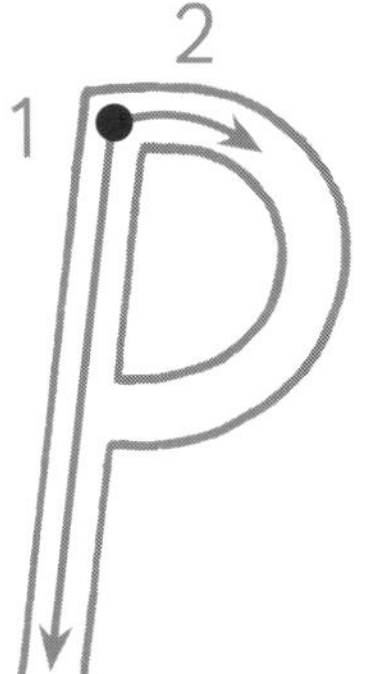

Circle your best letter.

Pp

Name

Initial and end sounds

Lesson 12 • Worksheet 3

1 Add **p** and then say the word.

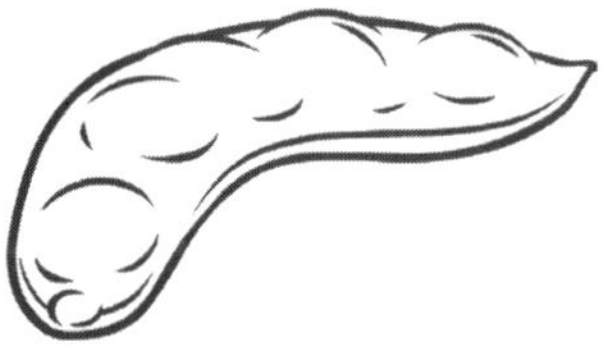

p eas

_____en

_____encil

_____enguin

ta _____

cu _____

mo _____

ma _____

2 Circle every **P**.

P	D	P	P	B
P	B	P	D	P

How many? _____

Circle every **p**.

p	p	p	b	g
j	b	p	a	p

How many? _____

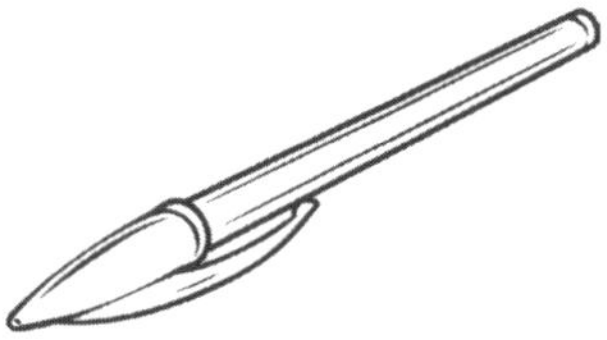

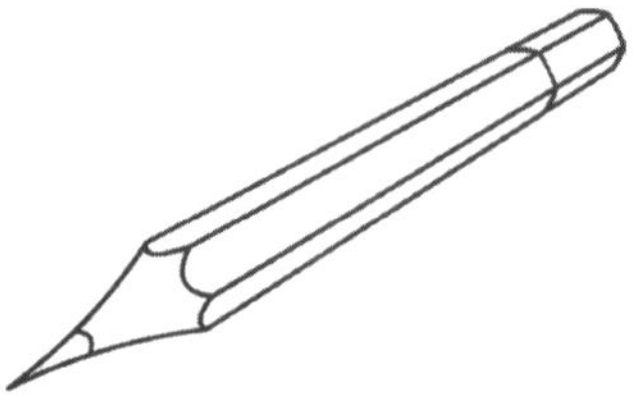

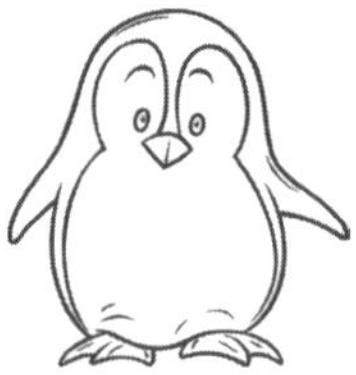

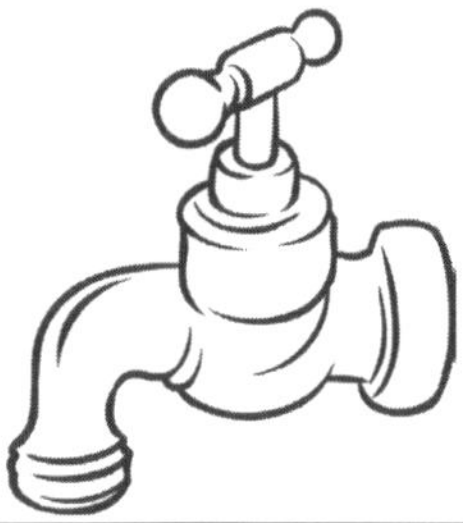

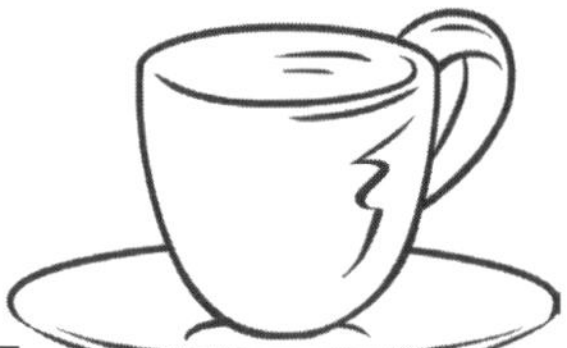

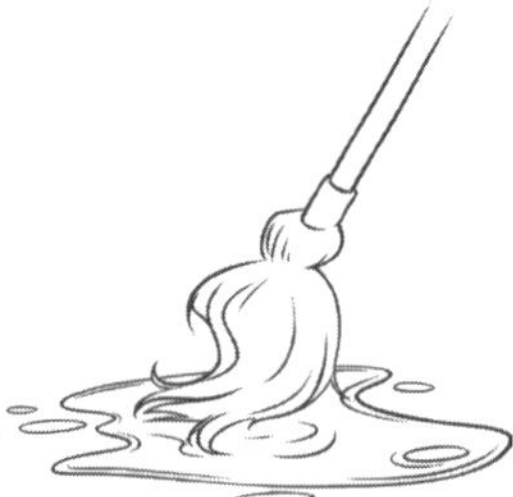

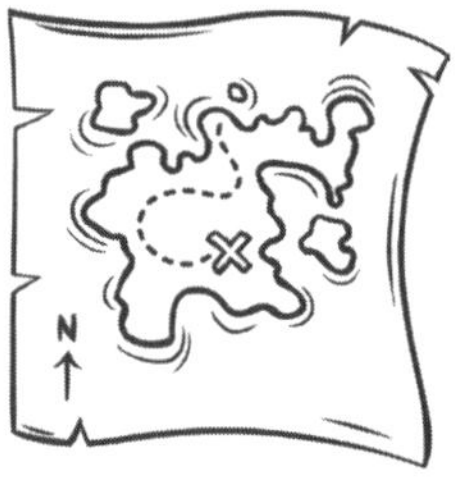

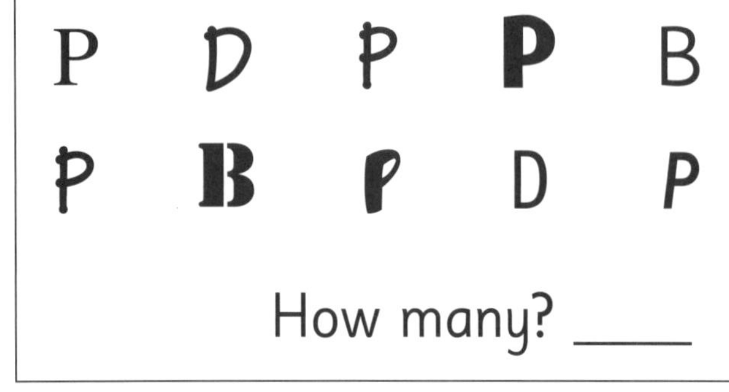

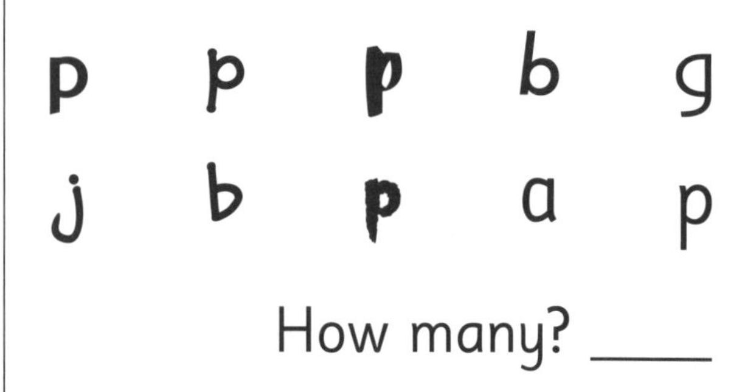

Name

Check

Pp

Lesson 12 · Worksheet 4

1 Circle the letter each picture **starts** with.

 p d	 n m	 c n	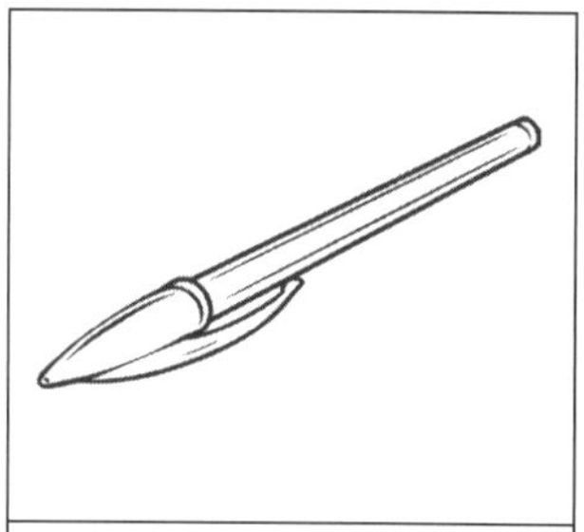 n p
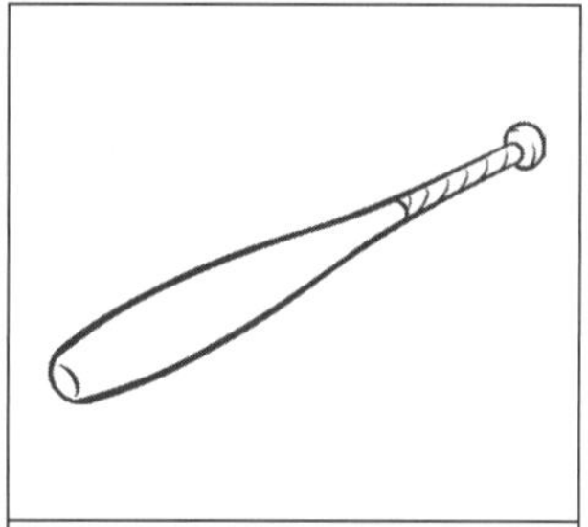 p b	 p g	 b p	 n m

2 Colour the pictures that **end** with **p**.

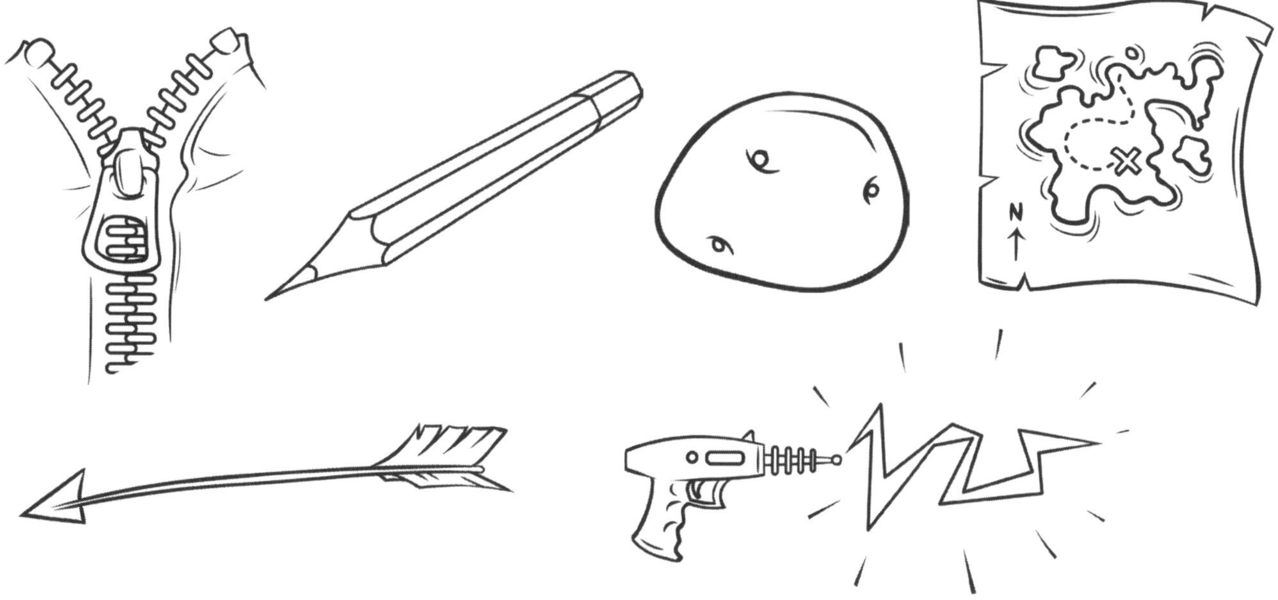

Lesson 13 the sound **ap**

Learning objectives

Children will:

- identify the rime ap.
- identify words that contain ap.
- blend onsets and rimes to make a word.

Australian Curriculum Content Descriptions

Sound and letter knowledge

ACELA1439 identify and manipulate sounds (phonemes) in spoken words

Expressing and developing ideas

ACELA1435 learn that word order in sentences is important for meaning

ACELA1438 build word families using onset and rime

Interpreting, analysing and evaluating

ACELY1649 navigate a text correctly, starting at the right place and reading in the right direction, returning to the next line as needed, matching one spoken word to one written word

Sight words

I, am, a

Word families

zap, map, cap, tap, nap, rap, lap, gap, apron

Vocabulary words

Sam, pats, cat, bat, fat, sat

ESL/ELL

The correct pronunciation of /p/ can be reinforced using ap words. Students may find it fun to exaggerate the pronunciation as the lips come together and then release with a sound like a pop.

Extra assistance

When making word family lists, teach students to run through the alphabet and try each letter as a starting sound, looking for the "real" words. For example:

lap map nap ~~oap~~ –> this is not a real word

Classroom activities

Brainstorm

Brainstorm a list of words that end with the ap sound. Start with single letter onsets, going through the letters they know first. Then ask if anyone knows of any other beginnings such as fr and fl.

Which Hat?

Place three hats on the floor with the labels ap, am and at. Discuss the sounds. Have pictures of objects that have ap, am or at in them. Each student chooses one and works out which hat it must go in. Discuss their choice with the class.

Reading Eggs Lesson sequence	**TEACH Content and skills**	**PRACTISE Children will:**	**APPLY**
Hear: *Animated Lesson*	Introduce the sound ap through words and the song *Sam's Nap.*	identify and read ap in isolation and in words.	**Worksheet 1** Word family
Write: *Make a Sentence*	Recognise correct word order for a sentence.	choose the correct words to make a sentence.	**Worksheet 2** Read and write
Find: *Word family, Rhyming Squares, Alien Planets, Missing Sound and Golden Goose*	Identify the correct onset letter to complete a word. Identify rhyming words. Recognise a given word.	choose the correct initial letter to make a word. Find rhyming words. Find the given word in a group.	**Worksheet 3** Vocabulary
Vocabulary: *Label It, Blend a Word and Tiles*	Build vocabulary skills: Match pictures to words. Blend and recognise words.	recognise key vocabulary. Blend sounds to read and make words.	**Worksheet 4** Check
Read: *Book*	Read aloud book.	listen, follow the reading and read along.	**Reading Eggs Story book** I am Sam

Related Reading Eggs Activities, Interactives, Songs and Books

Reading Eggs Playroom

Puzzle Table:
Swap parts,
Shape puzzle

Music Café

Sam's Nap

Reading Eggs Puzzle Park

Alphabet Match

Reading Eggs Posters

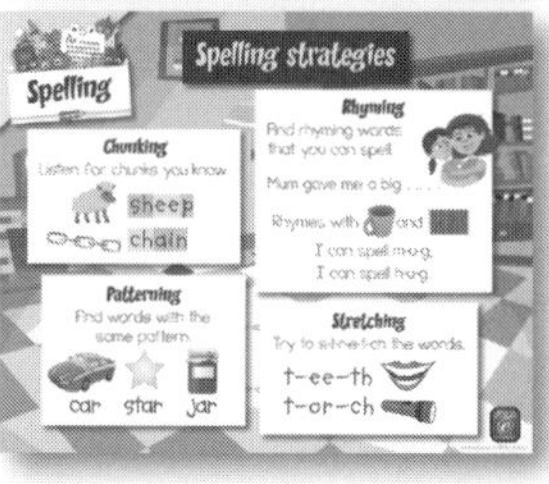

Reading Eggs Library Books

My Program Books

Alphabet Flashcards

Game 7 – Making words ending with ap.

Teacher Toolkit

Targeting Handwriting Interactively

Spelling Activities

Reading Eggs Apps

Eggy Alphabet

Eggy Phonics 1

Critter Card

Happy nap

ap

Name

Word family

Lesson 13 • Worksheet 1

1 Finish the **ap** words.

2 Colour the **ap** pictures.

3 Finish the sentences.

Name

Read and write

Complete each sentence with a word from the box.

has a Sam cat

Sam pats a ________.

Sam ________ a bat.

Sam pats ______ fat cat.

________ pats a rat.

ap

Name

Vocabulary

Lesson 13 • Worksheet 3

1 Join each letter to the word machine. Write each word you make.

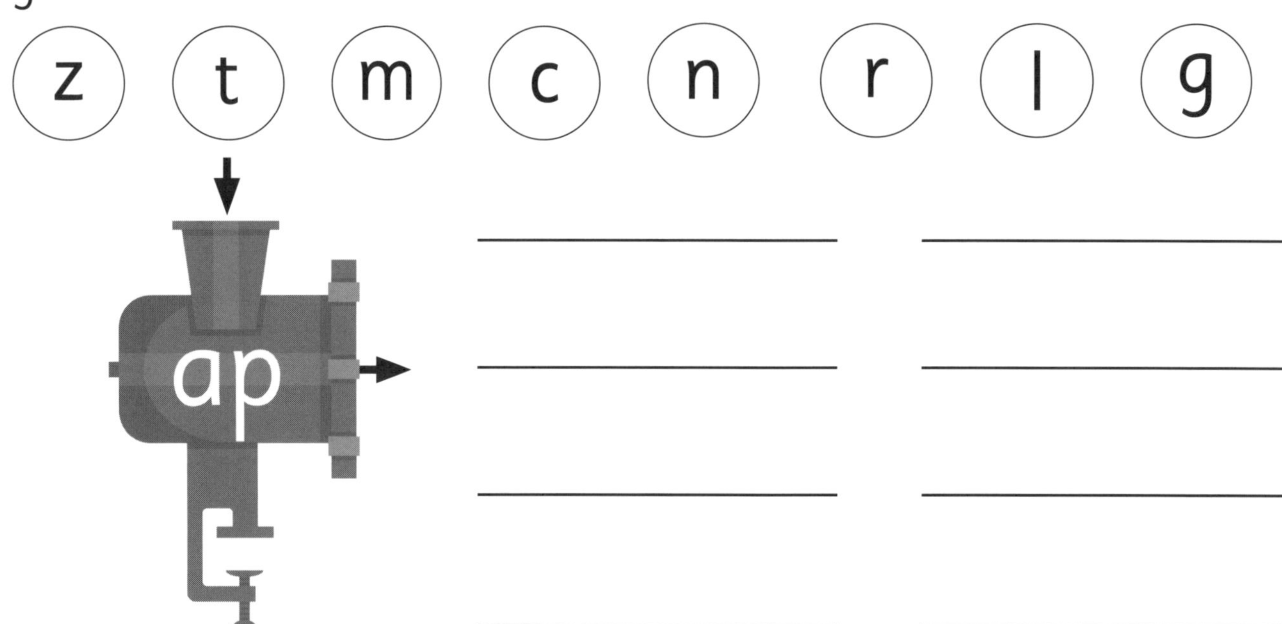

2 Join the words that rhyme.

Name

Check

ap

Lesson 13 • Worksheet 4

Match each word to a picture.

ant

bee

cap

bat

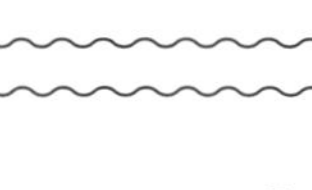

mat

tap

map

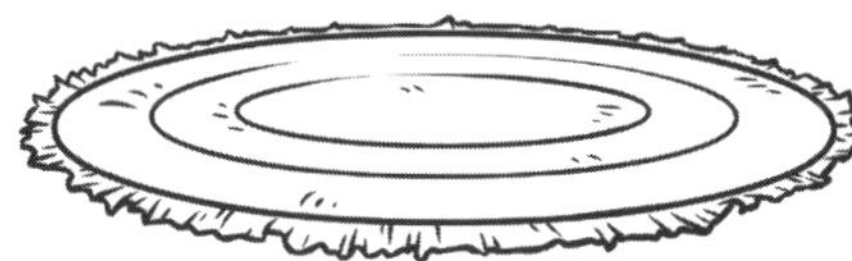

sat

Lesson 14 the letter **h**

Learning objectives

Children will:

- identify the sound h.
- identify words that contain h.
- recognise and write h and H.

Australian Curriculum Content Descriptions

Sound and letter knowledge

ACELA1439 identify and manipulate sounds (phonemes) in spoken words

ACELA1440 identify familiar and recurring letters and the use of upper and lower case in written texts

Creating texts

ACELY1653 follow clear demonstrations of how to construct each letter, learn to construct lower case letters

Expressing and developing ideas

ACELA1758 recognise the most common sound made by each letter of the alphabet, including consonants and short vowel sounds

Vocabulary words

house, hum, hook, hope, hen, hand, ham, hole, hammer, heart, hair, horse, helmet, head, hamburger, hat, hive

ESL/ELL

Some students who speak Middle Eastern languages may pronounce /h/ with a throaty sound. Spanish and French-based languages often make the h sound silent. Practise saying simple, recognisable words that start with /h/ like ham, hand and head.

Extra assistance

To practise proper formation of the sound /h/ the mouth should be open (not wide) with the tongue low in the mouth. There is a continuous blow of air but no sound from the throat.

Classroom activities

Letter Pictures

Provide the students with a piece of paper that has a large h in the middle.

- trace over the h with a pencil
- draw things that start with h around the letter and colour them in

Which Hat?

Place three hats on the floor with the labels h, p and n. Discuss the sounds. Have a pile of objects or pictures of objects that start with h, p and n. Each student chooses one and works out which hat it must go in. Discuss their choice with the class.

Reading Eggs Lesson sequence	TEACH Content and skills	PRACTISE Children will:	APPLY
Hear: *Animated Lesson*	Introduce the sound /h/ through words and the song *He's with Her.*	identify and read /h/ sound in isolation and in words.	**Worksheet 1** Phonemic awareness
Write: *Dot-to-Dot*	Reinforce correct letter formation of lower case h.	write the letter h.	**Worksheet 2** Handwriting
Find: *Letter Grid, Mark Your Letter and Trains*	Recognise h in upper and lower case.	locate lower case h and upper case H.	**Worksheet 3** Initial sounds
Vocabulary: *Letter Book, Word Windows and Label It*	Build vocabulary skills: Blend and recognise words. Match pictures to words.	blend sounds to read words and recognise them.	**Worksheet 4** Check
Read: *Book*	Read aloud book.	listen, follow the reading and read along.	**Reading Eggs Alphabet book** h

Related Reading Eggs Activities, Interactives, Songs and Books

Reading Eggs Playroom

Alphabet Activities

Book Shelf Song

Books:
Humpty Dumpty,
Hickory Dickory Dock,
Hey Diddle Diddle

Dress Up Corner:
Hero dress ups

Music Café

He's with Her

Reading Eggs Puzzle Park

Alphabet Match

Reading Eggs Posters

Reading Eggs Library Books

My Program Books

Alphabet Flashcards

Game 4 – Make the critters with the h cards.

Teacher Toolkit

Targeting Handwriting Interactively

Alphabet Activities

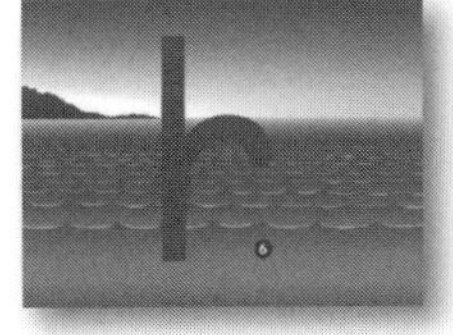

Reading Eggs Apps

Eggy Alphabet

Critter Card

Horse hee heepo

Hh

Lesson 14 • Worksheet 1

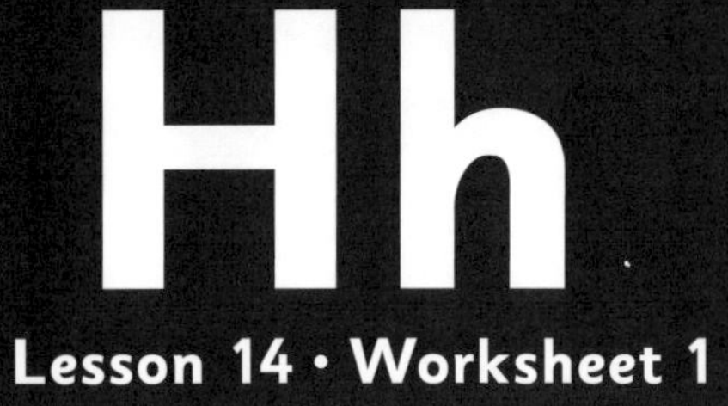

Name

Phonemic awareness

Circle the thing in each row that begins with **h**. Colour them.

h	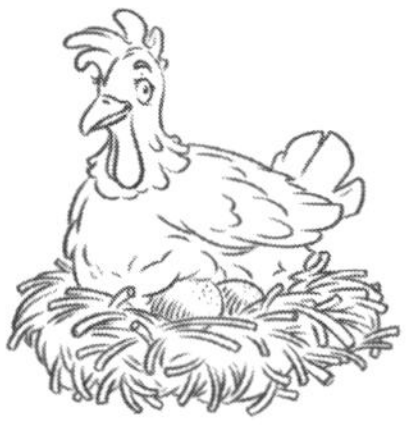	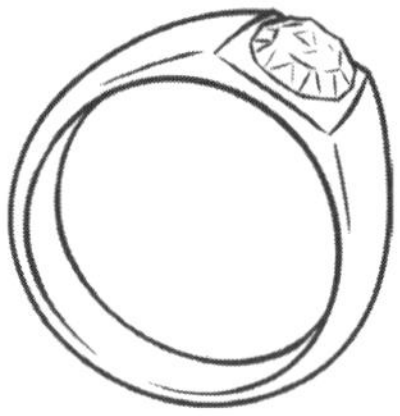	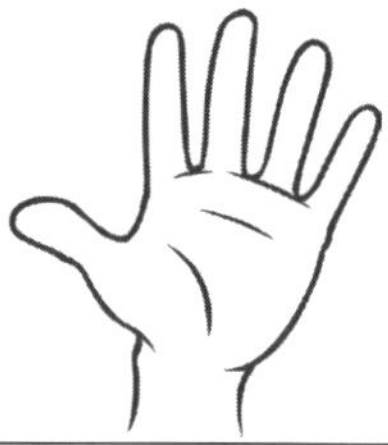
h	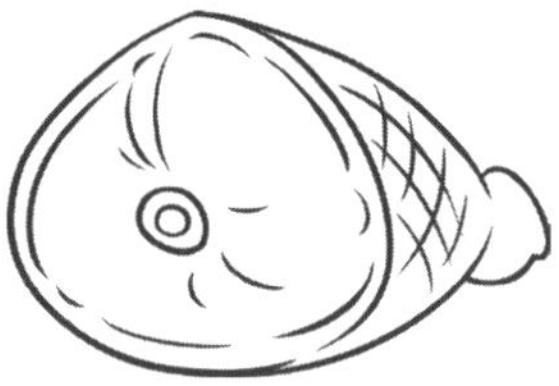	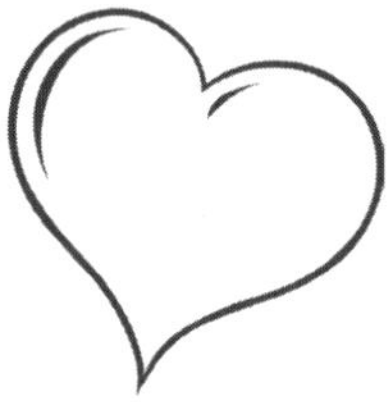	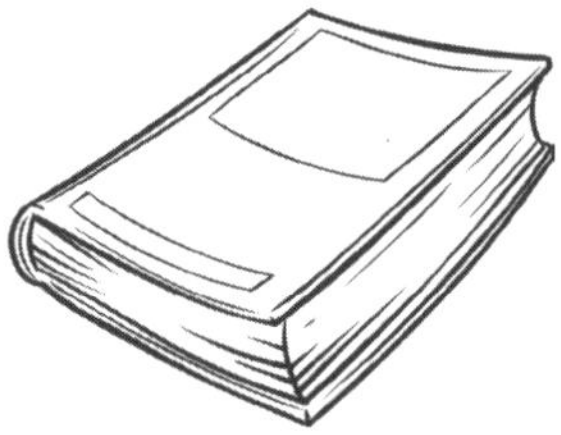
h	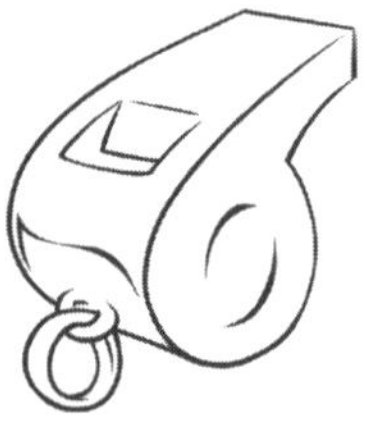	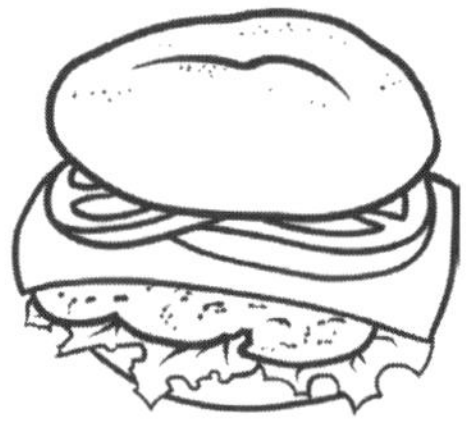	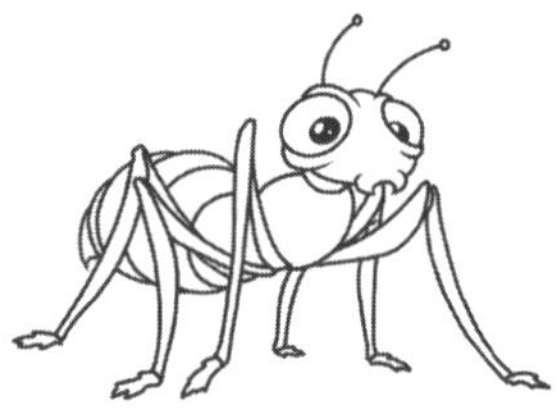
h	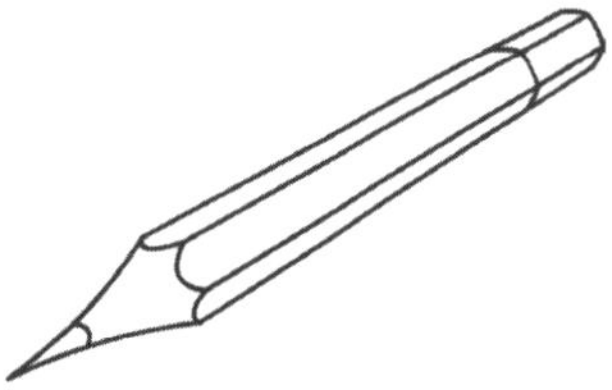	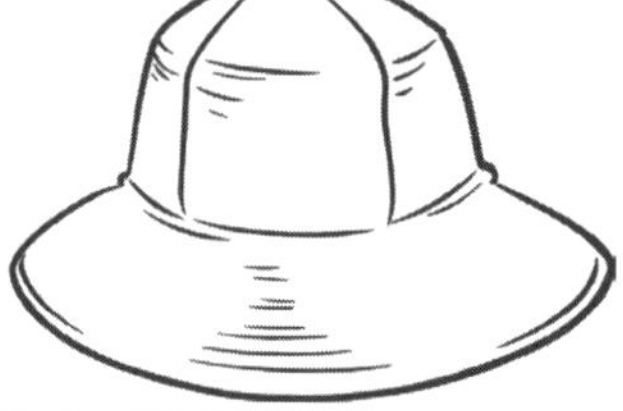	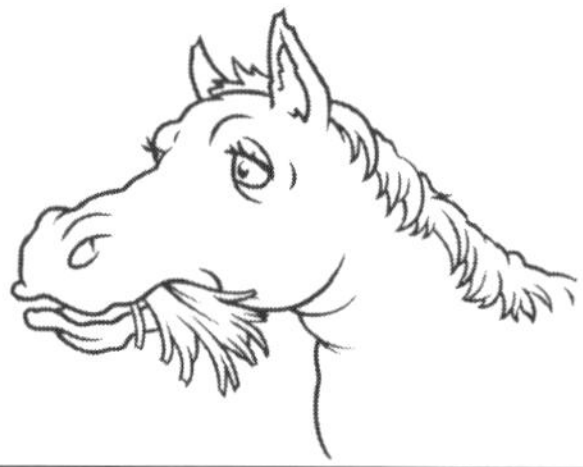
h	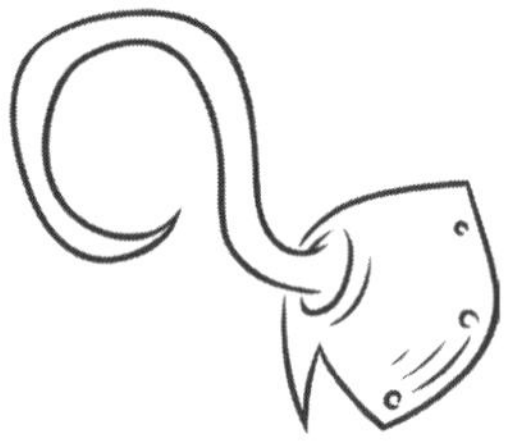	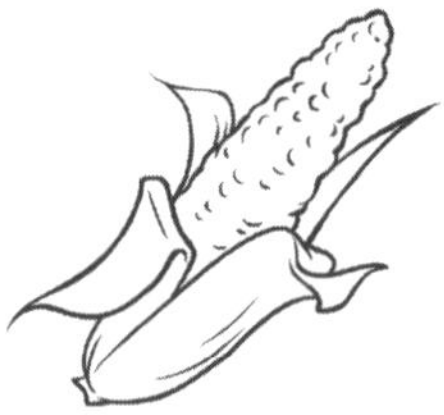	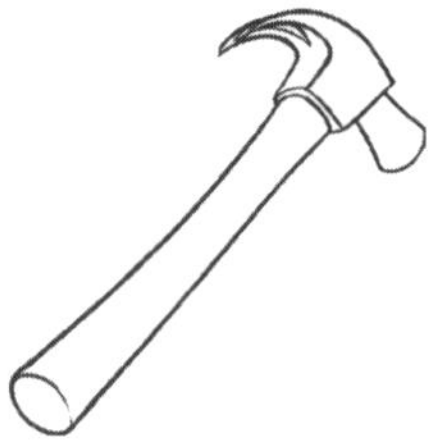
h	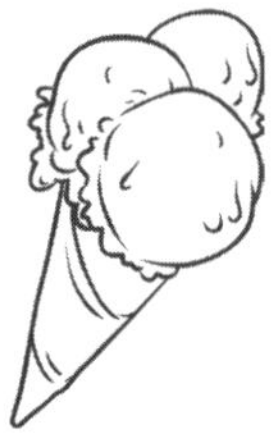	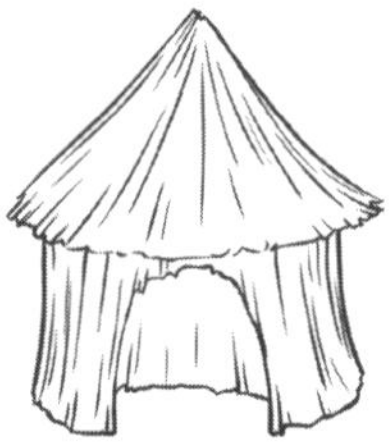	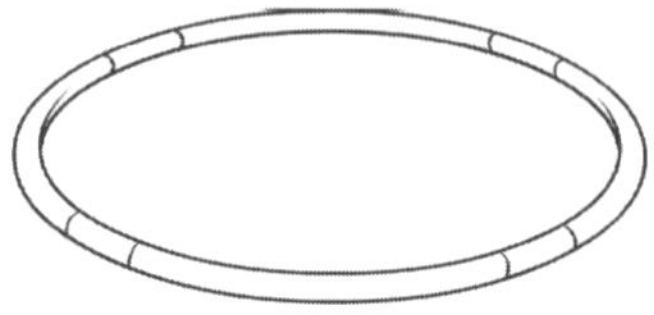

Name

Handwriting

Hh

Lesson 14 • Worksheet 2

1 Trace Horse hee heepo's friends.

2 Trace and write.

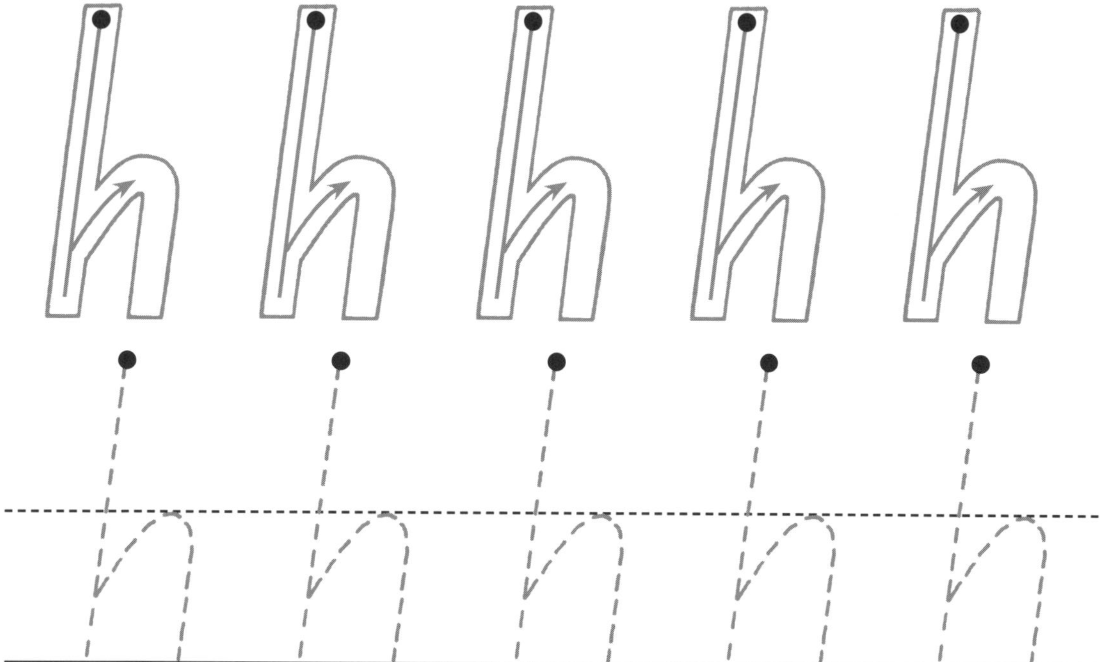

3 Trace and write.

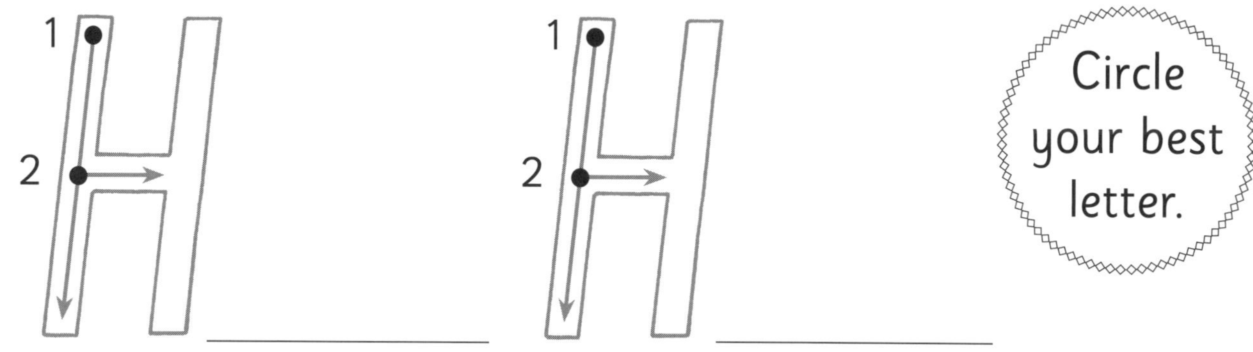

Hh

Lesson 14 • Worksheet 3

Name

Initial sounds

1 Add **h**. Read the word.

h am	____ en
____ at	____ ammer
____ and	____ ook
____ ut	____ orse

2 Draw hats on heads.

Name

Check

1 Match each letter to a picture.

2 Circle every **H**.

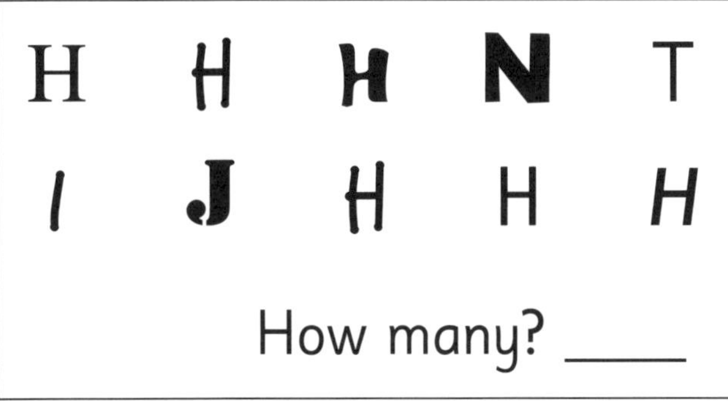

How many? ____

Circle every **h**.

h m h t h
h n o h y

How many? ____

3 Trace and write.

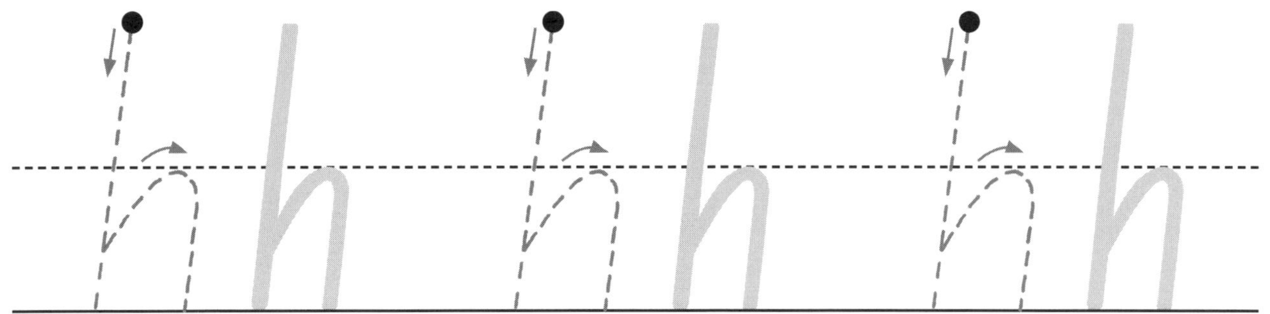

Lesson 15 the letter r

Learning objectives

Children will:

- identify the sound r.
- identify words that contain r.
- recognise and write r and R.

Australian Curriculum Content Descriptions

Sound and letter knowledge

ACELA1439 identify and manipulate sounds (phonemes) in spoken words

ACELA1440 identify familiar and recurring letters and the use of upper and lower case in written texts

Creating texts

ACELY1653 follow clear demonstrations of how to construct each letter, learn to construct lower case letters

Expressing and developing ideas

ACELA1758 recognise the most common sound made by each letter of the alphabet, including consonants and short vowel sounds

Vocabulary words

rice, raspberry, robot, rose, rabbit, raft, radio, ring, rope, rug, ruler, rock, rat, rake, referee, rectangle

ESL/ELL

Many students from an Asian language background will have trouble distinguishing between /r/ and /l/.

Practise listening to these sounds and separating them out by asking students which word is right:

My car goes on the road. / My car goes on the load.

I hurt my rip. / I hurt my lip.

Extra assistance

Some students may confuse the sounds /r/ and /l/ in pronunciation as well. Give them opportunities to practise saying the sound /r/ with tongue twisters.

Round and round the rugged rocks the ragged rascal ran.

Roberta ran rings around the Roman ruins.

Classroom activities

Trace It

Trace the letter r with fingers while saying rrrrr. Trace it in the air, on the floor, on someone's back, on paper using finger paint, in a tray of sand or on a tablet using a drawing app.

All Change!

Students sit in a circle with an object or picture in their hands that starts with b, c, f, m, p, r, s or t (make sure at least two students have each letter). The teacher calls out a word starting with one of those letters and the students whose objects start with that letter have to jump up and swap places.

Reading Eggs Lesson sequence	**TEACH Content and skills**	**PRACTISE Children will:**	**APPLY**
Hear: *Animated Lesson*	Introduce the sound /r/ through words and the song *Reading rrr.*	identify and read /r/ sound in isolation and in words.	**Worksheet 1** Phonemic awareness
Write: *Dot-to-Dot*	Reinforce correct letter formation of lower case r.	write the letter r.	**Worksheet 2** Handwriting
Find: *Letter Grid, Mark Your Letter*	Recognise r in different fonts in both upper and lower case.	locate lower case r and upper case R.	**Worksheet 3** Initial sounds
Vocabulary: *Blend a Word, Letter Book, Label It, Send a Letter and In the Box*	Build vocabulary skills: Blend and recognise words. Match pictures to words.	blend sounds to read words and recognise them. Match pictures to their initial letter.	**Worksheet 4** Check
Read: *Book*	Read aloud book.	listen, follow the reading and read along.	**Reading Eggs Alphabet book** r

Related Reading Eggs Activities, Interactives, Songs and Books

Reading Eggs Playroom

Alphabet Activities

Book Shelf Song

Books:
Alphabet Song,
Row Row Row Your Boat,
Little Peter Rabbit

My Wall:
Make my Room

Music Café

Reading rrr

Reading Eggs Puzzle Park

Alphabet Match

Reading Eggs Posters

Reading Eggs Library Books

Teacher Toolkit

Targeting Handwriting Interactively

Alphabet Activities

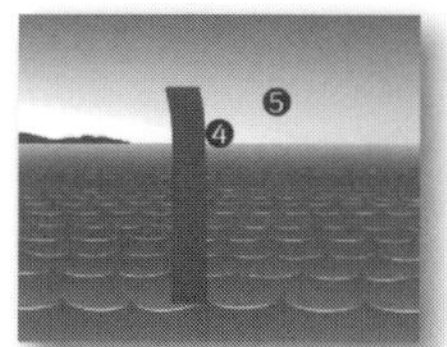

My Program Books

Reading Eggs Apps

Eggy Alphabet

Alphabet Flashcards

Game 4 – Make the critters using the r cards.

Critter Card

Red rabbit

Name

Phonemic awareness

1 Colour the pictures that begin with **r**.

2 Match each letter to a picture.

Name

Handwriting

Rr

Lesson 15 • Worksheet 2

1 Run over to the raspberries and rice.

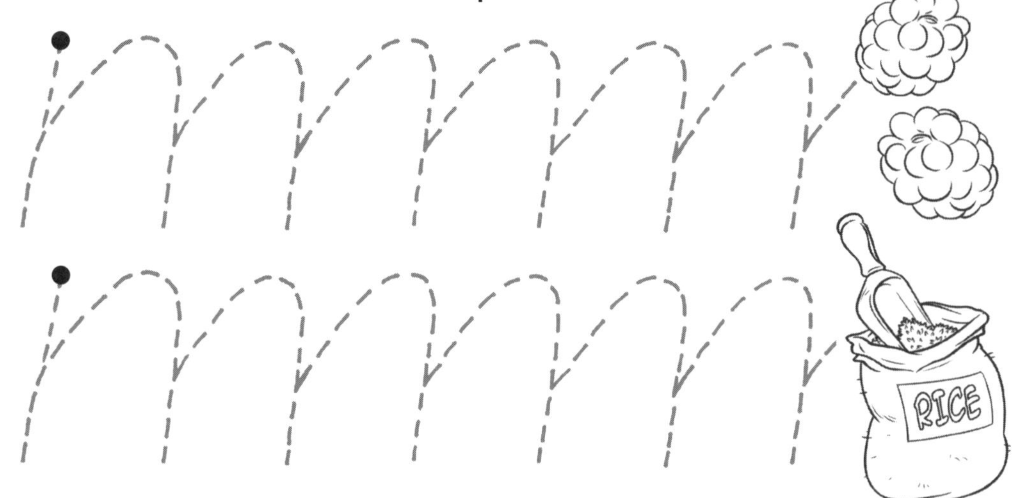

R is for Red rabbit.

2 Trace and write.

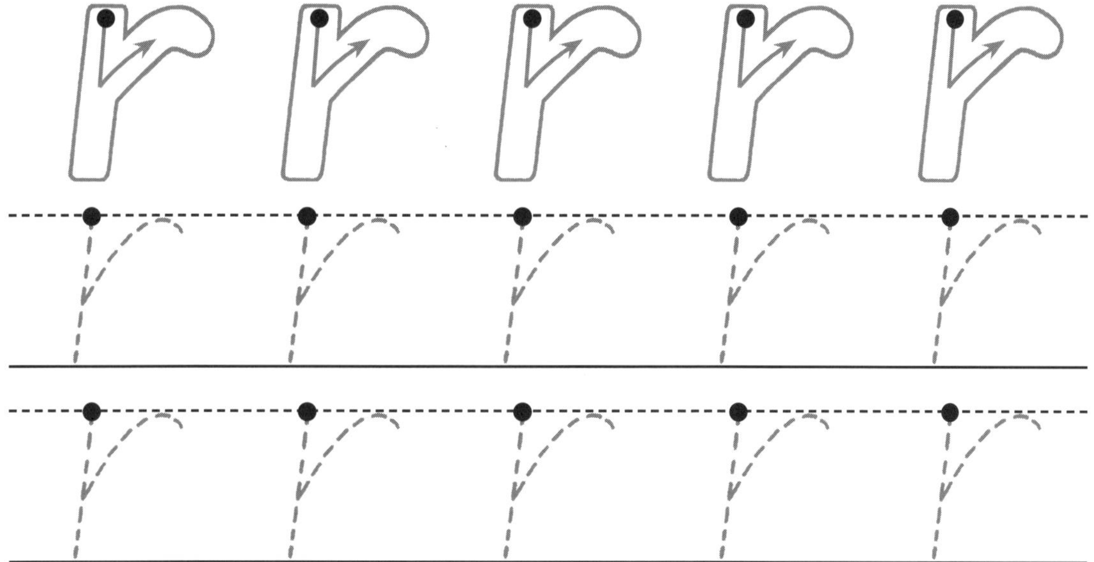

3 Trace and write.

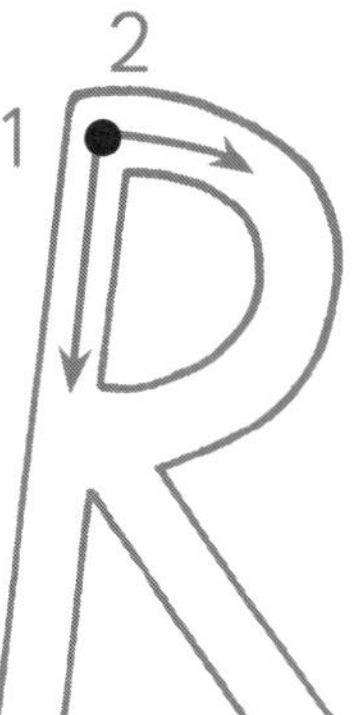

Circle your best letter.

Rr

Lesson 15 • Worksheet 3

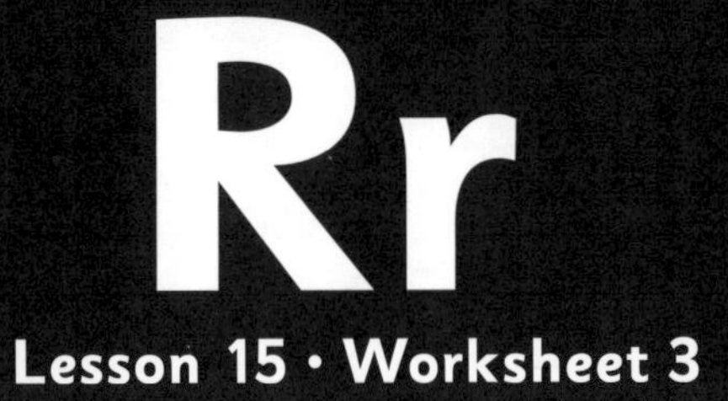

Name

Initial sounds

1 Add **r** and read the word.

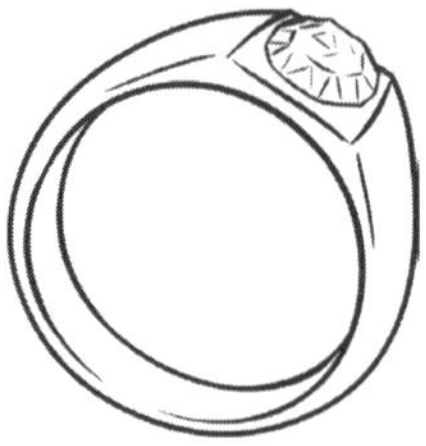

___r___ing

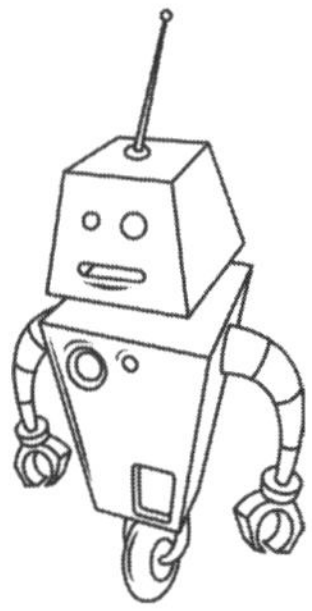

______obot

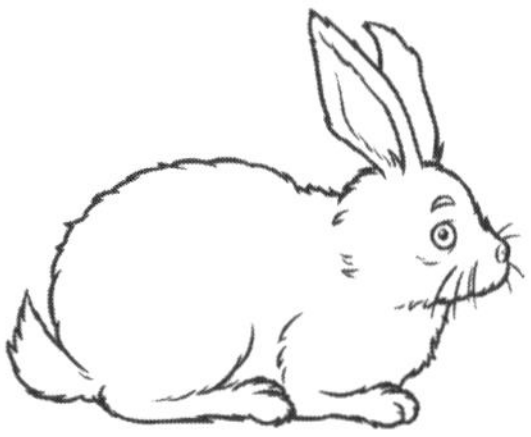

______abbit

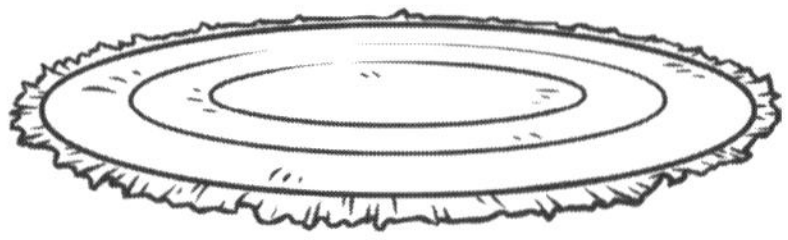

______ug

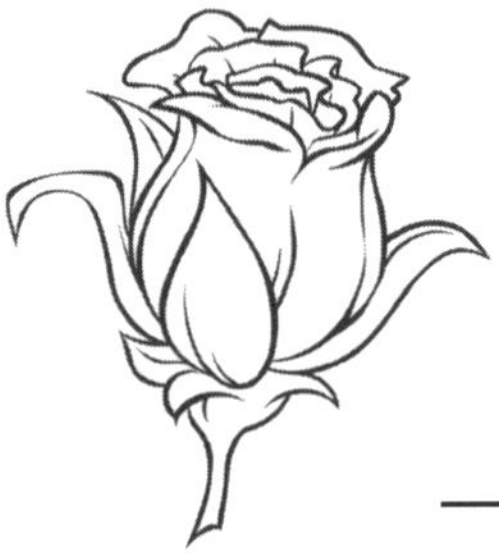

______ose

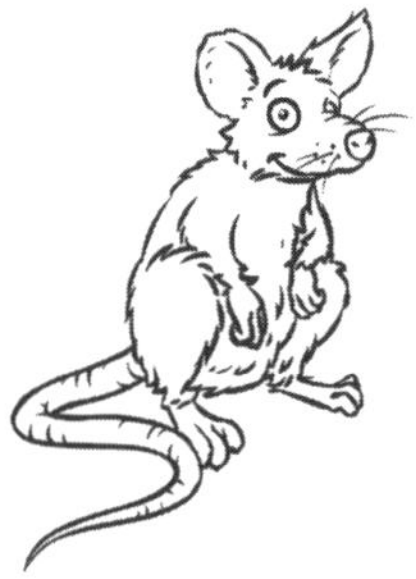

______at

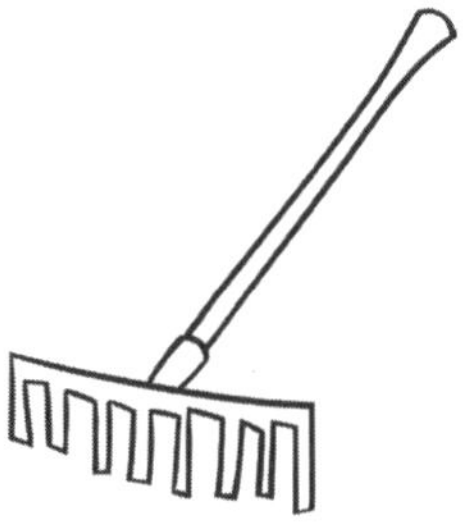

______ake

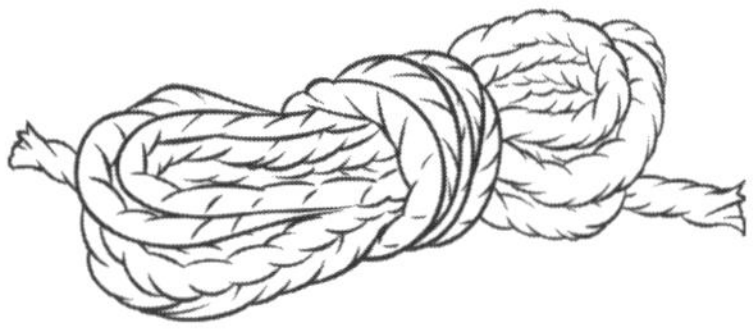

______ope

2 Draw a rainbow.

Name

Check

Rr

Lesson 15 • Worksheet 4

1 Trace and write.

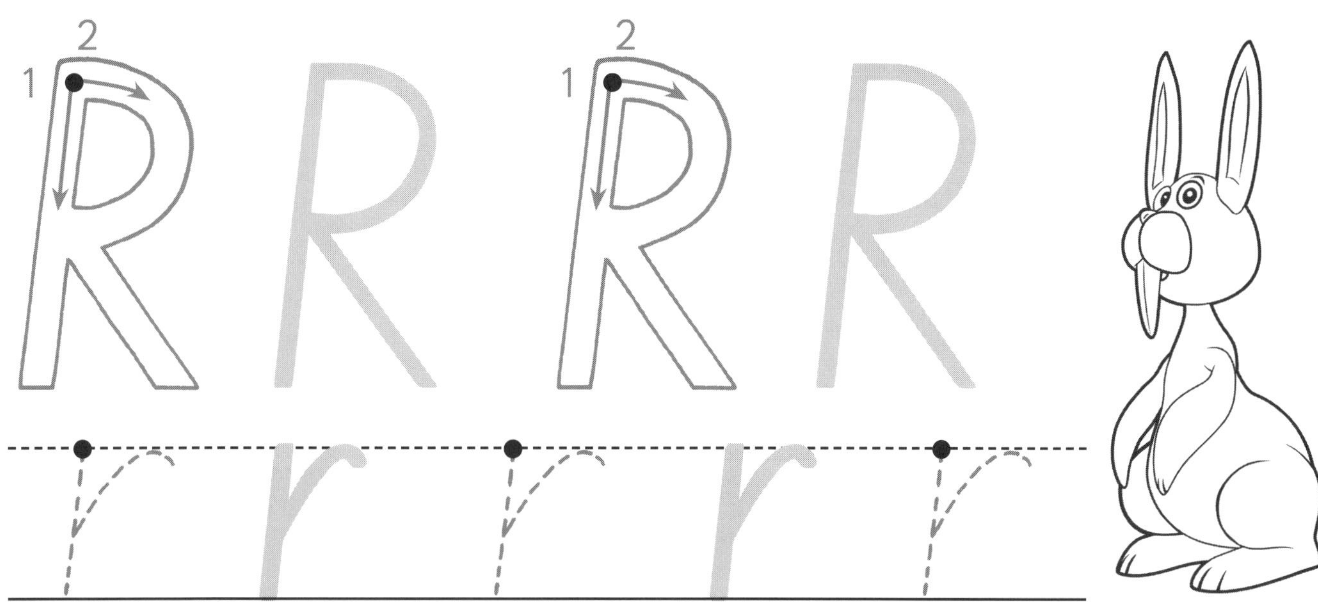

2 Circle every **R**.

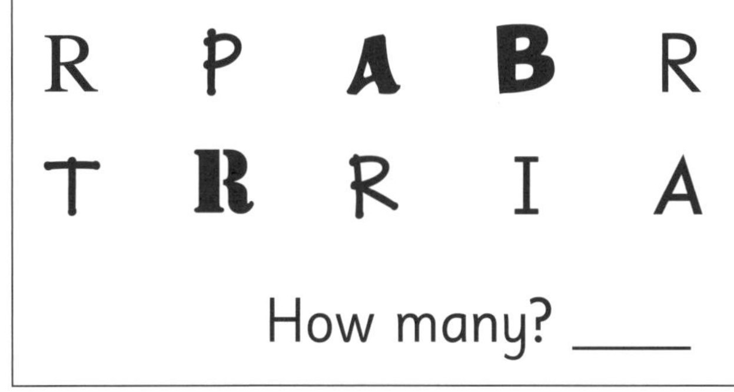

Circle every **r**.

3 Circle the beginning sound.

r s

p r

t r

r f

Lesson 16 the sound **an**

Learning objectives

Children will:

- identify the sound an.
- identify words that contain the rime an.
- write an words.

Australian Curriculum Content Descriptions

Sound and letter knowledge

ACELA1439 identify and manipulate sounds (phonemes) in spoken words

Expressing and developing ideas

ACELA1435 learn that word order in sentences is important for meaning

ACELA1438 build word families using onset and rime

ACELA1758 recognise the most common sound made by each letter of the alphabet, including consonants and short vowel sounds

Interpreting, analysing and evaluating

ACELY1649 navigate a text correctly, starting at the right place and reading in the right direction, returning to the next line as needed, matching one spoken word to one written word

Sight words

an, I, am, can, a

Word families

an, man, can, ran, van, pan, hand, dance, land, ant, fan

Vocabulary words

Sam, bat, cat, rat

ESL/ELL

Many languages do not distinguish between long and short vowel sounds. Give students opportunities to practise pronunciation with pairs of words, eg man and mane, can and cane, lad and laid, or tongue twisters.

Can a man fan the van?

I ran from the pan to the man.

Extra assistance

To help students sound out simple consonant-vowel-consonant words like man and van, the idea of a head, body and tail can be used. For visual learners this could be done using cut-outs of animal heads, bodies and tails on which they write the letters. For kinaesthetic learners it could involve nodding, wriggling and stamping as they sound the word out.

Reading Eggs Lesson sequence	TEACH Content and skills	PRACTISE Children will:	APPLY
Hear: *Animated Lesson*	Introduce the rime an through words and the song *Changing with an.*	identify the sound an in isolation and in a word.	**Worksheet 1** Word family
Write: *Make a Sentence*	Recognise correct word order for a sentence.	choose the correct words to make a sentence.	**Worksheet 2** Read and write
Find: *Climb the Ladder, Rhyming Squares, Trains*	Recognise the word can. Identify rhyming words. Recognise letters in both upper and lower case.	find the given word. Find images of rhyming words. Match lower case and upper case letters.	**Worksheet 3** Initial sounds
Vocabulary: *Label It, Blend a Word, Word family, Tiles*	Build vocabulary skills: Blend and recognise words. Identify the correct onset letter to complete the word.	blend sounds to read words and recognise them. Match words to pictures.	**Worksheet 4** Vocabulary
Read: *Book*	Read aloud book.	listen, follow the reading and read along.	**Reading Eggs Story book** Sam can bat

Classroom activities

Which One?

Put a list of words on the board and ask students if you use the word an or a in front of each word, or neither. Use singular and plural nouns starting with vowels and consonants, but also a couple of verbs and adjectives. See if the children can come up with the rules for using a or an.

Find the Start

Give pairs of students a pair of words with the first letter missing. Ask them to figure out which letter could be the starter for both the given words, for example: _an & _at, _an & _am, _an & _ap and so on. Discuss their answers as a class. Was there more than 1 possible answer for any pairs of words?

Related Reading Eggs Activities, Interactives, Songs and Books

Reading Eggs Playroom

Book Shelf Song

Books:

The Ants Go Marching

Animal Corner:

Animal games

Music Café

Changing with an

Reading Eggs Puzzle Park

Alphabet Match

Reading Eggs Posters

Reading Eggs Library Books

My Program Books

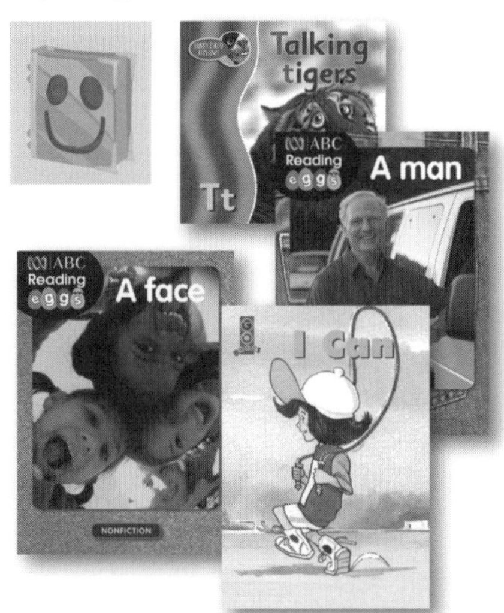

Alphabet Flashcards

Game 7 – Making words using the an cards.

Teacher Toolkit

Targeting Handwriting Interactively

Alphabet Activities

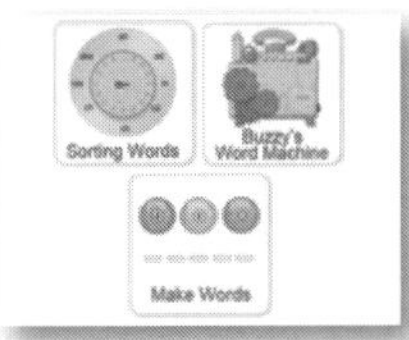

Reading Eggs Apps

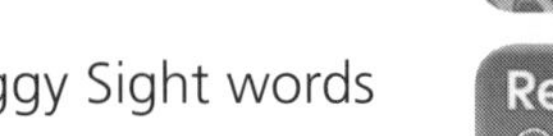

Eggy Alphabet

Eggy Sight words

Critter Card

Ratacanbat

Lesson 16 • Worksheet 1

Name

Word family

1 Join each letter to the word machine.
Write each word you make.

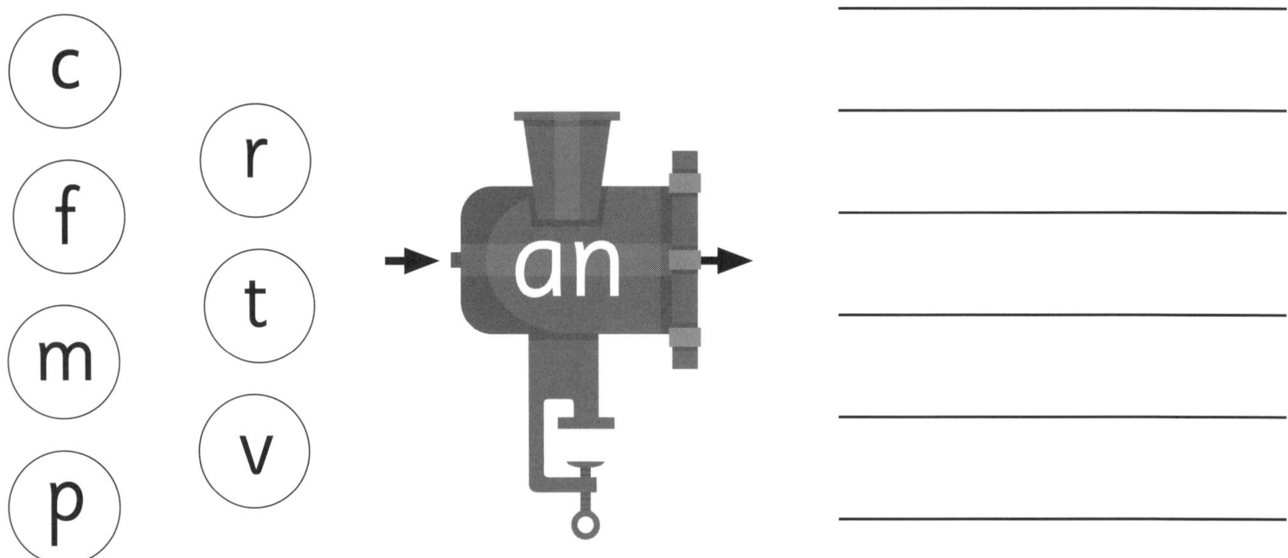

2 Colour the **an** pictures and write their label.

Name

Read and write

1 Choose a word and finish the sentence.

Sam cat

A ________ can bat.

________ can pat.

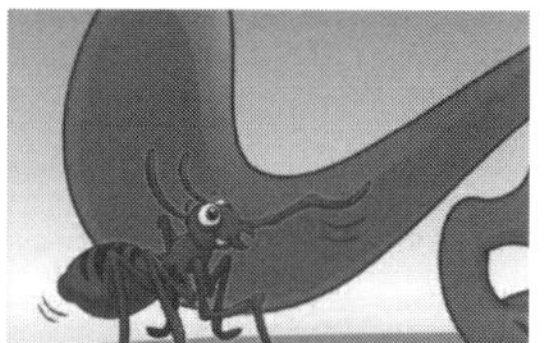

2 Read the questions and circle the answer.

Can a man pat? Yes No

Can a fan nap? Yes No

Can a pan zap? Yes No

Can a hand tap? Yes No

3 Finish the sentences.

I can ________ .

I can ________ .

Lesson 16 • Worksheet 3

Name

Initial sounds

1 Finish the **an** words.

2 Circle the initial sounds.

Name

Vocabulary

an

Lesson 16 · Worksheet 4

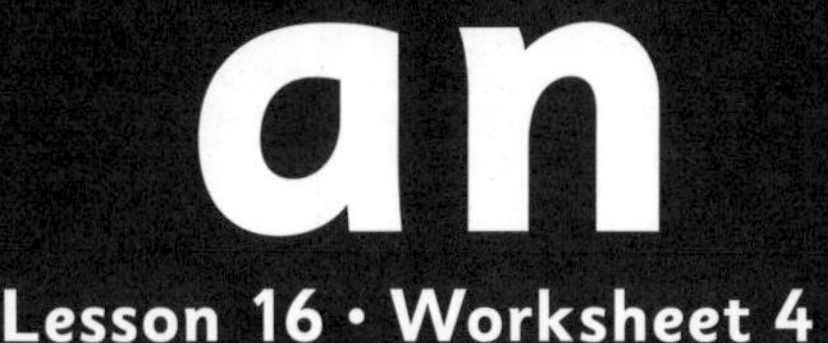

1 Colour the rhyming words.

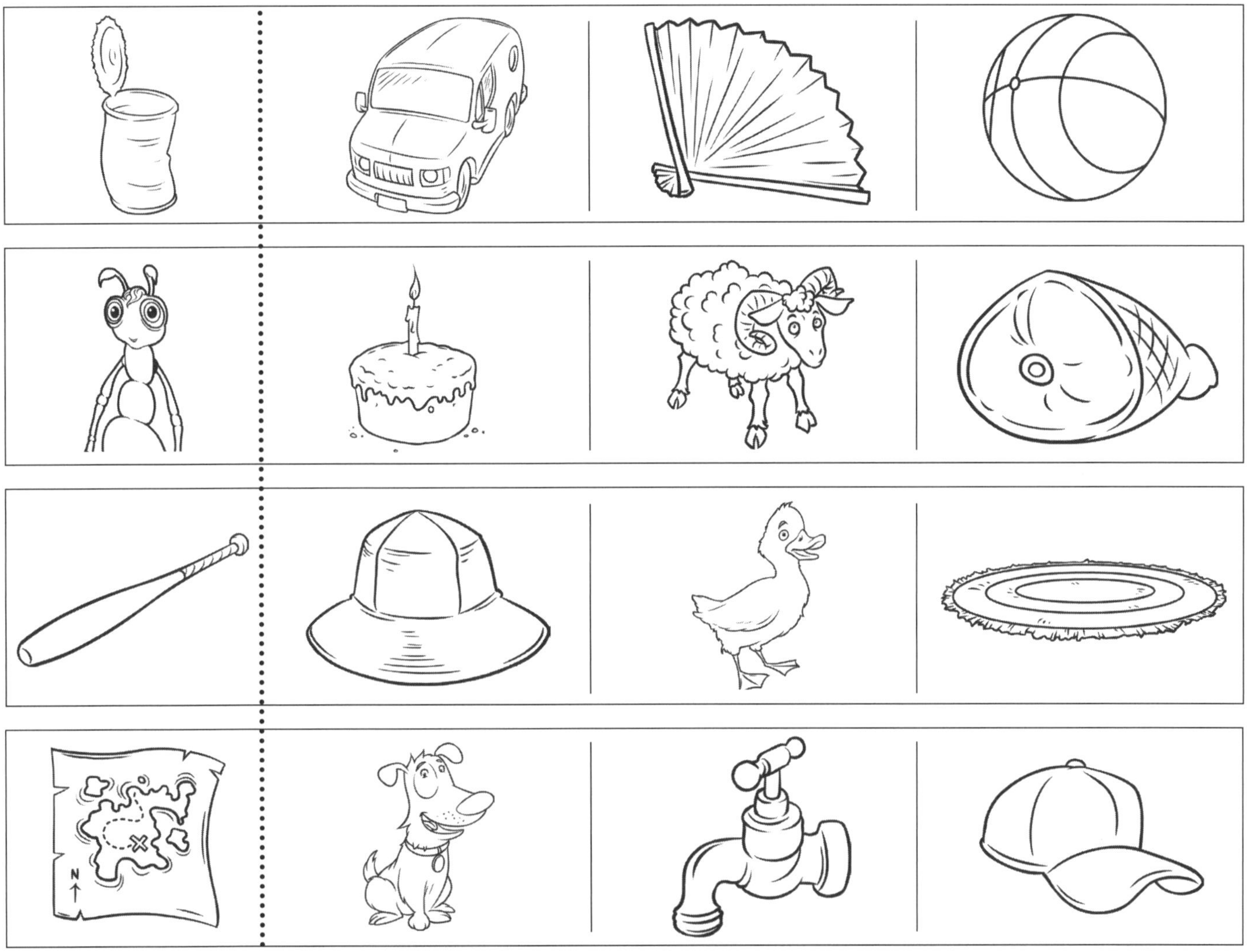

2 How many other rhyming words can you think of?

____

____

____

Lesson 17 the letter **z**

Learning objectives

Children will:

- identify the sound z.
- identify words that contain z.
- recognise and write z and Z.

Australian Curriculum Content Descriptions

Sound and letter knowledge

ACELA1439 identify and manipulate sounds (phonemes) in spoken words

ACELA1440 identify familiar and recurring letters and the use of upper and lower case in written texts

Creating texts

ACELY1653 follow clear demonstrations of how to construct each letter, learn to construct lower case letters

Expressing and developing ideas

ACELA1758 recognise the most common sound made by each letter of the alphabet, including consonants and short vowel sounds

Vocabulary words

zero, zebra, zigzag, zucchini, zoom, zip, zoo, zap

ESL/ELL

Students who speak Spanish, Tagalog, Korean or Hmong may not distinguish between /z/ and /s/. Give them opportunities to practise pairs of words, eg sit and zit, zoo and sue, bus and buzz.

Extra assistance

To help students differentiate the sounds /z/ and /s/, have them put a hand on their throat. For /s/ we do not use the voice, just breath, so there should be no movement in the throat. When making a /z/, the voice is used and they can feel vibrations in the throat.

Classroom activities

Brainstorm

Brainstorm a list of words that start with the /z/ sound. Then make a second list of words that end with the /z/ sound. Illustrate them or act them out.

Throw it Away!

Sit in a circle with a box in the middle. Students each hold two items or pictures or words on cards. The teacher says a word. If the child has an object starting with the same first letter they throw it into the box. Discuss the objects in each round.

Reading Eggs Lesson sequence	TEACH Content and skills	PRACTISE Children will:	APPLY
Hear: *Animated Lesson*	Introduce the sound /z/ through words and the song *Zippy Z*.	identify and read /z/ sound in isolation and in words.	**Worksheet 1** Phonemic awareness
Write: *Dot-to-Dot*	Reinforce correct letter formation of lower case z.	write the letter z.	**Worksheet 2** Handwriting
Find: *Letter Grid, Mark Your Letter and Missing Sound*	Recognise z in both upper and lower case. Identify the correct onset letter to complete the word.	locate lower case z and capital Z. Choose the correct initial letter to make the an word.	**Worksheet 3** Initial and end sounds
Vocabulary: *Letter Book, Sound Streamers, Wheel of Words and In the Box*	Build vocabulary skills: Match pictures to words. Blend sounds to make words.	blend and read key vocabulary and match to pictures. Match pictures to their initial letter.	**Worksheet 4** Check
Read: *Book*	Read aloud book.	listen, follow the reading and read along.	**Reading Eggs Alphabet Book** z

Related Reading Eggs Activities, Interactives, Songs and Books

Reading Eggs Playroom

Alphabet Activities

Book Shelf Song

Books:
Alphabet Song

Puzzle Table

Play kitchen:
Making pizza

Music Café

Zippy Z

Reading Eggs Puzzle Park

Alphabet Match

Reading Eggs Posters

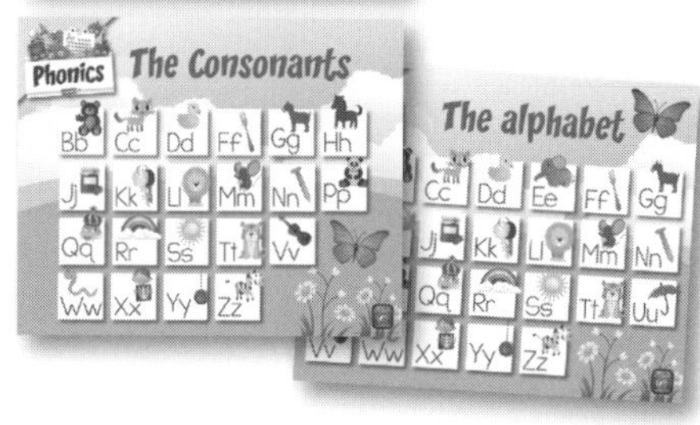

Reading Eggs Library Books

My Program Books

Alphabet Flashcards

Game 2 – Sound puzzles using z and other known letters.

Teacher Toolkit

Targeting Handwriting Interactively

Alphabet Activities

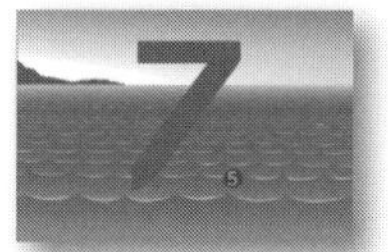

Reading Eggs Apps

Eggy Alphabet

Critter Card

Zebstar

Zz

Lesson 17 • Worksheet 1

Name

Phonemic awareness

Colour the pictures that start with **z**.

z z z z z z

Name

Handwriting

Zz

Lesson 17 • Worksheet 2

1 Trace Happy Nap's snores.

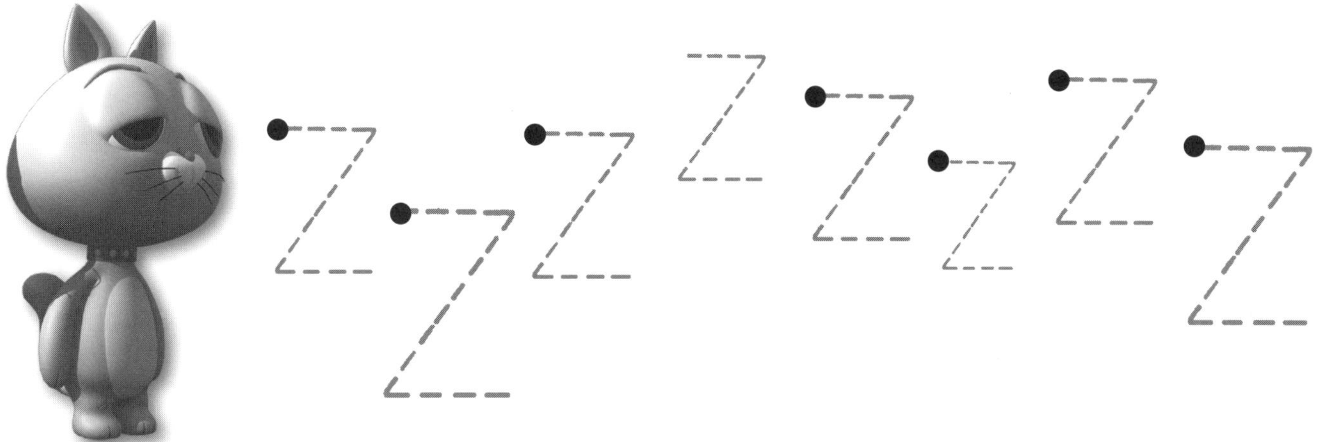

2 Trace and write.

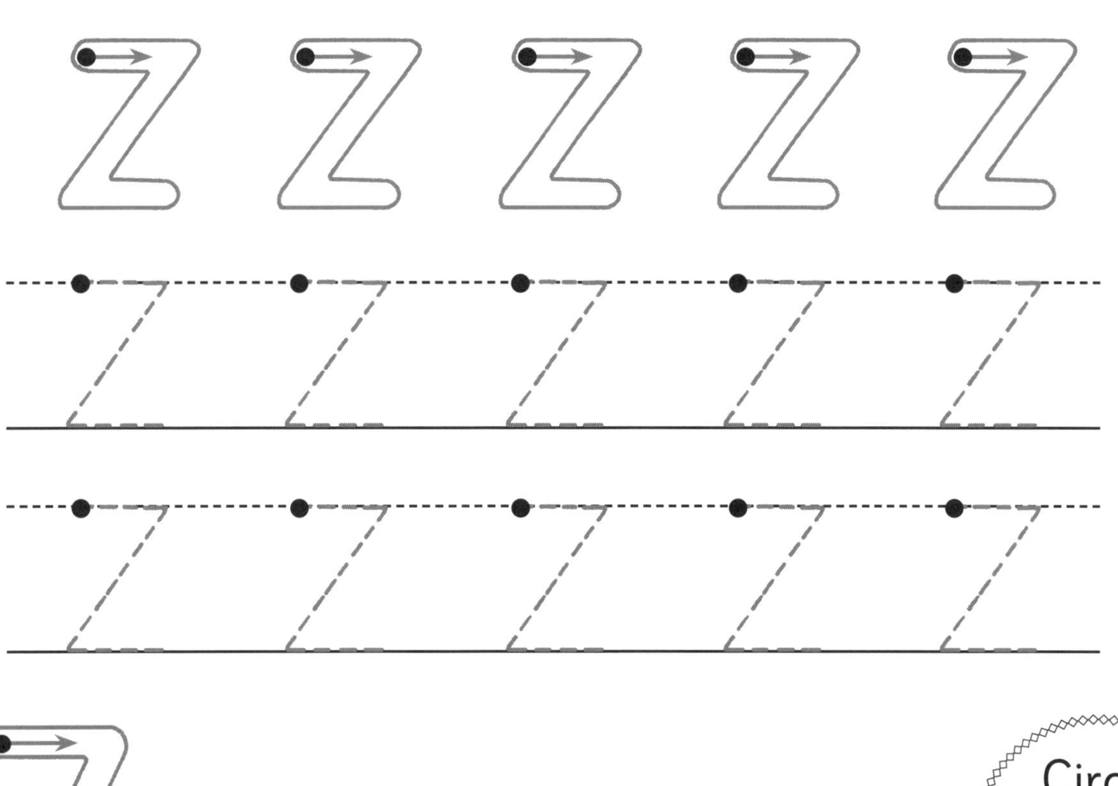

Circle your best letter.

Zz

Lesson 17 • Worksheet 3

Name

Initial and end sounds

1 Add **z** and read the word.

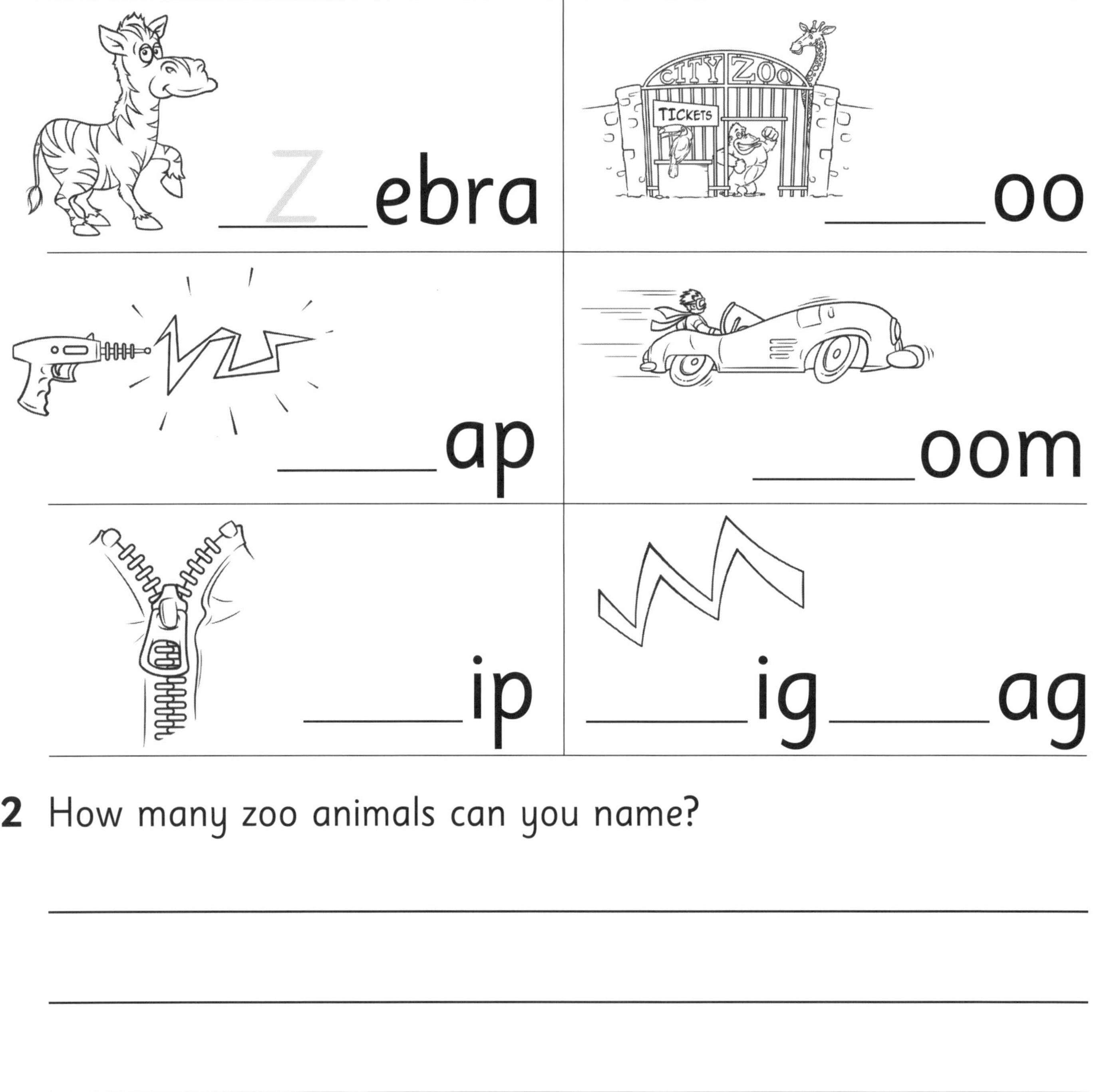

2 How many zoo animals can you name?

Name

Check

Zz

Lesson 17 • Worksheet 4

1 Trace.

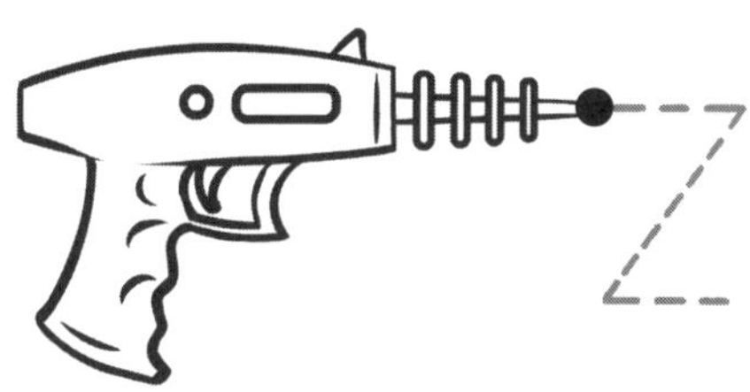

zap

2 Circle every **Z**.

Z	Z	S	Z	P
N	M	Z	I	Z

How many? ____

Circle every **z**.

z	m	z	t	s
z	p	s	z	z

How many? ____

3 Match each letter to a picture.

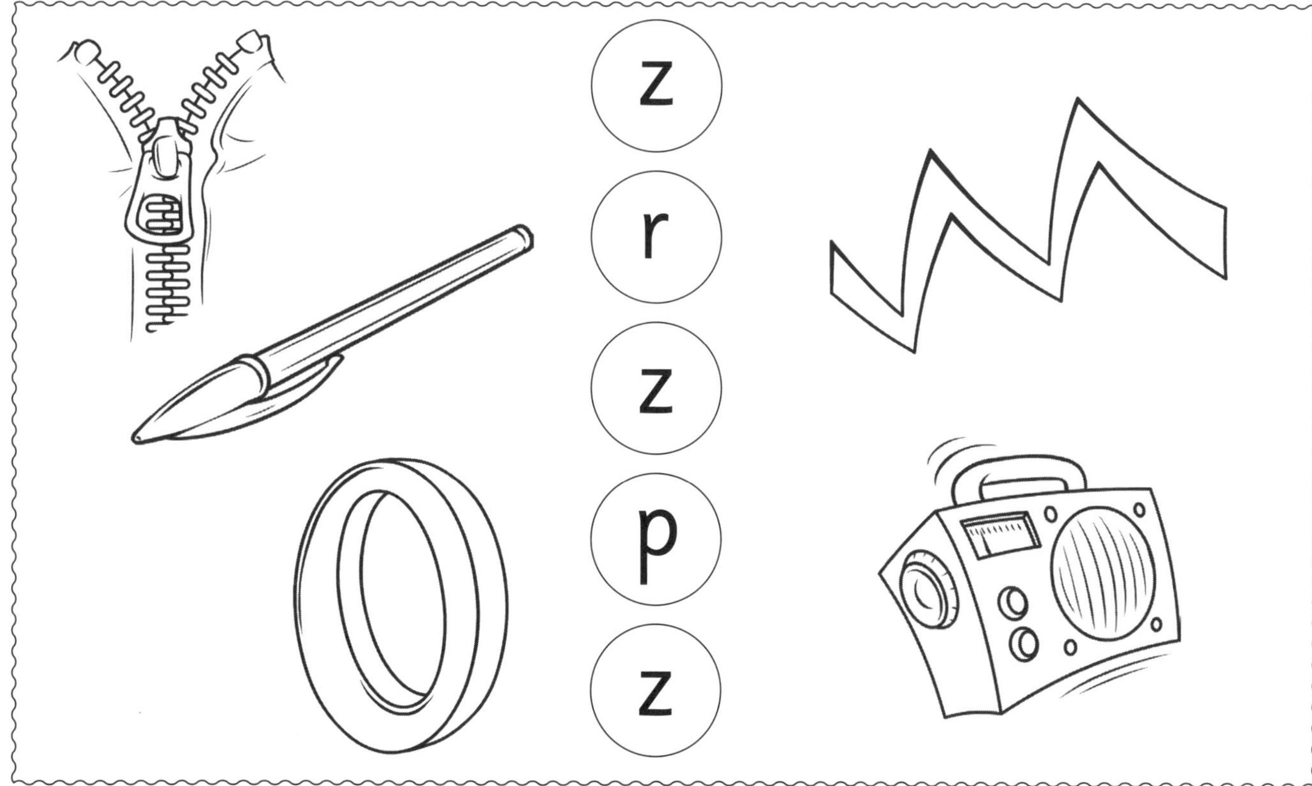

Lesson 18 the letter *e* and sound *ee*

Learning objectives

Children will:

- identify the sound ee.
- identify words that contain ee.
- recognise and write e and E.

Australian Curriculum Content Descriptions

Sound and letter knowledge

ACELA1439 identify and manipulate sounds (phonemes) in spoken words

ACELA1440 identify familiar and recurring letters and the use of upper and lower case in written texts

Creating texts

ACELY1653 follow clear demonstrations of how to construct each letter, learn to construct lower case letters

Expressing and developing ideas

ACELA1758 recognise the most common sound made by each letter of the alphabet, including consonants and short vowel sounds

Word families

cheek, bee, cheese, queen, knee, jeep, seed, leek, sheep, tree, see, weed, teepee, tee, three

Vocabulary words

egg, eat, engine, elbow, ear, eagle, envelope, elephant

ESL/ELL

Other languages often do not distinguish between long and short vowel sounds. Students may mix them up when reading aloud and speaking. Find games for them to play where correct pronunciation and identification of sounds is important, like Bingo with word pairs such as fell and feel, met and meet, and so on.

Extra assistance

In many languages each sound has its own letter or symbol, so some students will need help to know when a vowel is pronounced with a short or long sound. The pair of sounds represented by e and ee are one instance to practise and learn.

Classroom activities

Decorate the Letters

Provide the students with a piece of paper that has many different forms of letter e on it – some dotted, some in bubble writing, some solid letters, a couple of capitals:

- trace over the dotted letters with different coloured pencils, textas or crayons
- glue collage materials such as paper bits, leaves or wool to the solid letters
- colour in the bubble letters with dots, stripes or shapes

Reading Eggs Lesson sequence	**TEACH Content and skills**	**PRACTISE Children will:**	**APPLY**
Hear: *Animated Lesson*	Introduce the sound /ee/ through words and the song *1 and 2 makes ee.*	identify and read /ee/ sound in isolation and in words.	**Worksheet 1** Phonemic awareness
Write: *Dot-to-Dot*	Reinforce correct letter formation of lower case e.	write the letter e.	**Worksheet 2** Handwriting
Find: *Frog Hops, Missing Sound, Letter Grid and Golden Goose*	Recognise a given word. Identify the correct onset letter for a word. Recognise e in both upper and lower case.	find the given word in a group. Choose the correct initial letter to make the word. Locate lower case e and capital E.	**Worksheet 3** Middle and end sounds
Vocabulary: *Label It, Blend a Word, Word Windows and Break it Up*	Build vocabulary skills: Match pictures to words. Blend words. Identify the number of phonemes in a word.	blend sounds to read words. Match words to pictures. Identify the number of sounds in a word.	**Worksheet 4** Vocabulary
Read: *Book*	Read aloud book.	listen, follow the reading and read along.	**Reading Eggs Alphabet book** e

Classroom activities

Mix and Match

Put the consonant letters of the alphabet on the board in writing or magnetic letters. Write the sound ee on the board. Each student comes to the board and writes a word they can make using ee and some of the other letters. Discuss their words with the class.

Related Reading Eggs Activities, Interactives, Songs and Books

Reading Eggs Playroom

Alphabet Activities

Book Shelf Song Books:
Alphabet Song,
Baa Baa Black Sheep,
The Wheels on the Bus

Paint Easel: Reggie Egg colouring in

Music Café

1 and 2 makes ee

Reading Eggs Puzzle Park

Alphabet Match

Reading Eggs Posters

Reading Eggs Library Books

My Program Books

Alphabet Flashcards

Game 6 – Critter Concentration using e and other known letters.

Teacher Toolkit

Targeting Handwriting Interactively

Alphabet Activities

Reading Eggs Apps

Eggy Alphabet

Eggy Phonics 1

Critter Card

Eggyphant

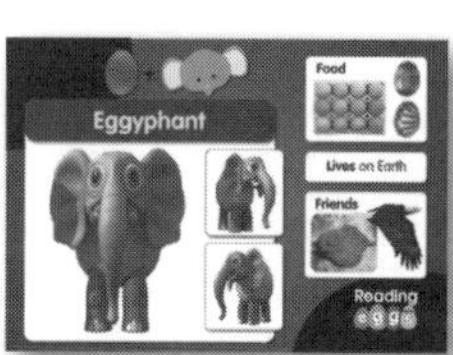

Name

Phonemic awareness

1 Colour the eggs that begin with **e**.

2 Add **e** and read the word.

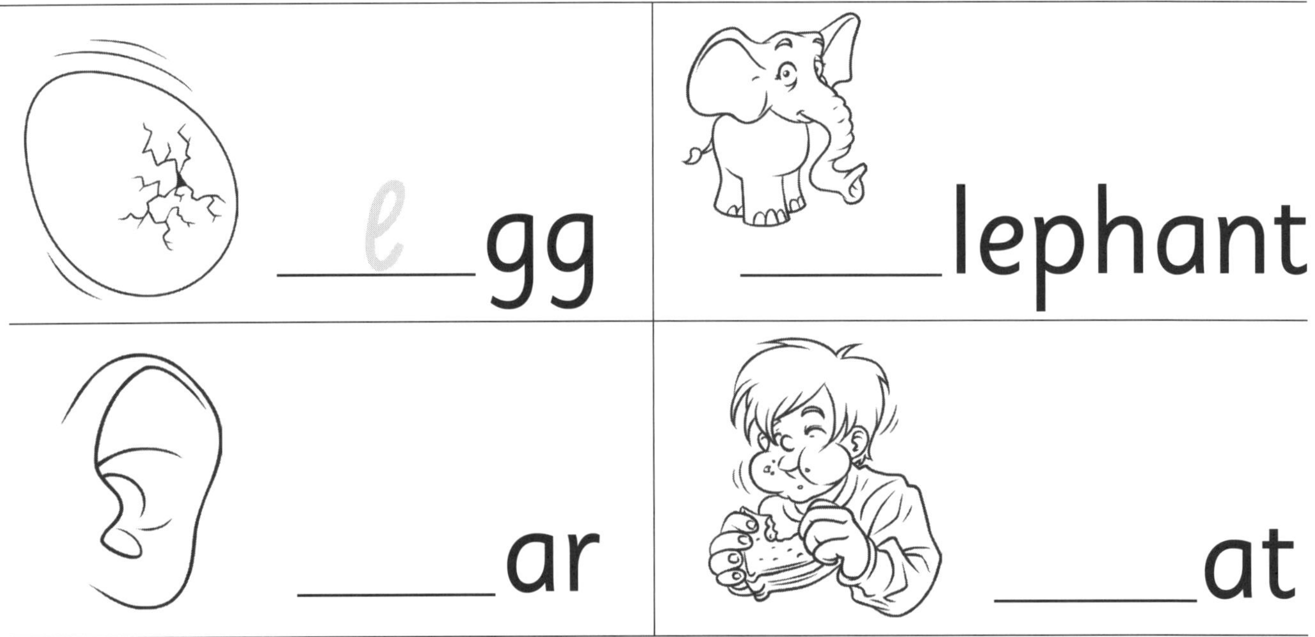

Name

Handwriting

Ee

Lesson 18 • Worksheet 2

1 Complete the ladders.

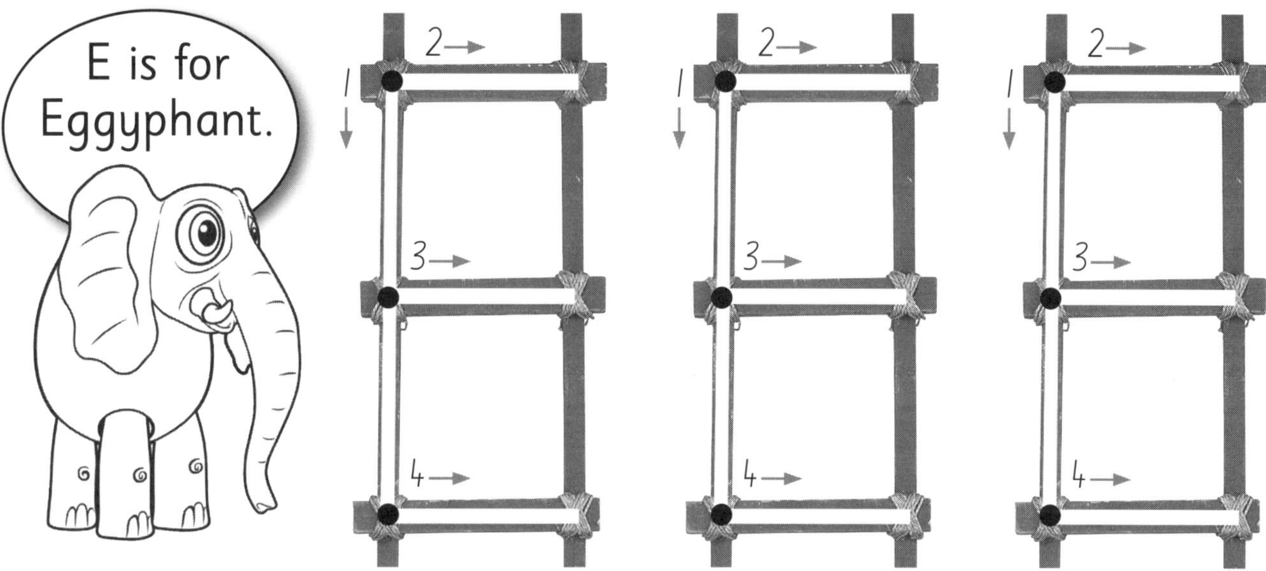

2 Trace and write.

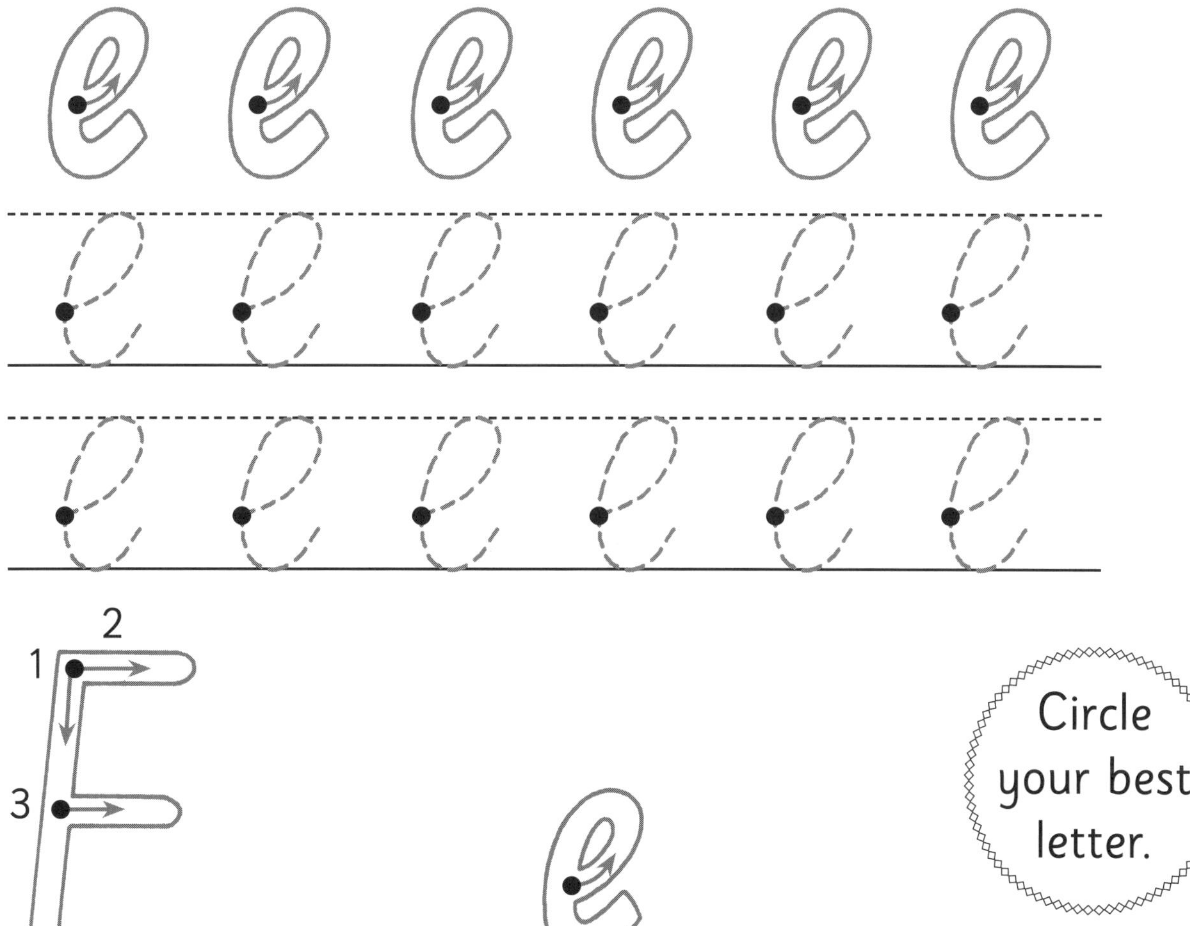

ee

Lesson 18 · Worksheet 3

Name

Middle and end sounds

1 Add **ee** and read the word.

b ________	t ________ th
s ________	tr ________
f ________ t	s ________ d
thr ________	sh ________ p

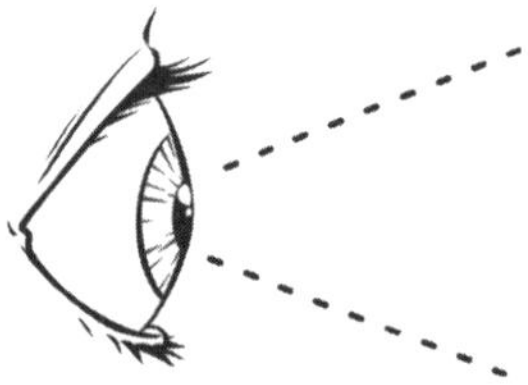

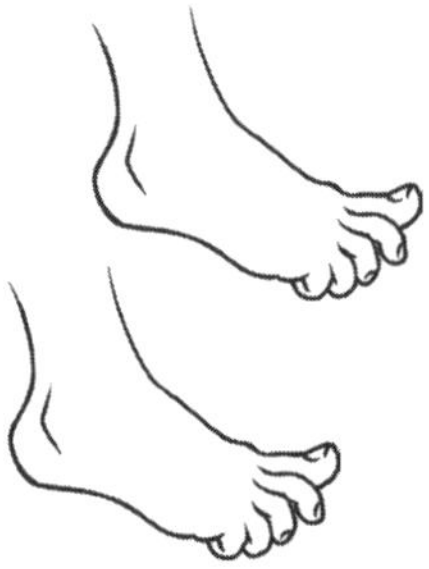

2 Draw more curls.

Name

Vocabulary

1 Join the jigsaw pieces together. Write the word.

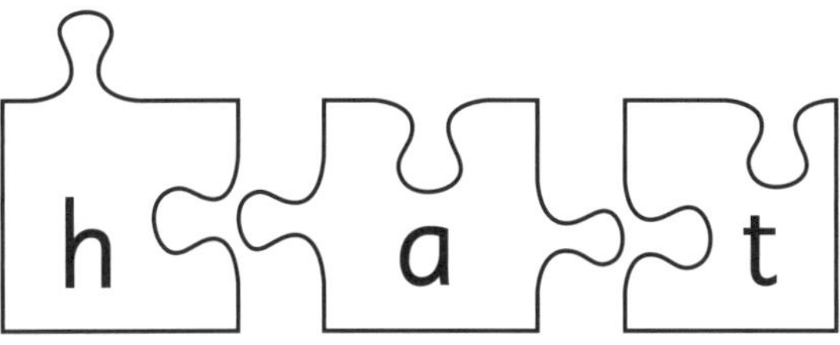

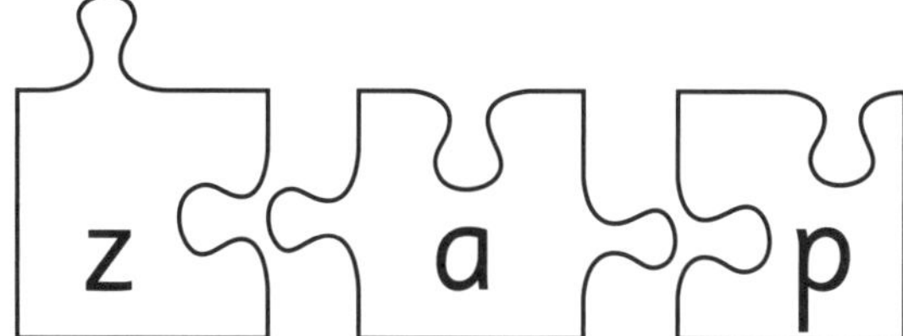

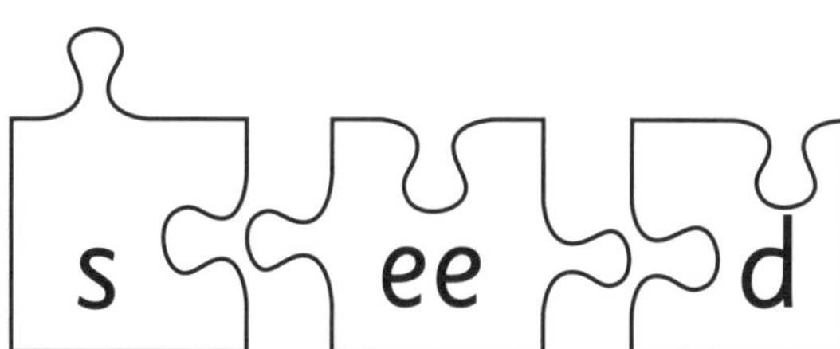

2 Colour the number of sounds in each word.

1 2 3

1 2 3

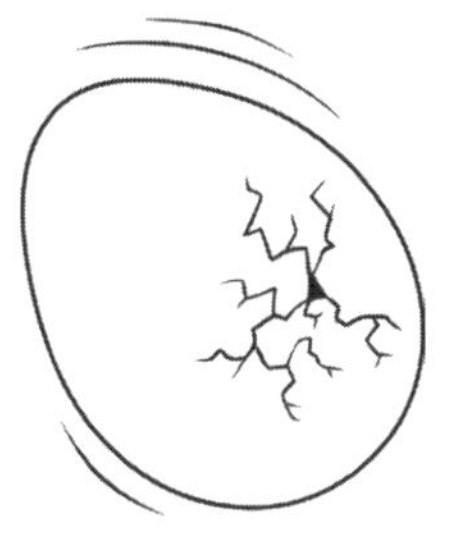

1 2 3

1 2 3

Lesson 19 the words **see** and **the**

Learning objectives

Children will:

- identify the sight words see and the.
- read and use the words see and the.
- review word families at, an, ap, am, ee.

Australian Curriculum Content Descriptions

Sound and letter knowledge

ACELA1439 identify and manipulate sounds (phonemes) in spoken words

Expressing and developing ideas

ACELA1435 learn that word order in sentences is important for meaning

ACELA1758 recognise the most common sound made by each letter of the alphabet, including consonants and short vowel sounds

Interpreting, analysing and evaluating

ACELY1649 navigate a text correctly, starting at the right place and reading in the right direction, returning to the next line as needed, matching one spoken word to one written word

Sight words

the, I, at, can, am, see

Word families

at, hat, sat, rat, cat, mat, fat, man, pan, can, fan, ran, tap, zap, map, cap, see, bee, am, Sam

ESL/ELL

English language learners need to understand that in the English language there are 26 letters, but there are actually 44 sounds. So far students will have encountered long and short vowel sounds (with the letters a, e and i), and the word *the* may be the first word they learn with a blend in it, introducing a new idea about sounds.

Extra assistance

Learning sight words is invaluable for all students, as these are words that occur frequently in all types of texts. They are often tricky words to sound out as they may not stick to the rules. Knowing sight words 'on sight' makes fluent reading easier.

Classroom activities

Can you use it?

Put a list of words on the board and ask students if you can put the word *the* in front of each word. Use singular and plural nouns, verbs and adjectives. See if the children can explain why some words work and some don't.

Mind the Gap!

Write this sentence on the board: I can see ___. Ask students to read this sentence by themselves, write it down and fill in the gap with a word of their own. Discuss their individual sentences as a group.

Reading Eggs Lesson sequence	TEACH Content and skills	PRACTISE Children will:	APPLY
Hear: *Animated Lesson*	Introduce the words the and see through words and the song *Sam can see*.	identify and read the words the and see in isolation and in sentences.	**Worksheet 1** Sight words
Write: *Pick up Bricks*	Recognise correct word order for a sentence.	put the words in the correct order to make a sentence.	**Worksheet 2** Writing sentences
Find: *Honey Bees, Send a Letter, Letter Lights and Missing Sound*	Recognise a given word. Recognise letters in upper and lower case. Identify the correct letter to complete the word.	find the given word in a group. Match lower case and capital letters. Choose the correct letter to make the word.	**Worksheet 3** Missing sounds
Vocabulary: *Sound Streamers, Fishing Boats, Tiles and Time for 20*	Build vocabulary skills: Identify sounds in words. Read and identify simple words. Match aural and written words.	sound out and select letters to make words. Match words to their picture. Find the word being said aloud.	**Worksheet 4** Word families
Read: *Book*	Read aloud book.	listen, follow the reading and read along.	**Reading Eggs Story book** Sam can see

Related Reading Eggs Activities, Interactives, Songs and Books

Reading Eggs Playroom

Alphabet Activities

Book Shelf Song

Books:
Alphabet Song

Play Mat:
Word blocks

Music Café

Sam can see

Reading Eggs Puzzle Park

Alphabet Match

Reading Eggs Posters

Reading Eggs Library Books

My Program Books

Alphabet Flashcards

Game 7 – Making words using known letters.

Teacher Toolkit

Targeting Handwriting Interactively

Alphabet Activities

Reading Eggs Apps

Eggy Sight words

Critter Card

Zeewee

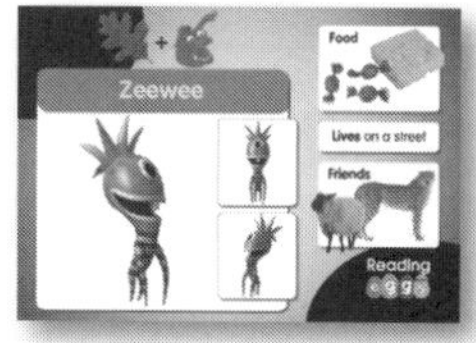

see the

Lesson 19 • Worksheet 1

Name

Sight words

1 Use **the** or **see** to finish the sentences.

I can ________ the cat.

I can see ________ hat.

I can ________ ________ bee.

2 Colour **the** in green and **see** in brown.

can	can	the	the	the	the	am	am
can	the	the	the	the	the	the	am
can	the	the	the	the	the	the	am
am	am	the	the	the	the	am	am
am	am	am	see	see	can	can	can
at	can	can	see	see	at	can	can
at	can	can	see	see	at	at	at
at	can	see	see	see	see	at	at

I can see the ________ .

Name

Writing sentences

Finish each sentence. Use the words in the box.

man a the Sam can
hat see am cat I

I can see ____________________
____

Sam can ____________________
____

The man ____________________
____

see the

Lesson 19 • Worksheet 3

Name

Missing sounds

Finish the words.

s ________	t ________
f ________	h ________
b ________	m ________
p ________	s ________

Name

Colour the word families: **at** in blue, **an** in red, **ee** in green.

Lesson 20 Review

Learning objectives

Children will:

- review the sounds n, p, h, r, e, z, at, ap, an and ee.
- revise the words see, the and can.
- identify and read the word you.

Australian Curriculum Content Descriptions

Sound and letter knowledge

ACELA1439 identify and manipulate sounds (phonemes) in spoken words

ACELA1440 identify familiar and recurring letters and the use of upper and lower case in written texts

Expressing and developing ideas

ACELA1435 learn that word order in sentences is important for meaning

ACELA1758 recognise the most common sound made by each letter of the alphabet, including consonants and short vowel sounds

Interpreting, analysing and evaluating

ACELY1649 navigate a text correctly, starting at the right place and reading in the right direction, returning to the next line as needed, matching one spoken word to one written word

Sight words

see, the, can, you, I

Word families

see, bee, bat, cat, hat, Sam, man

Vocabulary words

bees, bats, cats

ESL/ELL

As students learn more letters, be sure to give them lots of opportunities to revise the letters they have already learnt. A lot of games traditionally played with a pack of cards or with numbers can be played using letter cards with both the lower and upper case letters on them: Bingo, Snap, Go Fish and Concentration or Memory for example.

Extra assistance

Blending different onsets and rimes to make new words can cater for visual learners by using animal bodies for rimes and a variety of animal heads for the onsets. Students can have fun making crazy creatures while learning to blend and recognise words they know, reinforcing the idea of the onset and the rime.

Classroom activities

How does it end?

Give the students a letter each (b, c, f, h, m, n, p, r, s, t, z), either written on a card or a magnetic letter. Write the sounds at, am, ap, an and ee on the top of the board. Each student comes to the board and writes the words they can make using their initial letter and any of the endings. Discuss their words with the class.

Reading Eggs Lesson sequence	**TEACH Content and skills**	**PRACTISE Children will:**	**APPLY**
Hear: *Animated Lesson*	Revise words and sounds learnt so far with the song *Running revision*.	identify the words and sounds learnt so far.	**Worksheet 1** Phonemic awareness
Write: *Make a Sentence*	Recognise correct word order for a sentence.	choose the correct words to make a sentence.	**Worksheet 2** Read and write
Find: *Build a Wall, Trains, Jumping Astronauts*	Identify sight words. Recognise both upper and lower case letters.	match and find sight words. Match lower case and capital letters.	**Worksheet 3** Sight words
Vocabulary: *Blend a Word, Fishing Boats, Tiles, Rhyming Squares, Break it Up*	Build vocabulary skills: Blend and read simple words. Recognise rhyming words. Identify the number of phonemes in a word.	blend sounds to read and make words. Match words to their picture. Find images of rhyming words. Identify the number of sounds in a word.	**Worksheet 4** Vocabulary
Read: *Book*	Read aloud book.	listen, follow the reading and read along.	**Reading Eggs Story book** Can you see?

Classroom activities

Make your own questions

Students use their own words to complete the question, Can you see the __? For example: Can you see the floor? Can you see the car? Can you see the book?

Then they swap with another student and answer the questions with yes or no.

Related Reading Eggs Activities, Interactives, Songs and Books

Reading Eggs Playroom

Alphabet Activities

Book Shelf Song

Books:

Alphabet Song,

Row Row Row Your Boat,

Baa Baa Black Sheep

My Wall:

Make you!

Music Café

Running revision

Reading Eggs Puzzle Park

Alphabet Match

More than One

Reading Eggs Posters

Reading Eggs Library Books

Teacher Toolkit

Targeting Handwriting Interactively

Alphabet Activities

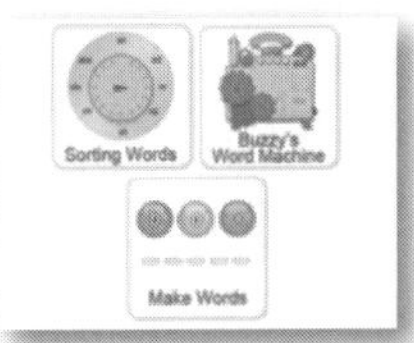

My Program Books

Reading Eggs Apps

Eggy Alphabet

Alphabet Flashcards

Game 5 – From a to z using known letters.

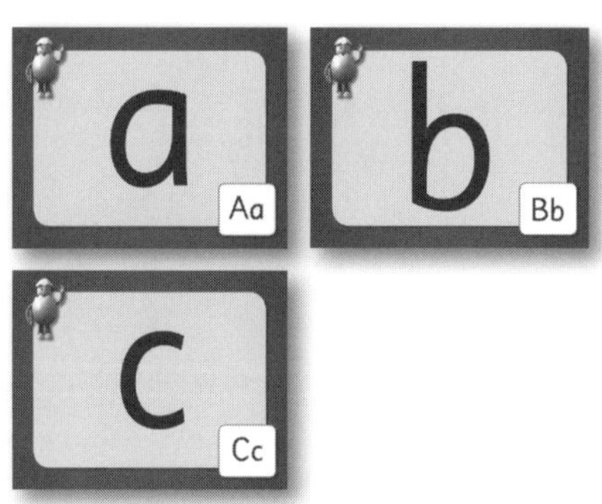

Critter Card

Fishtank castle

Review

Lesson 20 • Worksheet 1

Name

Phonemic awareness

1 Trace each letter. Match to a picture that starts with that letter.

2 Colour the letters you know.

a	b	c	d	e	f	g	h	i
j	k	l	m	n	o	p	q	r
s	t	u	v	w	x	y	z	★

Name

Read and write

Review

Lesson 20 • Worksheet 2

1 Put the words in the correct order.

bee. the See

____

hat. can
I the see

____

____

you fan?
Can see the

____

____

2 Put these words in correct order to make a question and answer.

see you
the Can
bats?

____

____

can I the
bats. see

____

____

Review

Lesson 20 · Worksheet 3

Name

Sight words

1 Finish the questions. Circle the answers.

Can ______ see Sam? Yes No

______ you see the bees? Yes No

Can you ______ the cats? Yes No

Can you see ______ bats? Yes No

2 Complete the sentences for yourself.

I can see ______________________.

I can see ______________________.

Name

Vocabulary

Review

Lesson 20 • Worksheet 4

Label the pictures.

1

2

1

3

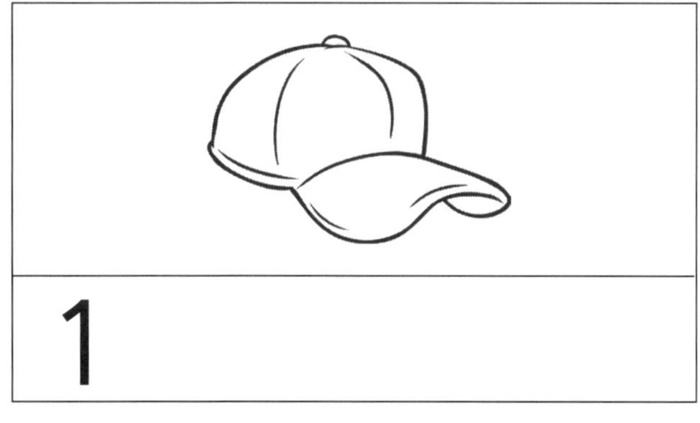

1

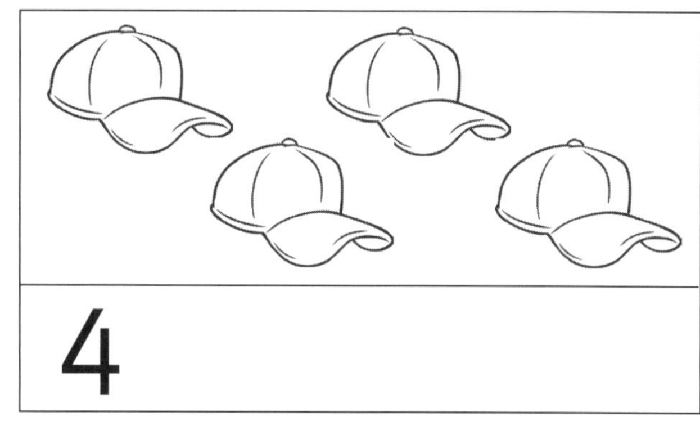

4

1

5

Lesson 21 the letter v

Learning objectives

Children will:

- identify the sound v.
- identify words that contain v.
- recognise and write v and V.

Australian Curriculum Content Descriptions

Sound and letter knowledge

ACELA1439 identify and manipulate sounds (phonemes) in spoken words

ACELA1440 identify familiar and recurring letters and the use of upper and lower case in written texts

Creating texts

ACELY1653 follow clear demonstrations of how to construct each letter, learn to construct lower case letters

Expressing and developing ideas

ACELA1758 recognise the most common sound made by each letter of the alphabet, including consonants and short vowel sounds

Sight words

see, the

Vocabulary words

van, vegetable, vet, violin, vase, vulture, volcano, vest

ESL/ELL

Students who speak Spanish may pronounce /v/ with a /b/ sound. Give them opportunities to hear the difference. Ask students to raise their hand when they hear a /v/ sound. Then say various words, enunciating clearly: van, ban, vegemite, bellow, vegetable, boat, and so on.

Extra assistance

Students learning a second language need to practise. Choral responses, where groups of students recite the same word, phrase, sentence or sound, are an effective tool to build familiarity with new sounds and vocabulary. Have the students repeat /v/ words after you to practise pronunciation.

Classroom activities

Buzzy Bee

Sit in a circle. Everyone says, 'Buzzy Bee, Buzzy Bee, what have you got in your hive for me? Something beginning with v!' Then students take turns around the circle naming something that begins with the sound /v/.

Bingo!

Give students a laminated board with 10 squares on it. Ask them to write a letter in each square from the list v, b, f, p (use whiteboard markers). Hold up pictures of items starting with v, b, f, p and say the name of the item in the picture. Students put a cross on that initial letter on their board. First one to 10 calls out 'bingo' and wins!

Reading Eggs Lesson sequence	**TEACH Content and skills**	**PRACTISE Children will:**	**APPLY**
Hear: *Animated Lesson*	Introduce the sound /v/ through words.	identify and read /v/ sound in isolation and in words.	**Worksheet 1** Phonemic awareness
Write: *Dot-to-Dot*	Reinforce correct letter formation of lower case v.	write the letter v.	**Worksheet 2** Handwriting
Find: *Letter Grid, Leaping Penguins, Letter Lights, Golden Goose*	Recognise v in both upper and lower case. Identify key vocabulary.	locate lower case v and capital V. Find the given word in a group.	**Worksheet 3** Initial sounds
Vocabulary: *Blend a Word, Letter Book, Label It, Sound Streamers*	Build vocabulary skills: Blend, read and recognise words. Match pictures to their initial letter and to words.	blend and read key vocabulary and match to pictures. Match pictures to their initial letter.	**Worksheet 4** Check
Read: *Book*	Read aloud book.	listen, follow the reading and read along.	**Reading Eggs Alphabet book** v

Related Reading Eggs Activities, Interactives, Songs and Books

Reading Eggs Playroom

Alphabet Activities

Book Shelf Song

Books:
Alphabet Song,
1-2-3-4-5

Play Mat:
Words with blocks

Music Café

Very Dirty Monsters

Reading Eggs Puzzle Park

Alphabet match

More than one

Reading Eggs Posters

Reading Eggs Library Books

My Program Books

Alphabet Flashcards

Game 3 - Sound hunt with the letter v.

Teacher Toolkit

Targeting Handwriting Interactively

Alphabet Activities

Reading Eggs Apps

Eggy Alphabet

Critter Card

Village van

Vv

Lesson 21 · Worksheet 1

Name

Phonemic awareness

Colour the pictures that start with **v**.

Name

Handwriting

Vv

Lesson 21 • Worksheet 2

1 Trace each bird's beak.

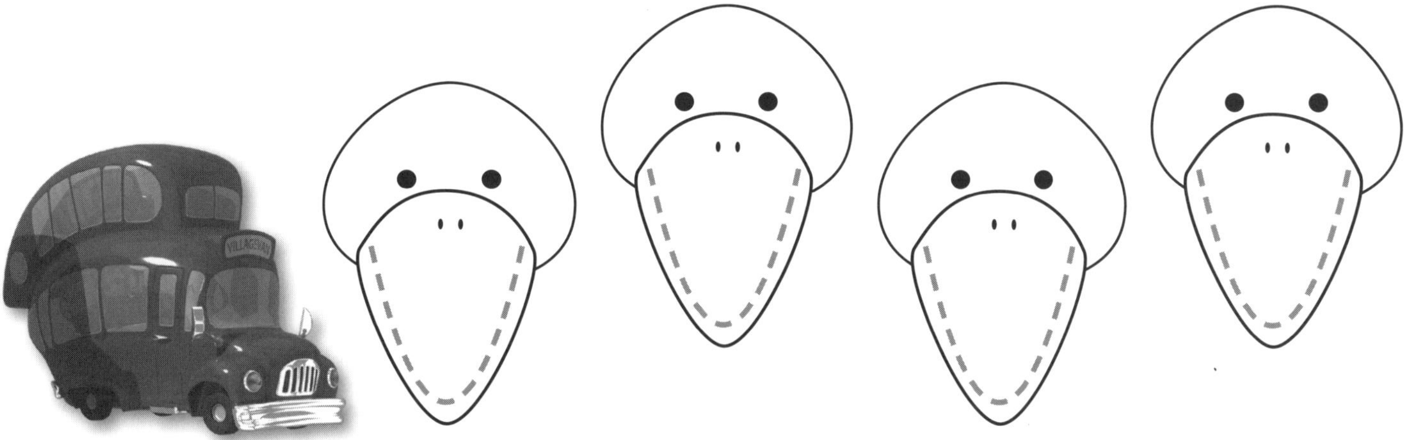

2 Trace and write.

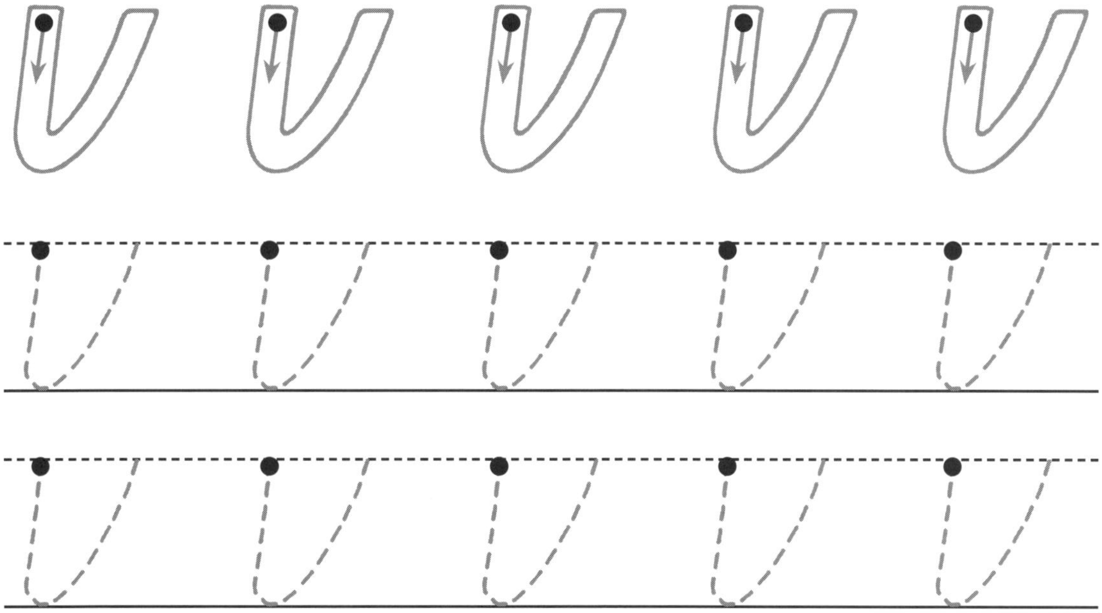

Circle your best letter.

Vv

Lesson 21 • Worksheet 3

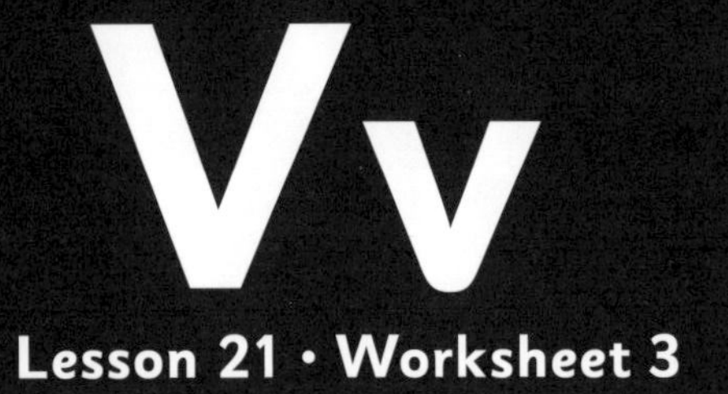

Name ______________________

Initial sounds

1 Add **v** and read the word.

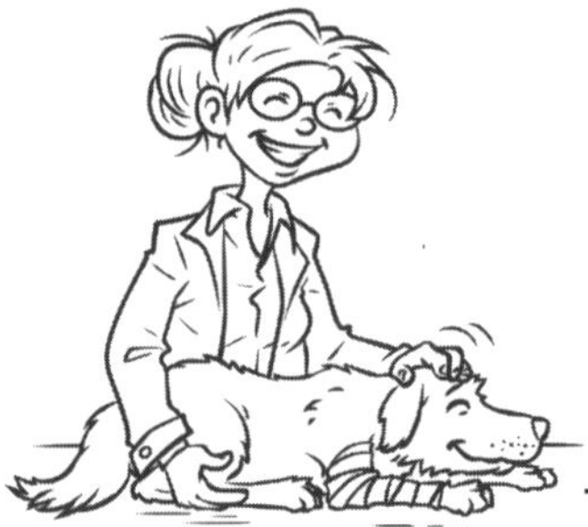

__v__et

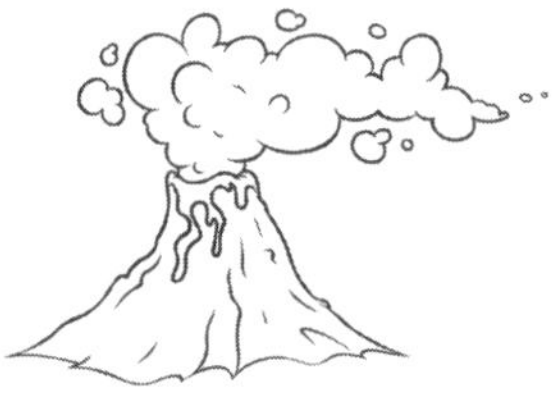

____olcano

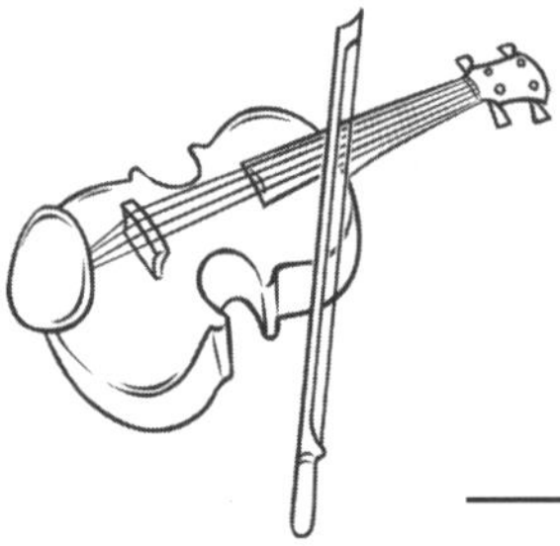

____iolin

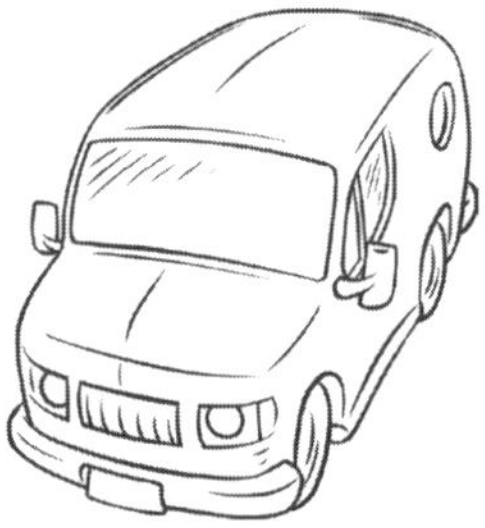

____an

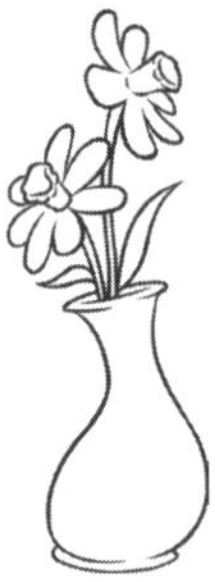

____ase

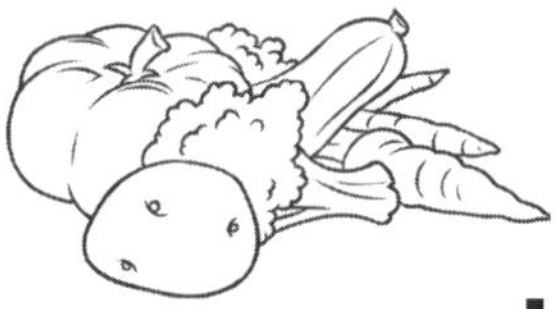

____egetables

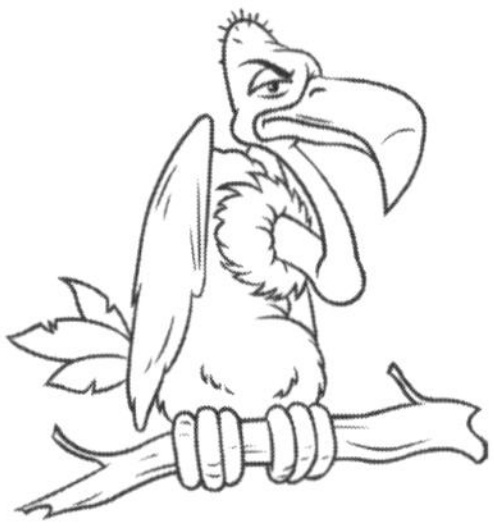

____ulture

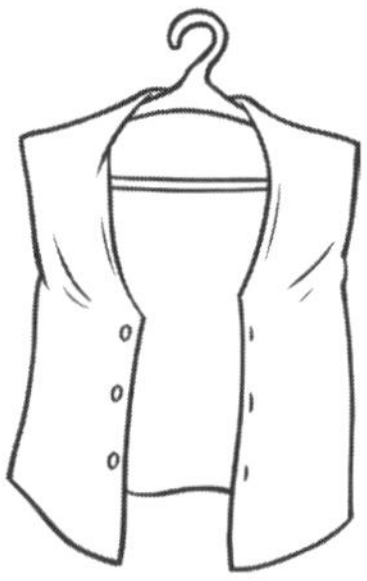

____est

2 How many vegetables can you name?

____

____

Name

Check

Vv

Lesson 21 · Worksheet 4

1 Circle every **V**.

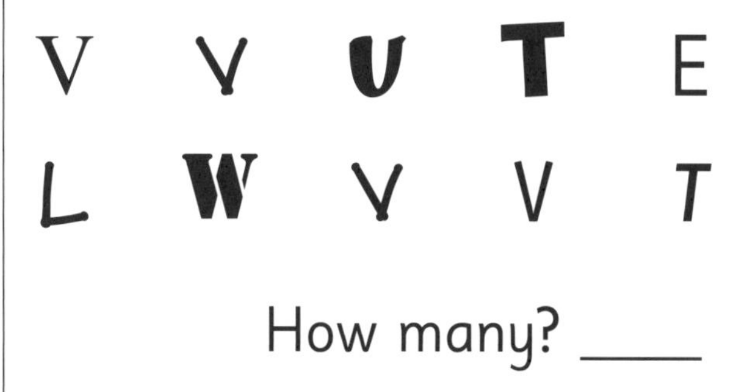

Circle every **v**.

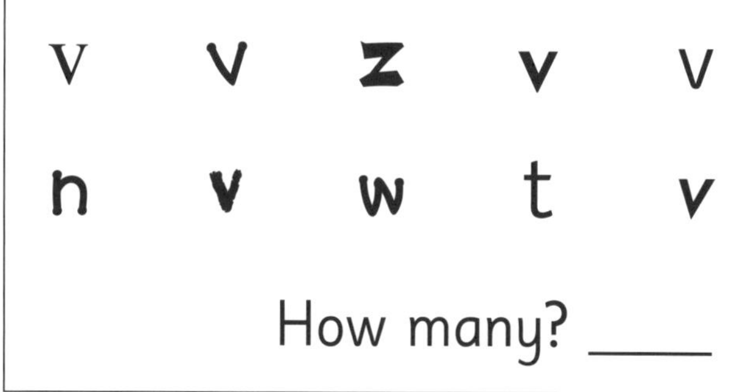

2 Which words have a **v** in them?

3 Match each letter to a picture.

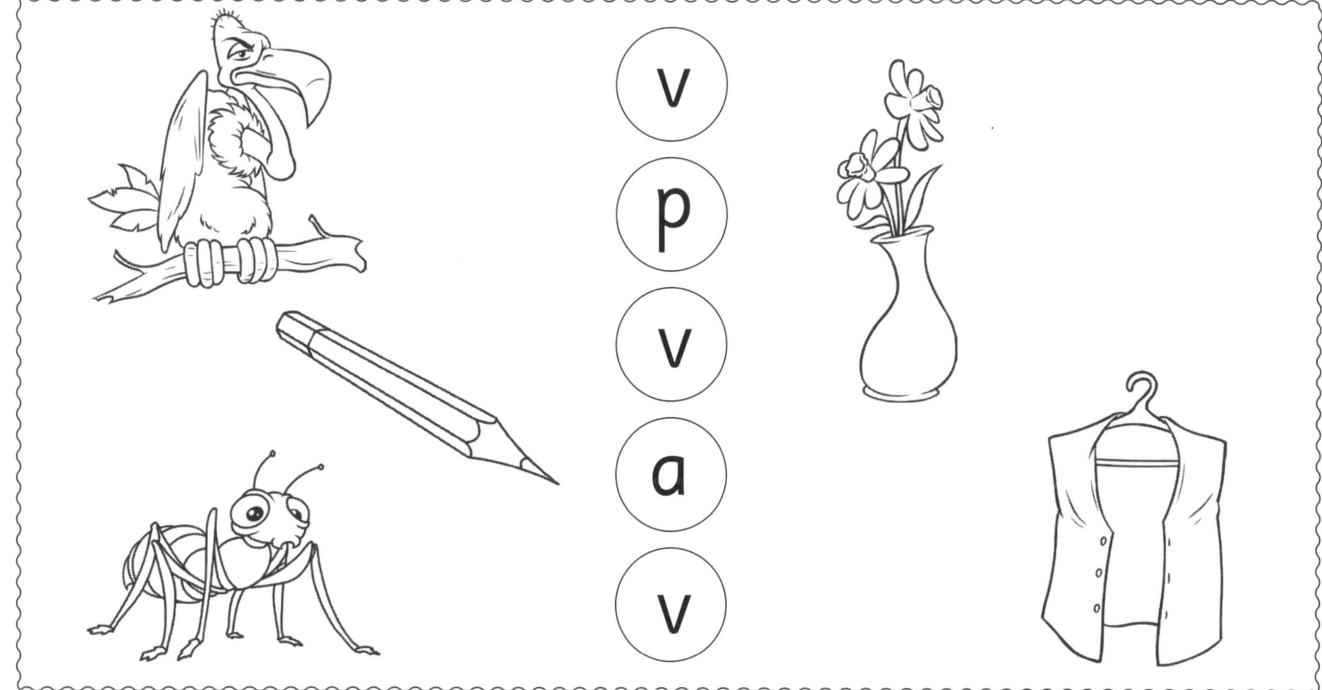

Lesson 22 and

Learning objectives

Children will:

- identify the rime and.
- identify words that contain and.
- read and write the word and.

Australian Curriculum Content Descriptions

Sound and letter knowledge

ACELA1439 listen to the sounds a student hears in the word, and write letters to represent those sounds, identify onset and rime in one-syllable spoken words

Expressing and developing ideas

ACELA1435 learn that word order in sentences is important for meaning

ACELA1438 build word families using onset and rime

ACELA1758 write consonant-vowel-consonant words by writing letters to represent the sounds in the spoken words

know that spoken words are written down by listening to the sounds heard in the word and then writing letters to represent those sounds

Sight words

and, see, the

Word families

band, sand, hand, land, mat, rat, hat, bee, bat, cat, Sam

ESL/ELL

Some students may have trouble with a final blend like nd. They may only pronounce the first consonant – the n. Be sure to pronounce the and words clearly and ask them to do the same.

Extra assistance

A game to encourage correct enunciation of the blend nd is to lay out pairs of cards with pictures from the and word family and play Memory. They only get to keep their matching pair if they can say the word correctly.

Classroom activities

Change the Start

Put the sound and on the board in magnetic letters. Put all the letters of the alphabet around it. Students take turns to make and words by simply changing the initial phoneme.

Sentence Shuffle

Write an enlarged version of the sentence See the mat and the rat and the hat and the bee and the bat and the cat and Sam. Read it with the children and discuss how the word and joins the items together. Reproduce each word on smaller pieces of card so students can make the sentence themselves. Encourage them to play around with word order and discover that they can swap the nouns around.

Reading Eggs Lesson sequence	TEACH Content and skills	PRACTISE Children will:	APPLY
Hear: *Animated Lesson*	Introduce the word and through words and pairs that go together.	identify and read the word and in isolation and in a group.	**Worksheet 1** Sight words
Write: *Make a Sentence*	Recognise correct word order for a sentence.	choose the correct words to make a sentence.	**Worksheet 2** Writing sentences
Find: *Send a Letter, Word family, Island Hop*	Recognise a given word. Identify the correct onset letter to complete the word.	find the given word in a group. Choose the correct initial letter to match the word to the picture.	**Worksheet 3** Word family
Vocabulary: *Blend a Word, Word Windows, Rhyming Squares, Tiles, Picture Picker*	Build vocabulary skills: Blend and recognise words. Identify rhyming words. Read sentences and match to pictures.	blend sounds to read and make words. Find images of rhyming words. Match the picture to the sentence.	**Worksheet 4** Vocabulary
Read: *Book*	Read aloud book.	listen, follow the reading and read along.	**Reading Eggs Story book** The band

Related Reading Eggs Activities, Interactives, Songs and Books

Reading Eggs Playroom

Book Shelf Song Books:
The Grand Old Duke of York

Play Mat:
Words with Blocks

Music Café

He's with her

Reading Eggs Puzzle Park

Both ways

Read it

Reading Eggs Posters

Reading Eggs Library Books

My Program Books

Alphabet Flashcards

Game 7 – Making words with and.

Teacher Toolkit

Targeting Handwriting Interactively

Spelling Activities

Reading Eggs Apps

Eggy Alphabet

Critter Card

Sandy can

and

Lesson 22 • Worksheet 1

Name

Sight words

1 Write the word.

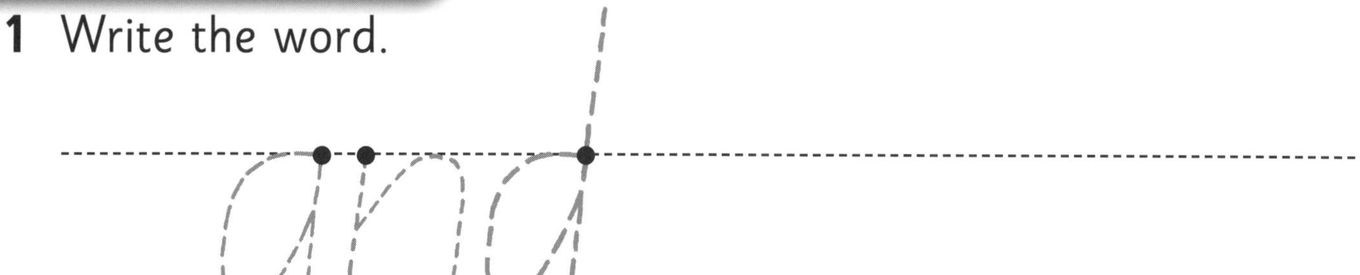

2 Use **and** to finish these sentences.

See the can __________ the fan.

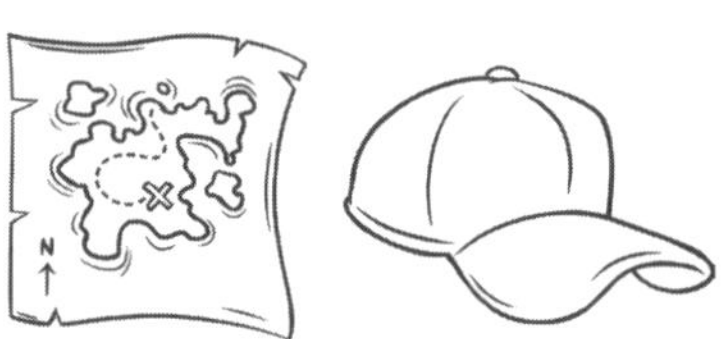

I can see a map __________ a cap.

3 Colour **and** brown, **the** grey and **see** blue.

see	the	the	the	the	the	the	see
see	see	the	the	the	the	see	see
see	see	see	the	the	see	see	see
see	see	see	and	and	see	see	see
see	see	and	and	and	and	see	see
see	and	and	and	and	and	and	see
and	and	and	and	and	and	and	and
and	and	and	and	and	and	and	and

Name

Writing sentences

and

Lesson 22 • Worksheet 2

Write the sentence. Draw a picture.

See and bat cat the

See the

tall thin and I am

and

Lesson 22 • Worksheet 3

Name

Word family

1 Finish each word. Colour the picture.

2 Put each letter in the word machine. Write the word you make.

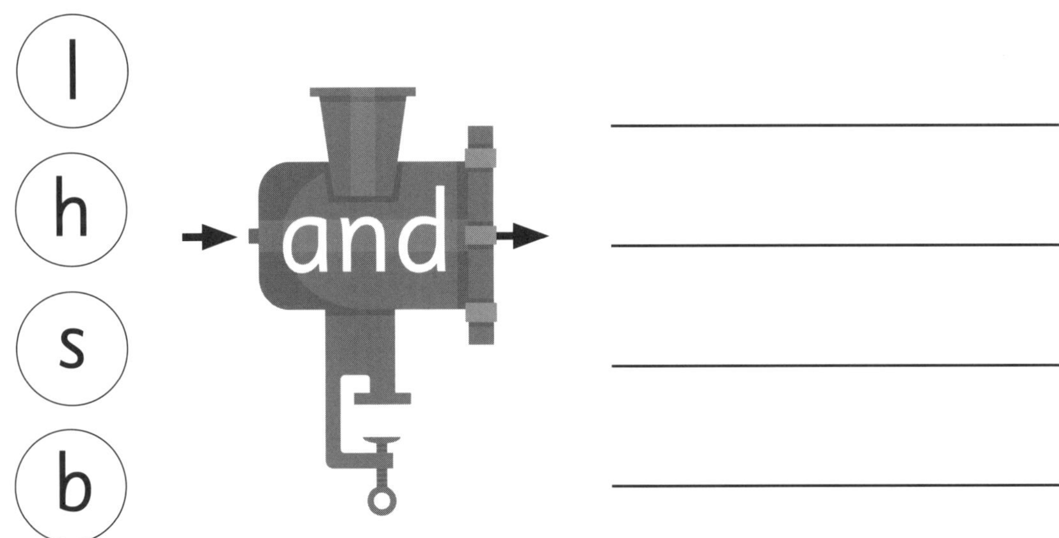

3 Finish the sentence using **and** words.

I see a ________ and

a ________ .

Name

Vocabulary

and

Lesson 22 • Worksheet 4

1 Colour the words that rhyme.

2 Write words that rhyme with Sam.

Lesson 23 the letter **d**

Learning objectives

Children will:

- identify the sound d.
- identify words that contain d.
- recognise and write d and D.

Australian Curriculum Content Descriptions

Sound and letter knowledge

ACELA1439 identify and manipulate sounds (phonemes) in spoken words

ACELA1440 identify familiar and recurring letters and the use of upper and lower case in written texts

Creating texts

ACELY1653 follow clear demonstrations of how to construct each letter, learn to construct lower case letters

ACELA1758 write consonant-vowel-consonant words by writing letters to represent the sounds in the spoken words

know that spoken words are written down by listening to the sounds heard in the word and then writing letters to represent those sounds

Sight words

you

Vocabulary words

door, dog, doll, dolphin, dinosaur, duck, dock, drum, dad, doctor, dragonfly

ESL/ELL

Some students may have trouble with the sounds /p/, /b/ and /d/. Let them practise the sounds using sets of words like pan, dan, ban, or pig, big, dig. Be sure to reinforce the initial sound.

Extra assistance

To differentiate /p/ and /d/, show students how the lips come together to make /p/ and stay open to make /d/. In /d/ the tongue starts behind the top teeth and pulls down, while in /p/ the tongue doesn't really move.

Classroom activities

Brainstorm

Brainstorm a list of words that start with the /d/ sound. Then make a second list of words that end with the /d/ sound. Can students think of any words that start *and* end with the /d/ sound?

Throw it Away!

Sit in a circle with a box in the middle. Students each hold two items or pictures or words on cards. The teacher says a word. If the child has an object starting with the same first letter they throw it into the box. Discuss the objects in each round.

Reading Eggs Lesson sequence	**TEACH Content and skills**	**PRACTISE Children will:**	**APPLY**
Hear: *Animated Lesson*	Introduce the sound /d/ through words and the songs *At Home with Jazz* and *Very Dirty Monsters*.	identify and read /d/ sound in isolation and in words.	**Worksheet 1** Phonemic awareness
Write: *Dot-to-Dot*	Reinforce correct letter formation of lower case d.	write the letter d.	**Worksheet 2** Handwriting
Find: *Letter Grid, Trains and Jumping Astronauts*	Recognise upper and lower case letters. Identify a given word.	locate lower case and capital letters. Find the given word in a group.	**Worksheet 3** Initial and end sounds
Vocabulary: *Today's Topic Words, Letter Book, Sound Streamers, In the Box and Word Windows*	Build vocabulary skills: Blend, read and recognise words. Match pictures to words.	blend and read key vocabulary and match to pictures. Match pictures to their initial letter.	**Worksheet 4** Check
Read: *Book*	Read aloud book.	listen, follow the reading and read along.	**Reading Eggs Alphabet book** d

Related Reading Eggs Activities, Interactives, Songs and Books

Reading Eggs Playroom

Alphabet Activities

Book Shelf Song

Books:
Alphabet Song,
Five Little Ducks

Paint Easel:
Drawing

Music Café

At Home with Jazz

Very Dirty Monsters

Reading Eggs Puzzle Park

Alphabet match

Both ways

Read it

Reading Eggs Posters

Reading Eggs Library Books

My Program Books

Alphabet Flashcards

Game 4 – Make the critters with the letter d.

Teacher Toolkit

Targeting Handwriting Interactively

Alphabet Activities

Reading Eggs Apps

Eggy Alphabet

Critter Card

Dogfin

Dd

Lesson 23 · Worksheet 1

Name

Phonemic awareness

1 Colour the pictures that begin with **d**.

2 Match each letter to a picture.

3 Circle every **D**.

D	D	A	D	D
C	D	B	0	J

How many? ____

Circle every **d**.

d	c	d	d	c
d	a	e	b	d

How many? ____

Name

Handwriting

Dd

Lesson 23 • Worksheet 2

1 Trace the dinosaurs.

2 Trace and write.

d d d d d

d d d d d

1 2 D d

Circle your best letter.

Dd

Lesson 23 • Worksheet 3

Name

Initial and end sounds

1 Add **d** and read the word.

2 Write words that end with **d**.

____

____

Name

Check

Dd

Lesson 23 • Worksheet 4

1 Circle the **beginning** sound.

p m d

t v s

h b d

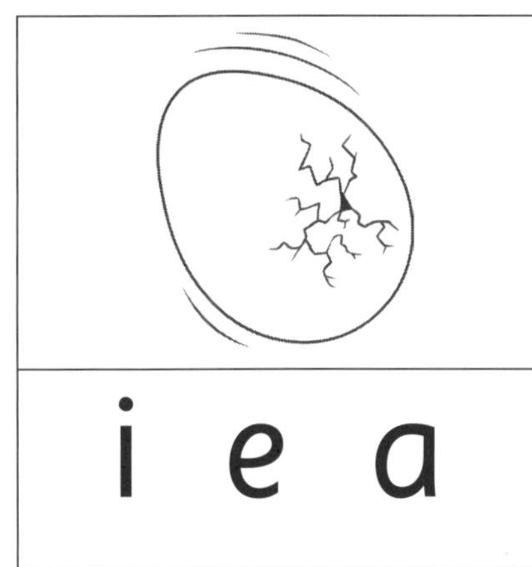

i e a

b n v

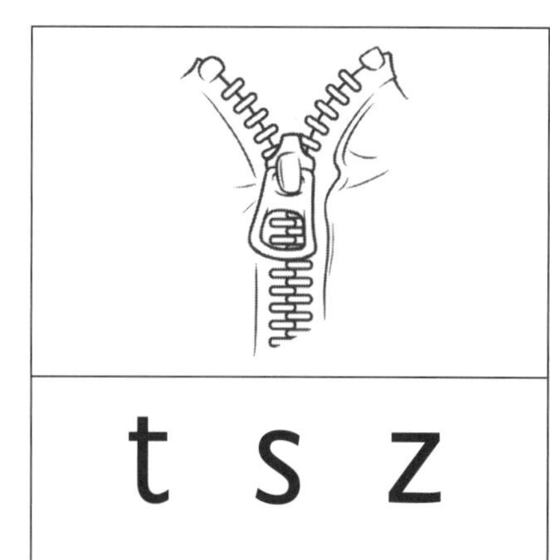

t s z

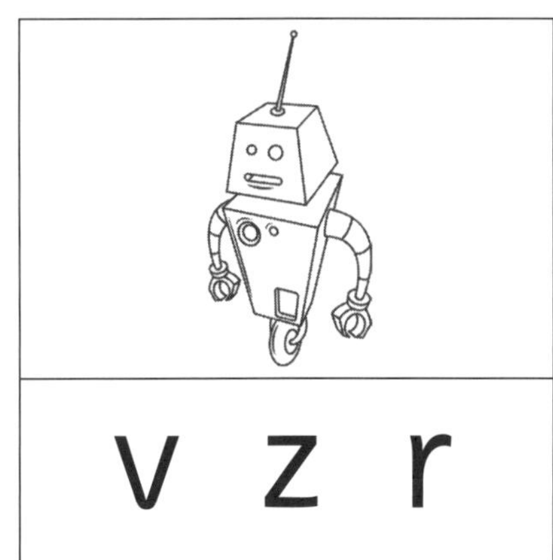

v z r

b p d

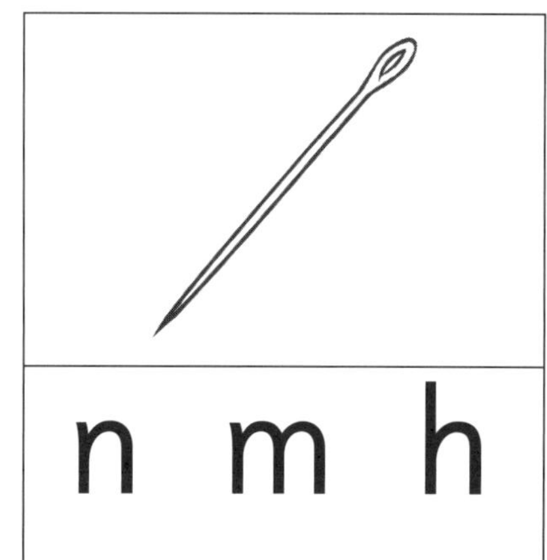

n m h

2 Write three words that use these letters.

a b c d e f h i m n p r s t v z

Lesson 24 the words **in** and **had**

Learning objectives

Children will:

- identify the words in and had.
- read the words in and had.
- revise other sight words.

Australian Curriculum Content Descriptions

Sound and letter knowledge

ACELA1439 listen to the sounds a student hears in the word, and write letters to represent those sounds identify and manipulate sounds (phonemes) in spoken words

Expressing and developing ideas

ACELA1435 learn that word order in sentences is important for meaning

ACELA1758 recognise the most common sound made by each letter of the alphabet, including consonants and short vowel sounds

Interpreting, analysing and evaluating

ACELY1649 navigate a text correctly, starting at the right place and reading in the right direction, returning to the next line as needed, matching one spoken word to one written word

Sight words

in, had, can, the, see, I, a

Word families

cat, rat, hat, sat, fat, nap

ESL/ELL

Many languages do not distinguish between long and short vowel sounds. Give students opportunities to practise pronunciation with pairs of words, eg mad and made, din and dine, or tongue twisters.

Extra assistance

In many languages each sound has its own letter or symbol, so some students will need help to know when a vowel is pronounced with a short or long sound.

Classroom activities

Sentence Shuffle

Write an enlarged version of the sentence The rat had a nap. and read it with the children. Reproduce each word on smaller pieces of card so students can make the sentence themselves and read it.

Mind the Gap!

Write this sentence on the board: I am in the ___. Ask students to read this sentence by themselves, write it down and fill in the gap with a word of their own. Discuss their individual sentences as a group.

Reading Eggs Lesson sequence	**TEACH Content and skills**	**PRACTISE Children will:**	**APPLY**
Hear: *Animated Lesson*	Introduce the words in and had through words and the song *Jazz's Dream*.	identify and read the words in and had in isolation and in a group.	**Worksheet 1** Initial and end sounds
Write: *Pick up Bricks*	Recognise correct word order for a sentence.	choose the correct words to make a sentence.	**Worksheet 2** Sight words
Find: *Kick a Goal, Climb the Ladder, Build a Wall, Letter Lights*	Identify a given word. Match letters in upper and lower case.	find the given word in a group. Locate lower case and capital letters.	**Worksheet 3** Read and write
Vocabulary: *Blend a Word, Missing Sound, Tiles, Picture Picker*	Build vocabulary skills: Blend and recognise words. Identify the correct onset letter to complete the word. Read sentences and match to pictures.	blend sounds to read and make words. Choose the correct initial letter to make the word match the picture. Find the picture to match the sentence.	**Worksheet 4** Writing sentences
Read: *Book*	Read aloud book.	listen, follow the reading and read along.	**Reading Eggs Story book** Cat and rat

Related Reading Eggs Activities, Interactives, Songs and Books

Reading Eggs Playroom

Book Shelf Song
Books:
The Grand Old Duke of York

Play Mat:
Words with Blocks

Paint Easel:
Colouring in

Music Café

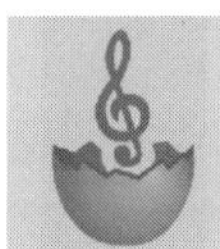

Jazz's Dream

Reading Eggs Puzzle Park

Both ways

Read it

Reading Eggs Posters

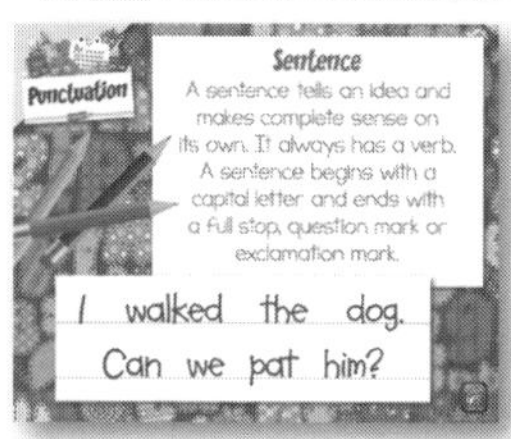

Reading Eggs Library Books

My Program Books

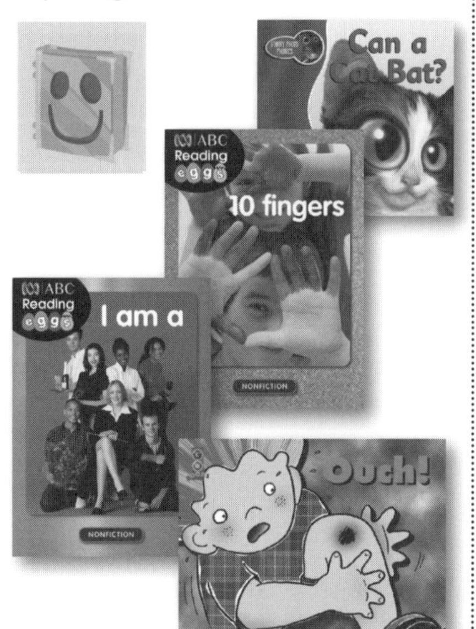

Alphabet Flashcards

Game 1 – Letter shape looking at the capitals and lowercase letters.

Teacher Toolkit

Targeting Handwriting Interactively

Spelling Activities

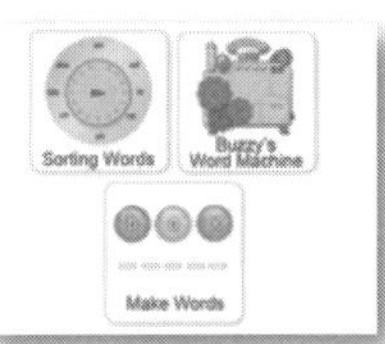

Reading Eggs Apps

Eggy Words

Critter Card

Jazz the cat

Initial and end sounds

Lesson 24 • Worksheet 1

Name

Draw lines to make words. Label each picture.

h	ap	
b	an	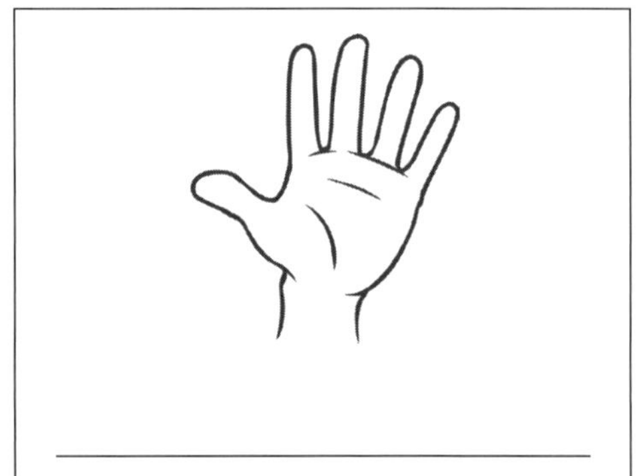
m	and	
c	ee	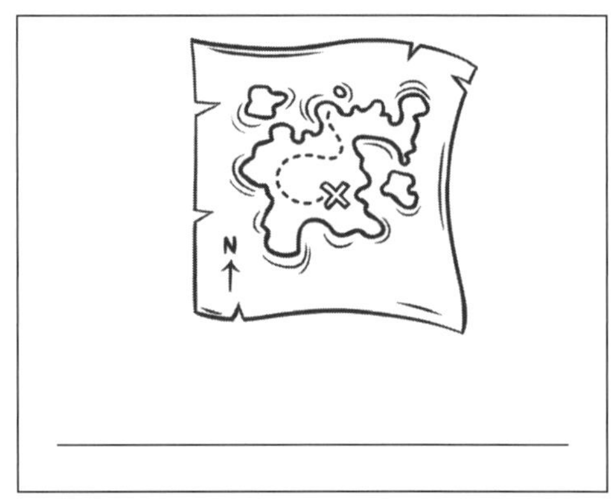

Name

Sight words

in had

Lesson 24 • Worksheet 2

1 Read and write.

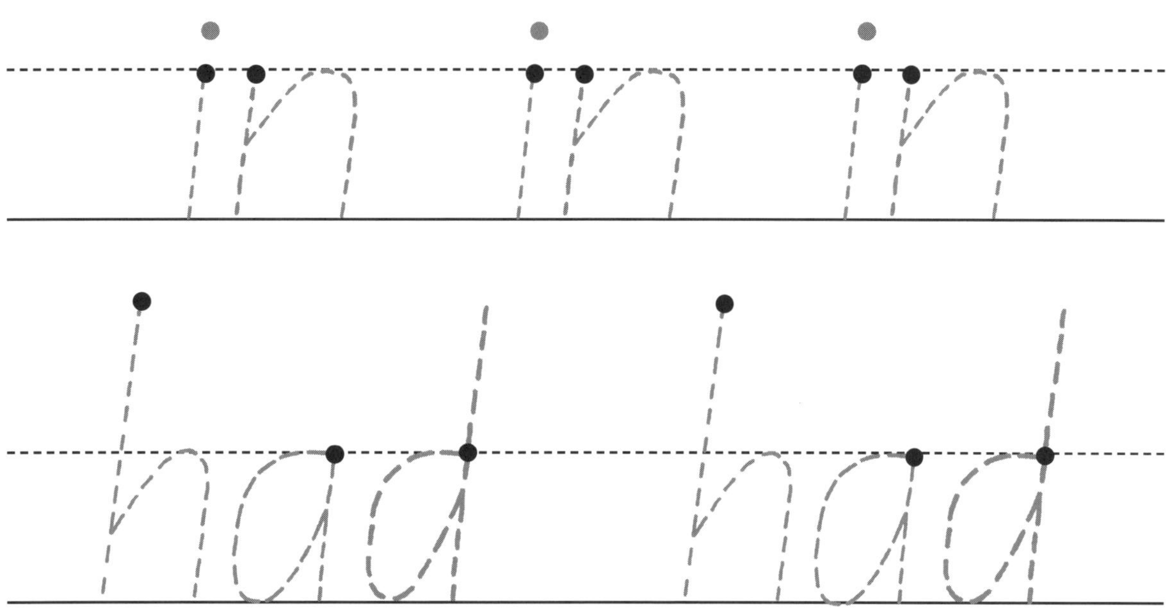

2 Use **in** or **had** to finish each sentence.

The rat ________ a hat.

The bee is ________ the tree.

The cat ________ a fan.

The egg is ________ the pan.

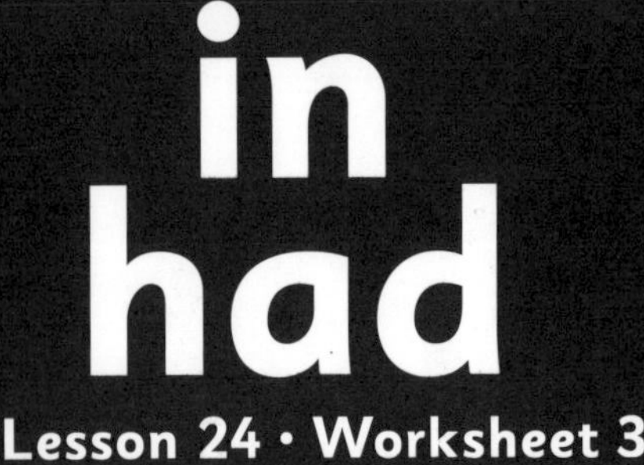

Name

Read and write

1 Use **in** and **had** to finish the sentences.

I am ________ a van.

The cat ________ a hat.

See the bat ________ the tree.

2 Draw a picture for each sentence.

The rat had a nap.	
I see the cat.	
See a rat in a hat.	

Name

Writing sentences

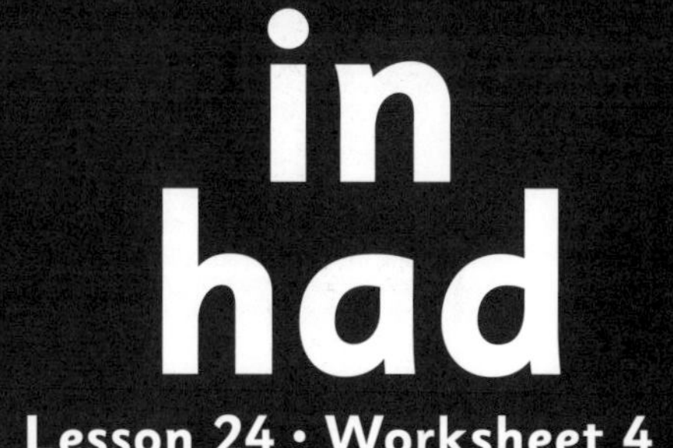

Make a sentence. Draw a picture.

am a I the in band.	

had man a nap. The	

the the and See tree bee.	

Lesson 25 the letter j

Learning objectives

Children will:

- identify the sound j.
- identify words that contain j.
- recognise and write j and J.

Australian Curriculum Content Descriptions

Sound and letter knowledge

ACELA1439 identify and manipulate sounds (phonemes) in spoken words

ACELA1440 identify familiar and recurring letters and the use of upper and lower case in written texts

Creating texts

ACELY1653 follow clear demonstrations of how to construct each letter, learn to construct lower case letters

Expressing and developing ideas

ACELA1758 recognise the most common sound made by each letter of the alphabet, including consonants and short vowel sounds

know that spoken words are written down by listening to the sounds heard in the word and then writing letters to represent those sounds

Sight words

see, you, the, can

Vocabulary words

jeep, jewel, jet, jelly, jug, jungle, jacket, jam, jar, jeans, jellybeans, juice, jump, juggle

ESL/ELL

Students who speak Spanish may pronounce the sound /j/ as /y/, saying yam instead of jam. Give them opportunities to hear the difference. Ask students to raise their hand when they hear a /j/ sound. Then say various words, enunciating clearly: juice, yellow, jelly, yard, and so on.

Extra assistance

For practise with pronunciation, give the students tongue twisters to try:

Jack jumped the jar of jellybeans.

The jar of jam was juggled jealously.

Classroom activities

Collage

Provide the students with a piece of paper that has a large j in the middle:

- trace over the j with a pencil.
- find things starting with j in an old magazine, cut out and glue around the j on the paper to create a collage.

Find the Letter

Give each student 3 cards with the letters j, d and v. Say a word and ask students to listen to the initial sound. They should hold up the card which makes that initial sound. Use clear, easily recognisable words such as:

jam dog van jump duck vet

Reading Eggs Lesson sequence	**TEACH Content and skills**	**PRACTISE Children will:**	**APPLY**
Hear: *Animated Lesson*	Introduce the sound /j/ through words and the song *Jazzy J*.	identify and read /j/ sound in isolation and in words.	**Worksheet 1** Phonemic awareness
Write: *Dot-to-Dot*	Reinforce correct letter formation of lower case j.	write the letter j.	**Worksheet 2** Handwriting
Find: *Letter Grid, Frog Hops, Golden Goose, Fishing Boats*	Recognise j in upper and lower case. Identify a given word.	locate lower case j and capital J. Find the given word in a group. Match word to picture.	**Worksheet 3** Initial sounds
Vocabulary: *Letter Book, Label It, Missing Sound*	Build vocabulary skills: Match pictures to words. Identify the correct onset letter to complete the word.	match words and pictures. Choose the correct initial letter to match the word to the picture.	**Worksheet 4** Check
Read: *Book*	Read aloud book.	listen, follow the reading and read along.	**Reading Eggs Alphabet book** j

Related Reading Eggs Activities, Interactives, Songs and Books

Reading Eggs Playroom

Alphabet Activities
Book Shelf Song
Books:
Alphabet Song,
Five Little Monkeys
Puzzle Table:
Jumbled Animals

Music Café

Jazzy J

Reading Eggs Puzzle Park

Alphabet match
Both ways
Read it

Reading Eggs Posters

Reading Eggs Library Books

My Program Books

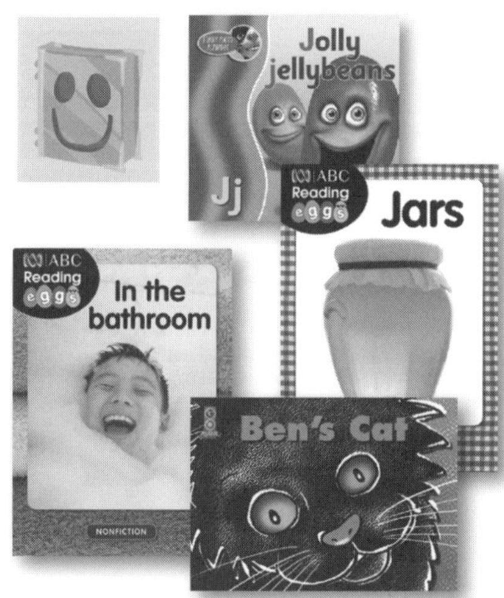

Alphabet Flashcards

Game 6 – Critter concentration using j and other known letters.

Teacher Toolkit

Targeting Handwriting Interactively

Alphabet Activities

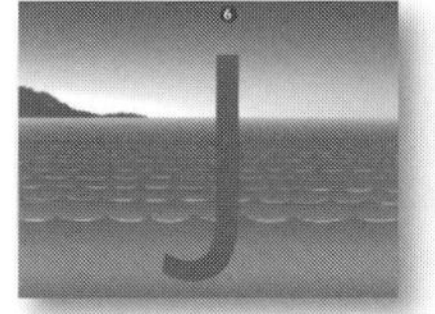

Reading Eggs Apps

Eggy Alphabet

Critter Card

Jelly jag

Jj

Lesson 25 • Worksheet 1

Name

Phonemic awareness

1 Colour the pictures that begin with **j**.

2 Match each letter to a picture.

3 Circle every **J**.

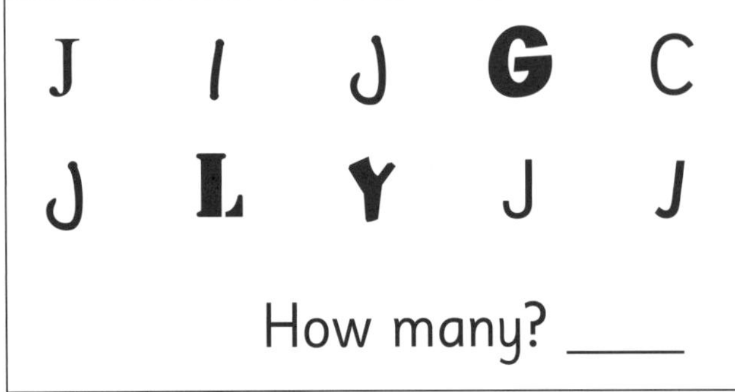

Circle every **j**.

j j j g j
i y j j b

How many? ____

Name

Handwriting

Jj

Lesson 25 • Worksheet 2

1 Trace the dotted lines.

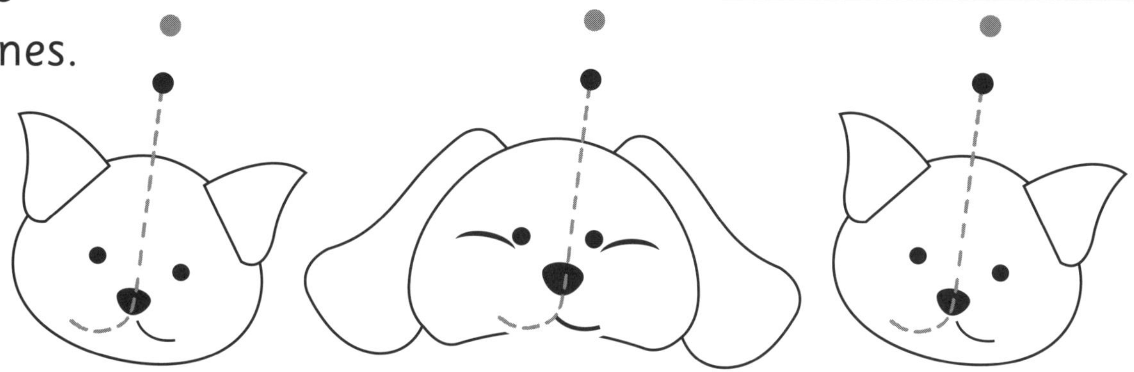

2 Trace and write.

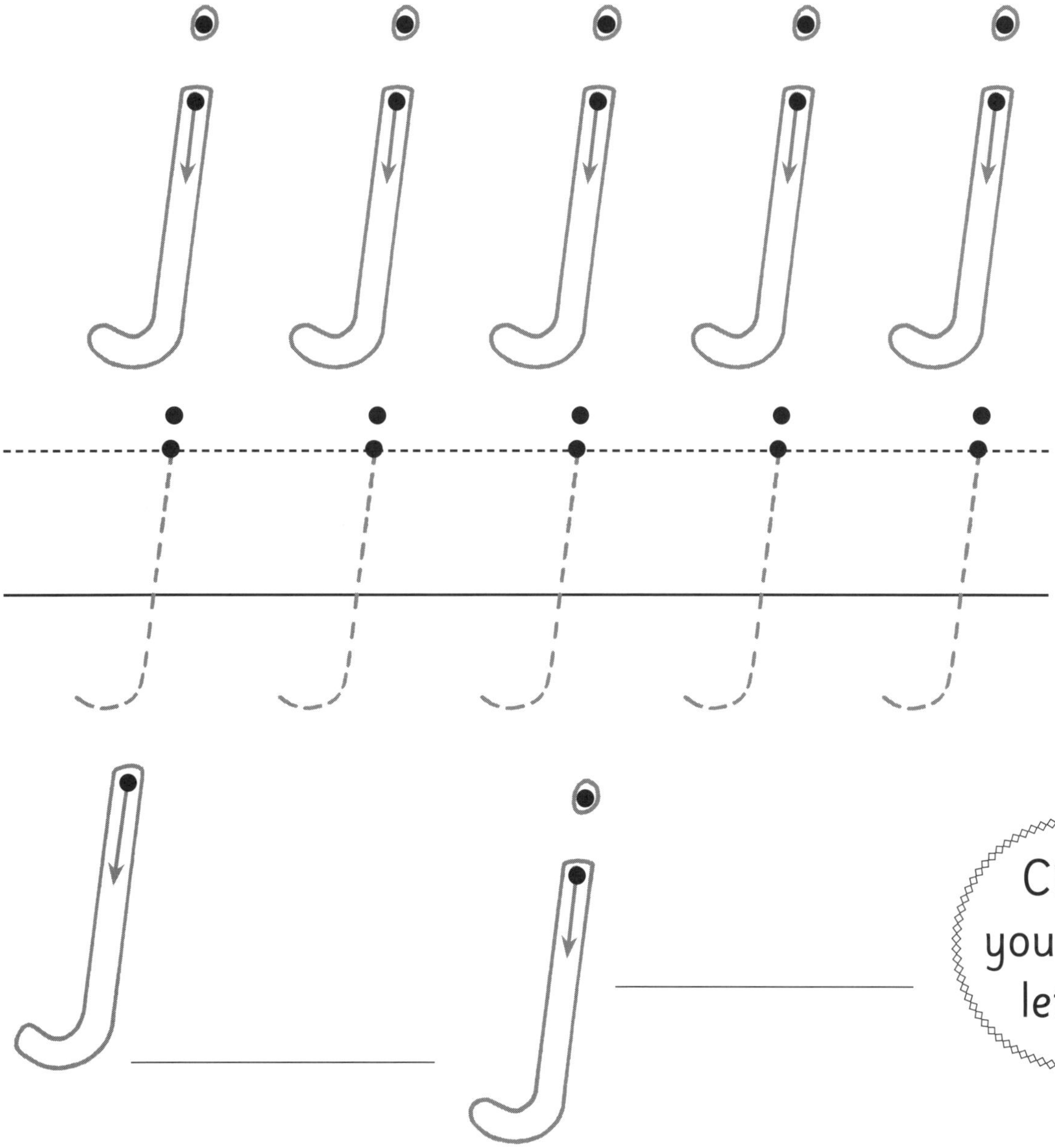

Circle your best letter.

Jj

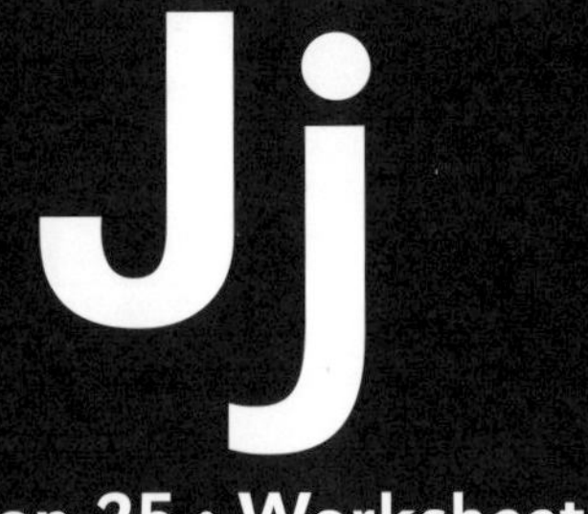

Lesson 25 · Worksheet 3

Name

Initial sounds

1 Add **j** and read the word.

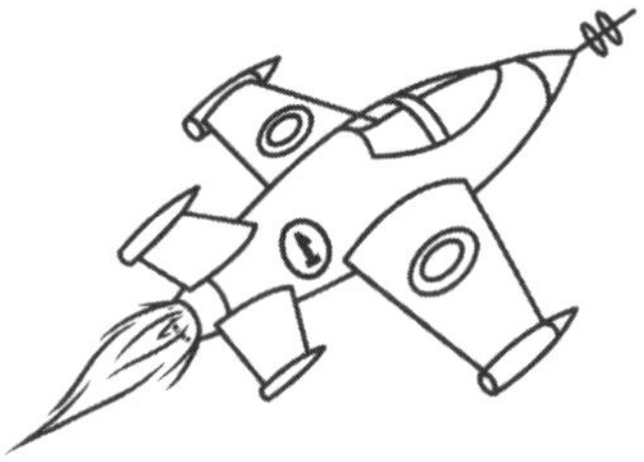

___j___et

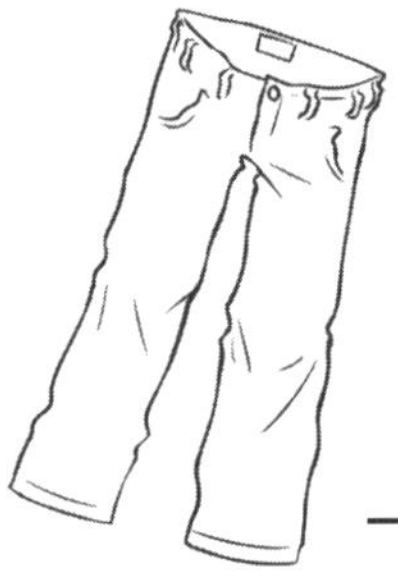

______eans

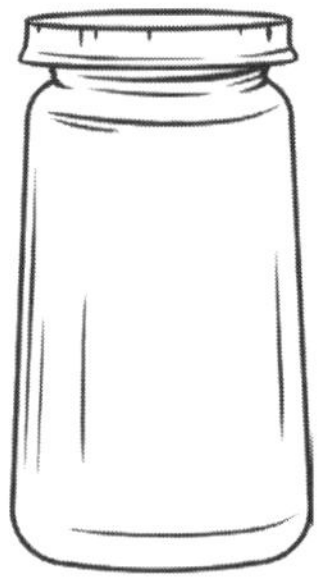

______ar

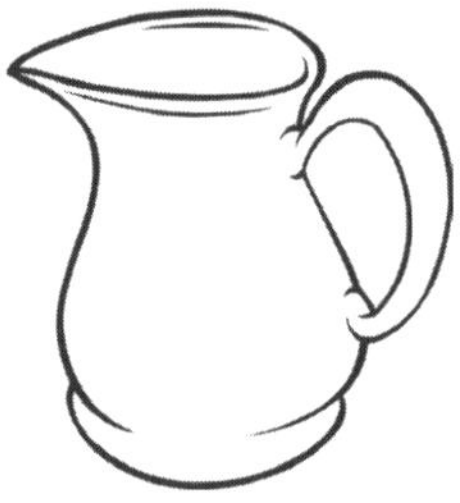

______ug

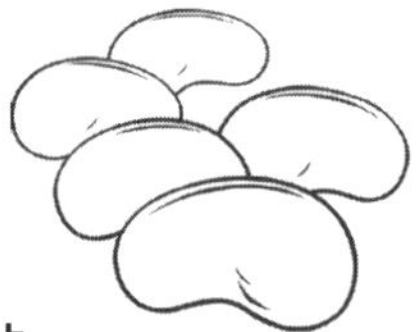

_____elly beans

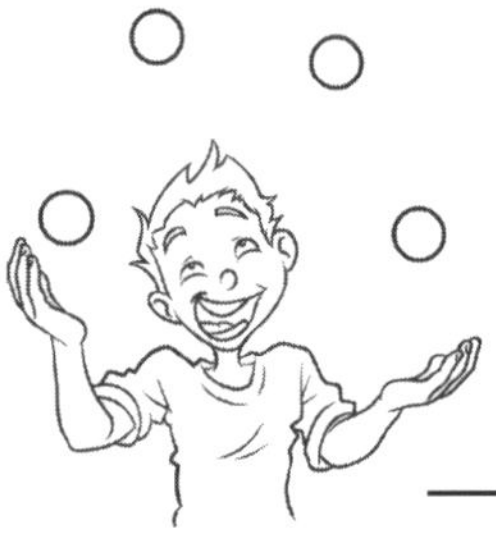

_____uggle

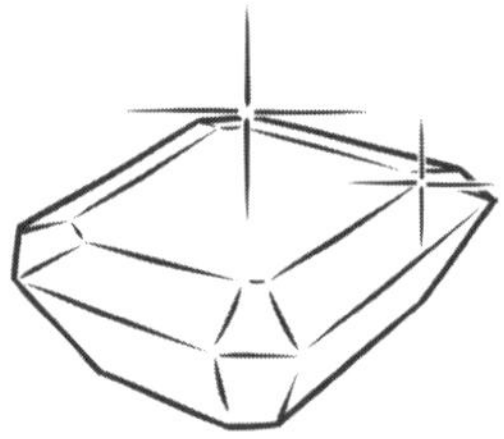

______ewel

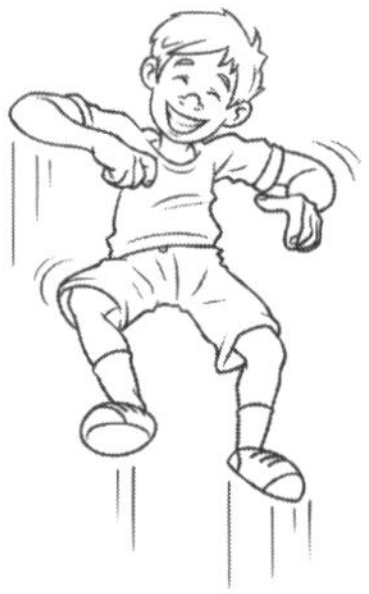

_____ump

2 How many types of jam can you name?

____

____

Name

Check

Jj

Lesson 25 · Worksheet 4

1 Circle the **beginning** sound.

p d	j v	z d

h r	v f	m n

2 Trace each letter and match to a picture.

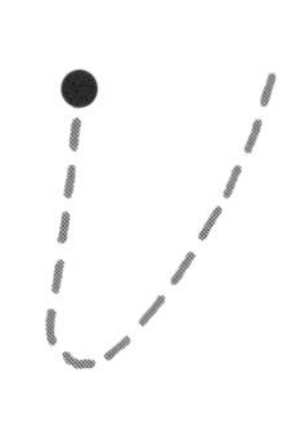

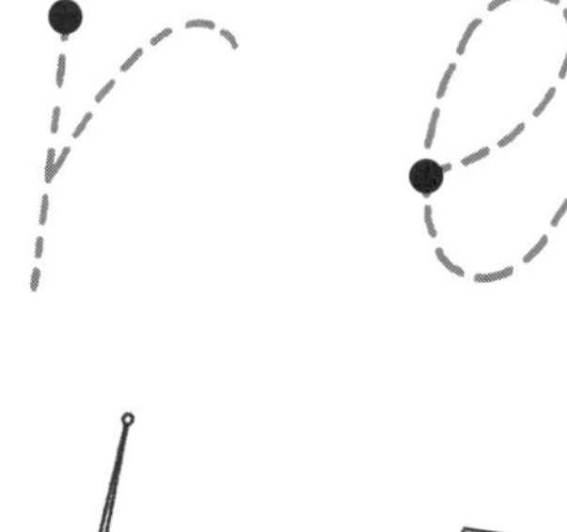

v z r e d j

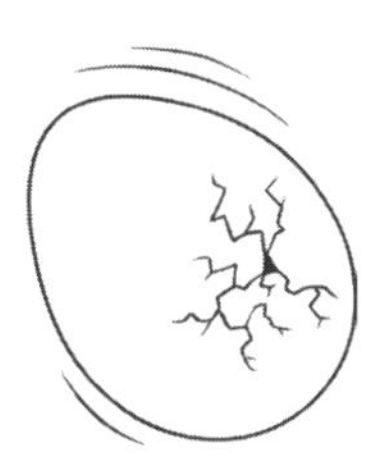

Lesson 26 the sound **ad**

Learning objectives

Children will:

- identify the rime ad.
- identify words that contain ad.
- recognise and write ad words.

Australian Curriculum Content Descriptions

Sound and letter knowledge

ACELA1439 listen to the sounds a student hears in the word, and write letters to represent those sounds; identify and manipulate sounds (phonemes) in spoken words

Expressing and developing ideas

ACELA1758 recognise the most common sound made by each letter of the alphabet, including consonants and short vowel sounds; write consonant-vowel-consonant words by writing letters to represent the sounds in the spoken words; know that spoken words are written down by listening to the sounds heard in the word and then writing letters to represent those sounds

Sight words

had, I, can, see

Word families

dad, bad, had, pad, mad, sad

Vocabulary words

cats, rats, bees, ants

ESL/ELL

The correct pronunciation of /d/ can be reinforced using ad words. Give the students pairs of sentences and ask them which word makes sense:

I love my dad. Or I love my dab.

I am feeling sad. Or I am feeling sap.

Extra assistance

When making word family lists, teach students to run through the alphabet and try each letter as a starting sound, looking for the "real" words. For example:

ad bad cad dad ~~ead~~ –> this is not a word

Classroom activities

How does it end?

Give the students a letter each (b, c, d, f, h, l, m, p, s and w), either written on a card or a magnetic letter. Write the sounds 'ad' and 'and' on the top of the board. Each student comes to the board and writes the words they can make using their initial letter and one or both endings. Discuss their words with the class.

Find the start

Give students a list of words with the first letter missing. Ask them to figure out which letter could be the starter for all the given words, for example:

_ad _and _ee _ap _at

Discuss the answers as a class. Was there more than one possible answer?

Reading Eggs Lesson sequence	TEACH Content and skills	PRACTISE Children will:	APPLY
Hear: *Animated Lesson*	Introduce the rime ad through words and the song *Add an ad*.	make ad words.	**Worksheet 1** Word family
Write: *Blend a Word, Rumble Jumble*	Blend and recognise words. Unjumble letters for a given word.	blend sounds to read words. Write a word from jumbled letters.	**Worksheet 2** Read and write
Find: *Word family, Alien Planets, Pet Store*	Identify the correct onset letter to complete the word. Recognise a given word. Identify plurals and numerals.	choose the correct initial letter to make the word. Find the given word in a group. Match number of pets to words.	**Worksheet 3** Plurals
Vocabulary: *Label It, Rhyming Squares, Break It Up, Wheel of Words*	Build vocabulary skills: Match pictures to words. Recognise rhyming words. Identify the number of phonemes in a word.	read key vocabulary and match to pictures. Find images of rhyming words. Identify the number of sounds in a word.	**Worksheet 4** Vocabulary
Read: *Book*	Read aloud book.	listen, follow the reading and read along.	**Reading Eggs Story book** Cats

Related Reading Eggs Activities, Interactives, Songs and Books

Reading Eggs Playroom

Book Shelf Song

Books:
Old Macdonald had a Farm,
Little Peter Rabbit

Play Mat:
Words with blocks

Music Café

Add an ad

Reading Eggs Puzzle Park

More than one

Both ways

Read it

Reading Eggs Posters

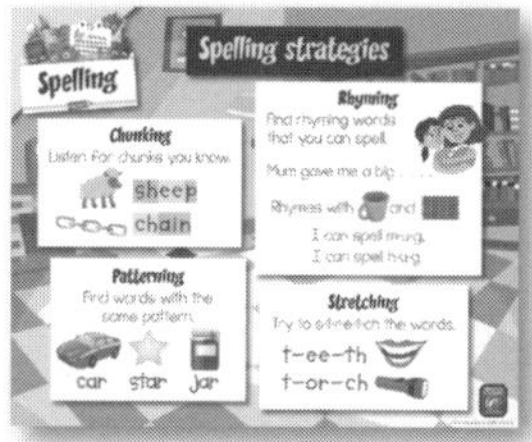

Reading Eggs Library Books

My Program Books

Alphabet Flashcards

Game 7 – Making words using ad.

Teacher Toolkit

Targeting Handwriting Interactively

Spelling Activities

Reading Eggs Apps

Eggy Sight words

Critter Card

Ladbug

ad

Lesson 26 • Worksheet 1

Name

Word family

1 Put each letter in the word machine. Write the word.

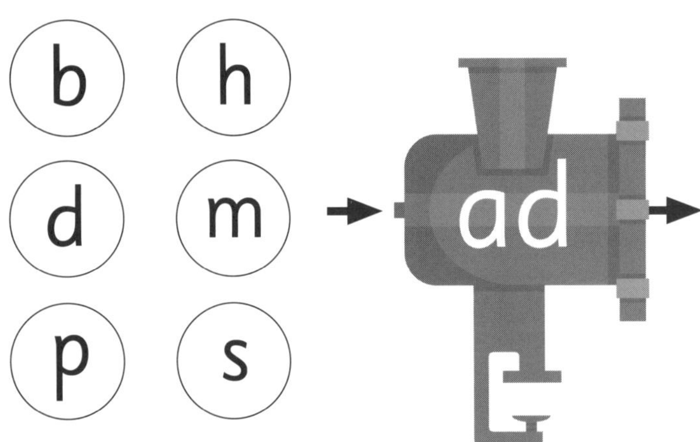

____

____

____

____

____

____

2 Finish the sentences with an **ad** word.

The man ________ a map.

The man is my ________.

No.1 Dad

I am ________.

I see a ________.

Name

Read and write

ad

Lesson 26 • Worksheet 2

Unjumble the letters and label each picture.

 ads ________	 scta ________
 tna ________	 nahd ________
 sbee ________	 dda ________
 nva ________	 pac ________

Plurals

Name

Lesson 26 • Worksheet 3

Label each picture. Use a number and a word from the box.
Add **s** for plurals!

1 2 3 4 rat bee cat ant

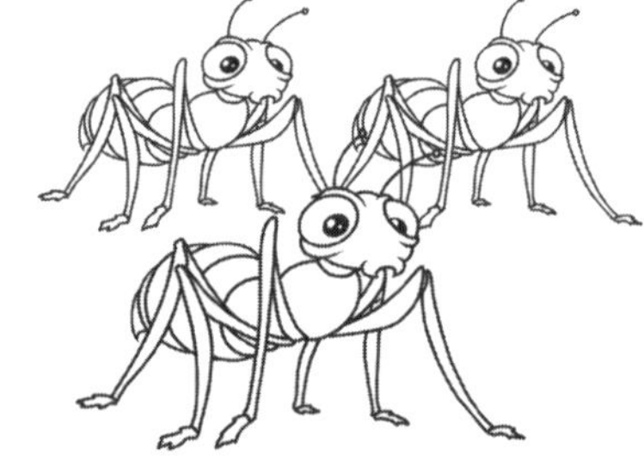

Name

Vocabulary

ad

Lesson 26 · Worksheet 4

1 How many sounds do you hear in each word? Colour the box.

had	and	bee
1 2 3 4	1 2 3 4	1 2 3 4
vans	**tree**	**maps**
1 2 3 4	1 2 3 4	1 2 3 4

2 Colour the rhyming words in each row.

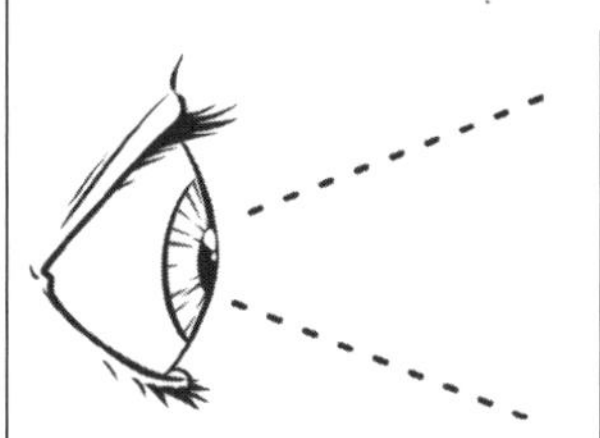

Lesson 27 the letter **o**

Learning objectives

Children will:

- identify the sound o.
- identify words that contain o.
- recognise and write o and O.

Australian Curriculum Content Descriptions

Sound and letter knowledge

ACELA1439 listen to the sounds a student hears in the word, and write letters to represent those sounds, identify and manipulate sounds (phonemes) in spoken words

ACELA1440 identify familiar and recurring letters and the use of upper and lower case in written texts

Creating texts

ACELY1653 follow clear demonstrations of how to construct each letter, learn to construct lower case letters

Expressing and developing ideas

ACELA1758 write consonant-vowel-consonant words by writing letters to represent the sounds in the spoken words; know that spoken words are written down by listening to the sounds heard in the word and then writing letters to represent those sounds

Vocabulary words

ostrich, oil, orange, oar, olive, octopus, old, on, otter, onion

ESL/ELL

Students who speak Spanish and some Asian languages at home may not distinguish between the short vowel sounds /o/, /u/ and /a/. Give them practice hearing and saying the sounds using word pairs: hot and hat, cod and cud etc.

Extra assistance

Use consonant-vowel-consonant words to reinforce vowel sounds. Give students a list of words with the consonants there and the vowels missing. Say the words out loud and the students have to fill in the middle sound. This is a good way to assess who is having trouble distinguishing them.

Classroom activities

Decorate the Letters

Provide students with a piece of paper that has a lot of the letter O on it in dotted writing. Students should trace over the dotted letters with different coloured pencils, textas or crayons, then draw on each O to turn it into something that has an o in it, such as an ostrich, octopus, olive, orange etc.

Which Hat?

Place three hats on the floor with the labels o, e and a. Discuss the sounds. Have a pile of objects or pictures of objects that start with o, e and a. Each student chooses one and works out which hat it must go in. Discuss their choice with the class.

Reading Eggs Lesson sequence	**TEACH Content and skills**	**PRACTISE Children will:**	**APPLY**
Hear: *Animated Lesson*	Introduce the sound /o/.	identify and read the /o/ sound in isolation.	**Worksheet 1** Phonemic awareness
Write: *Dot-to-Dot*	Reinforce correct letter formation of lower case o.	write the letter o.	**Worksheet 2** Handwriting
Find: *Letter Grid, In the Box, Trains*	Recognise o in upper and lower case. Match pictures to words.	locate lower case o and capital O. Match pictures to their initial letter.	**Worksheet 3** Missing sounds
Vocabulary: *Label It, Blend a Word, Sound Streamers, Letter Book, Rhyming Squares*	Build vocabulary skills: Blend and recognise key vocabulary. Identify sounds in words. Recognise rhyming words.	match pictures to words. Blend sounds to read words. Sound out and select letters to make words. Find images of rhyming words.	**Worksheet 4** Word families
Read: *Book*	Read aloud book.	listen, follow the reading and read along.	**Reading Eggs Alphabet book** o

Related Reading Eggs Activities, Interactives, Songs and Books

Reading Eggs Playroom

Alphabet Activities

Book Shelf Song

Books:
Alphabet Song,
Old Macdonald had a Farm

Music Café

Being on a boat

Reading Eggs Puzzle Park

Alphabet match

Both ways

Read it

Reading Eggs Posters

Reading Eggs Library Books

My Program Books

Alphabet Flashcards

Game 2 – Sound puzzles with known letters.

Teacher Toolkit

Targeting Handwriting Interactively

Alphabet Activities

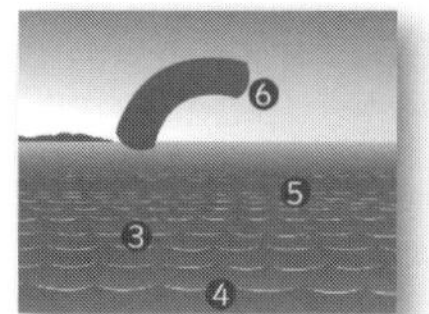

Reading Eggs Apps

Eggy Alphabet

Critter Card

Octo puss

Oo

Lesson 27 · Worksheet 1

Name

Phonemic awareness

1 Add **o** and read the word.

o range

____ctopus

____tter

____nion

2 Colour the right word. Cross out the wrong word.

bax

box

dot

dut

map

mop

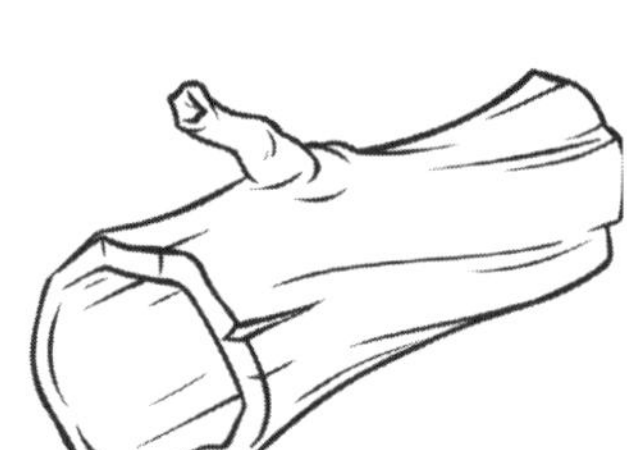

leg

log

Name

Handwriting

Oo

Lesson 27 • Worksheet 2

1 Buzz over to the honey.

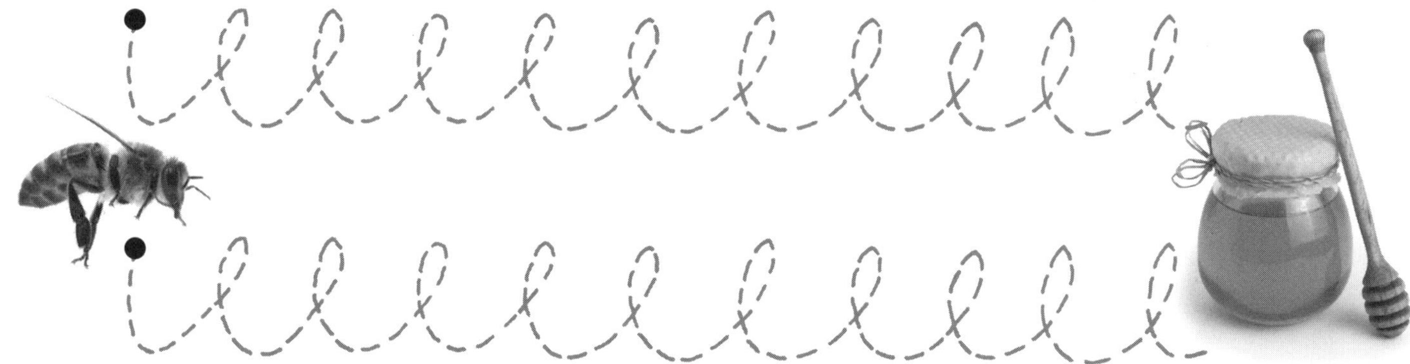

2 Trace and write.

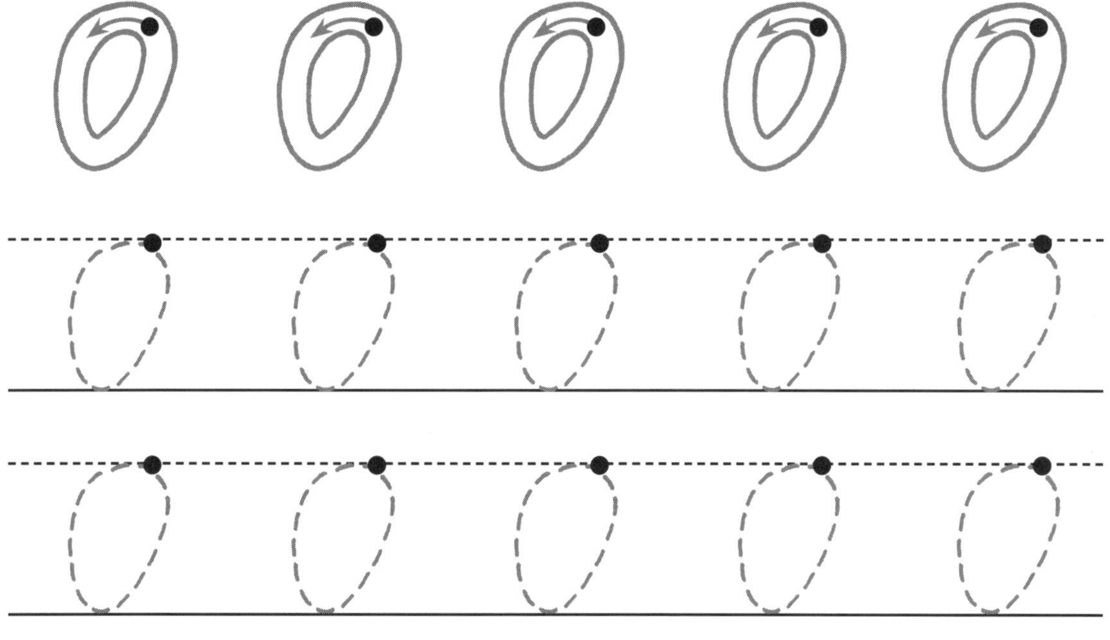

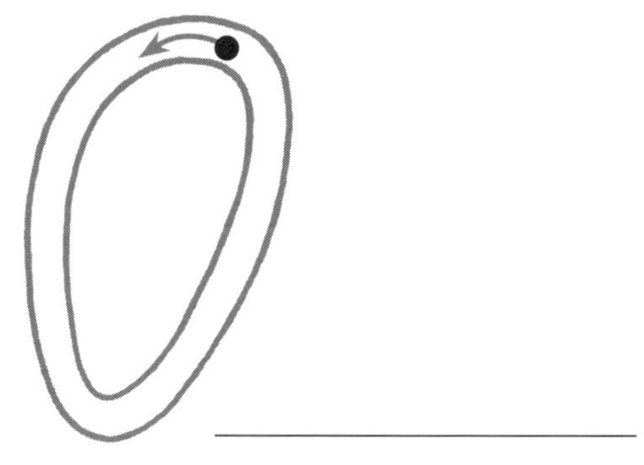

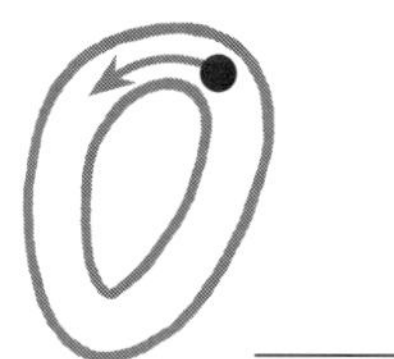

Circle your best letter.

Oo

Lesson 27 • Worksheet 3

Name

Missing sounds

1 Add **o** and read the word.

____live

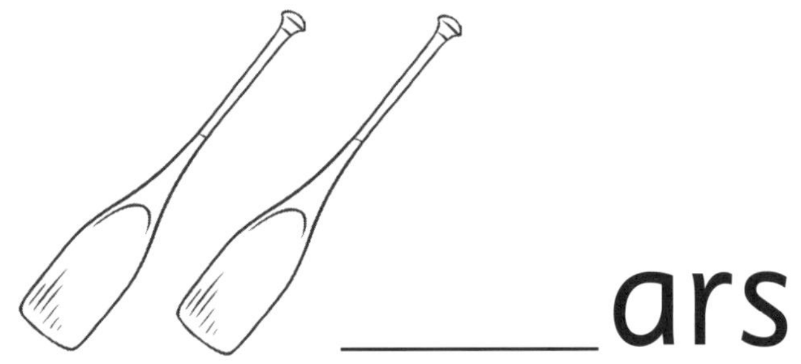

____ars

____strich

____range

b____x

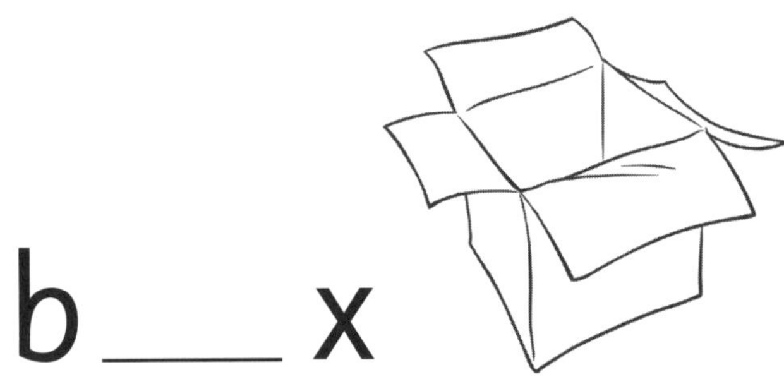

d____g

2 Circle every **O**.

O	P	C	O	O
O	O	D	Q	U

How many? ____

Circle every **o**.

o	o	a	o	e
b	o	c	p	o

How many? ____

Name

Word families

Lesson 27 • Worksheet 4

Label the pictures. Join the words that rhyme.

Lesson 28 the word **is**

Learning objectives

Children will:

- identify the word is.
- read and write the word is.
- recognise the words good and bad.

Australian Curriculum Content Descriptions

Sound and letter knowledge

ACELA1439 listen to the sounds a student hears in the word, and write letters to represent those sounds; identify and manipulate sounds (phonemes) in spoken words

Expressing and developing ideas

ACELA1435 learn that word order in sentences is important for meaning

ACELA1758 recognise the most common sound made by each letter of the alphabet, including consonants and short vowel sounds

Interpreting, analysing and evaluating

ACELY1649 navigate a text correctly, starting at the right place and reading in the right direction, returning to the next line as needed, matching one spoken word to one written word

Sight words

is, see, had, good, the, can, bad, an, a, I, am

Vocabulary words

ant, bat, cap, sad, bee

ESL/ELL

Many English language learners pronounce an i at the start of a word with an ee sound. 'Eet ees good.' Use pairs of sight word cards including some 'i' words like is, it, in, into, if, to play Memory. The students only get to keep the cards if they can pronounce the word properly.

Extra assistance

Other games that can be played with sight word cards to reinforce correct pronunciation are

- Go Fish, where they have to ask for a word card correctly
- Bingo, where they have to say the words when they are done
- Spelling Bee, where they have to say and spell the words

Classroom activities

Mind the Gap!

Write this sentence on the board: Sam ___ sad.

Ask students to read this sentence by themselves, write it down and fill in the gap with a word of their own. Discuss their individual sentences as a group.

Sentence Shuffle

Write an enlarged version of the sentence Matt is a bad ant and read it with the children. Reproduce each word on smaller pieces of card so students can make the sentence themselves and read it.

Reading Eggs Lesson sequence	TEACH Content and skills	PRACTISE Children will:	APPLY
Hear: *Animated Lesson*	Introduce the word is through words and the song *Jazz sings is.*	identify and read is in isolation and in a group.	**Worksheet 1** Sight words
Write: *Make a Sentence, Pick Up Bricks*	Recognise correct word order for a sentence.	choose the correct words to make a sentence.	**Worksheet 2** Vocabulary
Find: *Flock of Seagulls, Fishing Boats, Frog Hops, Golden Goose*	Recognise the given word.	locate the given word in a group.	**Worksheet 3** Writing sentences
Vocabulary: *Word Windows, Tiles, Picture Picker*	Build vocabulary skills: Blend and recognise words. Read and comprehend a sentence.	blend sounds to read and make words. Read a sentence and match to a picture.	**Worksheet 4** Read and write
Read: *Book*	Read aloud book.	listen, follow the reading and read along.	**Reading Eggs Story book** Matt the ant

Related Reading Eggs Activities, Interactives, Songs and Books

Reading Eggs Playroom

Play Mat:
Words with blocks

Paint Easel:
Write the words you know

Music Café

Jazz Sings Is

Reading Eggs Puzzle Park

Both ways

Read it

Reading Eggs Posters

Reading Eggs Library Books

My Program Books

Alphabet Flashcards

Game 5 – From A to Z with known letters.

Teacher Toolkit

Targeting Handwriting Interactively

Spelling Activities

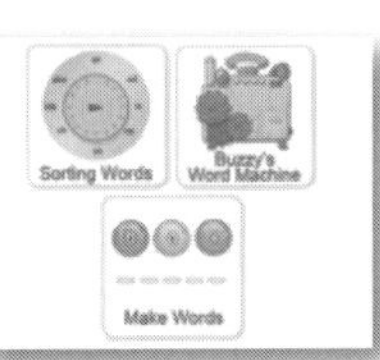

Reading Eggs Apps

Eggy Sight words

Critter Card

Issy me

is

Lesson 28 • Worksheet 1

Name

Sight words

1 Write the word.

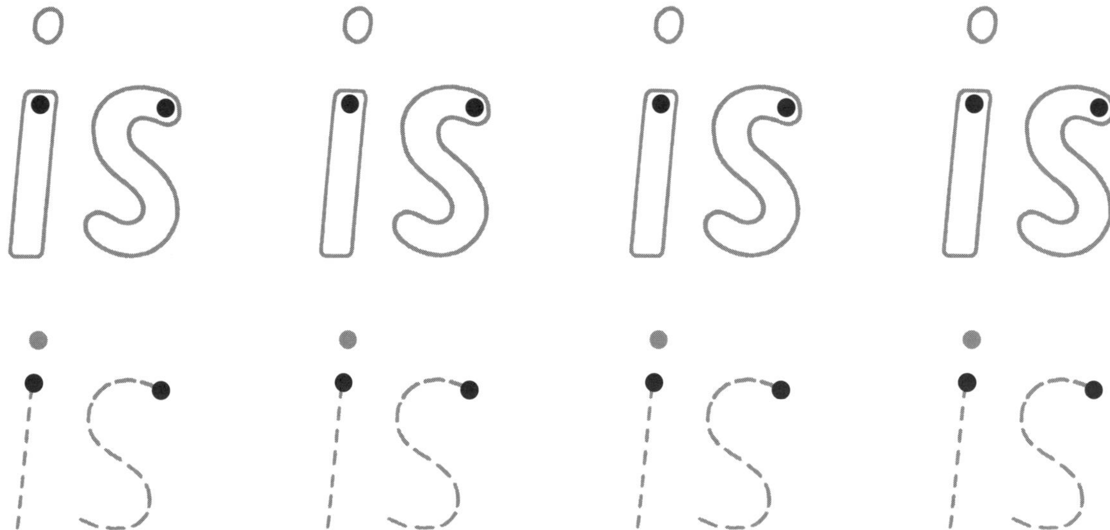

2 Finish the questions using a word from the box, then circle the answers.

Is   you   Can

_____ Sam a bad ant?   Yes   No

Can _____ run?   Yes   No

_____ you see a cat?   Yes   No

Name

Vocabulary

Lesson 28 · Worksheet 2

1 Good or bad? Join each picture to a word.

2 Colour **good** in blue and **bad** in red.

bee	bee	the	the	bad	bad	jam	jam
bee	good	the	bad	bad	bad	bad	jam
bee	can	the	bad	bad	the	the	jam
jam	good	the	bad	bad	bad	bad	jam
jam	good	jam	bad	bad	bad	bad	can
hat	good	can	bee	bee	bad	bad	can
hat	good	can	bad	bad	bad	bad	hat
hat	good	bee	bee	bad	bad	hat	hat

Lesson 28 · Worksheet 3

Name

Writing sentences

Unjumble the words to make sentences and then draw a picture.

man sad. is The		
The good. jam is		
in cat the The tree. is		

Name

Read and write

is

Lesson 28 · Worksheet 4

1 Read each sentence and match to a picture.

Sam can see the bee.

Matt is a bad ant.

2 Write your own sentence for this picture.

Lesson 29 the word **on**

Learning objectives

Children will:

- identify the word on.
- read and write the word on.
- revise word families.

Australian Curriculum Content Descriptions

Sound and letter knowledge

ACELA1439 listen to the sounds a student hears in the word, and write letters to represent those sounds; identify and manipulate sounds (phonemes) in spoken words

Expressing and developing ideas

ACELA1435 learn that word order in sentences is important for meaning

ACELA1758 recognise the most common sound made by each letter of the alphabet, including consonants and short vowel sounds

Interpreting, analysing and evaluating

ACELY1649 navigate a text correctly, starting at the right place and reading in the right direction, returning to the next line as needed, matching one spoken word to one written word

Sight words

on, the, is, see, can, you, had, a, an, and

Vocabulary words

bee, zap, mat, ant, sat

ESL/ELL

Students whose home language is Russian or Spanish may confuse the short /o/ sound with the long /oo/ sound. Give them practice hearing and saying the sounds using word pairs: cop and coop, hot and hoot etc.

Extra assistance

Learning sight words is invaluable for all students, as these are words that occur frequently in all types of texts. Knowing sight words 'on sight' makes fluent reading easier as students aren't having to sound them out as they read.

Classroom activities

Can you get on?

Put a list of words on the board and ask students if you can put the word on in front of each word. Use singular nouns with a or the, plural nouns, verbs and adjectives. See if the children can explain why some words work and some don't.

Make your own sentences

Write these sentence starters on the board and ask students to finish them. Then discuss the options for what something can be on and make a list.

I am on __
The cat is on __
The book is on __
The boat is on __

Reading Eggs Lesson sequence	TEACH Content and skills	PRACTISE Children will:	APPLY
Hear: *Animated Lesson*	Introduce the word on.	identify and read on in isolation and in a group.	**Worksheet 1** Sight words
Write: *Tiles*	Recognise sounds and match to letters.	identify letters to spell a word.	**Worksheet 2** Read and write
Find: *Alien Planets, Build a Wall, Missing Sound, Trains, Time for 20*	Recognise a given word. Identify the correct onset letter to complete the word. Recognise letters in upper and lower case.	find the given word in a group. Choose the correct initial letter to make the word. Locate lower case and capital letters.	**Worksheet 3** Initial sounds
Vocabulary: *Wheel of Words, Blend a Word, Picture Picker*	Build vocabulary skills: Blend and recognise key vocabulary. Read and comprehend a sentence.	match pictures to words. Blend sounds to read words. Read a sentence and match to a picture.	**Worksheet 4** Word families
Read: *Book*	Read aloud book.	listen, follow the reading and read along.	**Reading Eggs Story book** Zee the bee

Related Reading Eggs Activities, Interactives, Songs and Books

Reading Eggs Playroom

Book Shelf Song
Books:
Wheels on the bus,
Old Macdonald had a farm

Play Mat:
Words with blocks

Music Café

Being on a boat

Reading Eggs Puzzle Park

More than one
Both ways
Read it

Reading Eggs Posters

Reading Eggs Library Books

My Program Books

Alphabet Flashcards

Game 4 – Make the Critters with known letters.

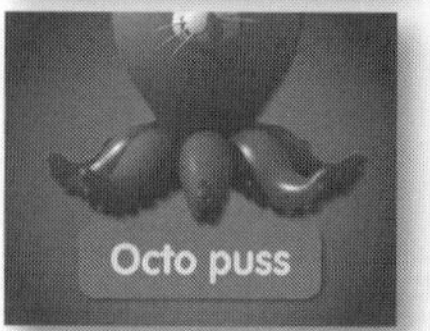

Teacher Toolkit

Targeting Handwriting Interactively

Spelling Activities

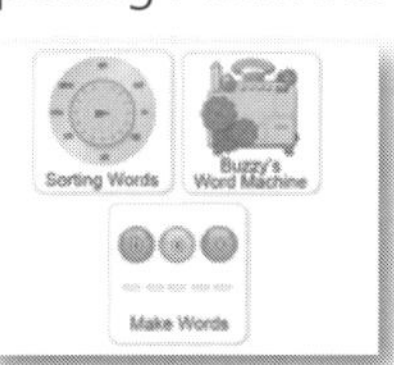

Reading Eggs Apps

Eggy Sight words

Critter Card

Zee the bee

on

Lesson 29 • Worksheet 1

Name

Sight words

1 Write the word.

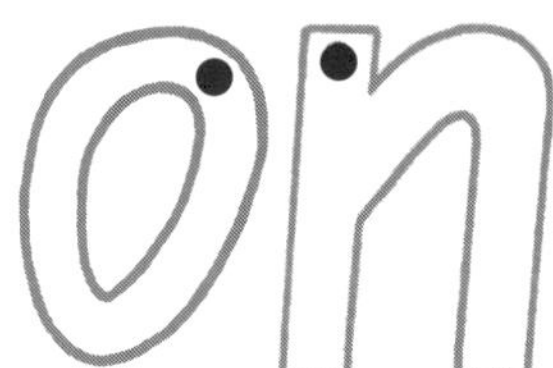

2 Complete the sentences with a word from the box

in on at

The bee is _____ the flower.

See a rat _____ a hat.

I am _____ school.

Name

Read and write

on

Lesson 29 · Worksheet 2

1 Read the sentence and draw a picture.

Sam the ant is on the mat.

Zee is a bee.

2 Write a sentence for each picture.

Initial sounds

Lesson 29 • Worksheet 3

Name

Make words. Match to a picture.

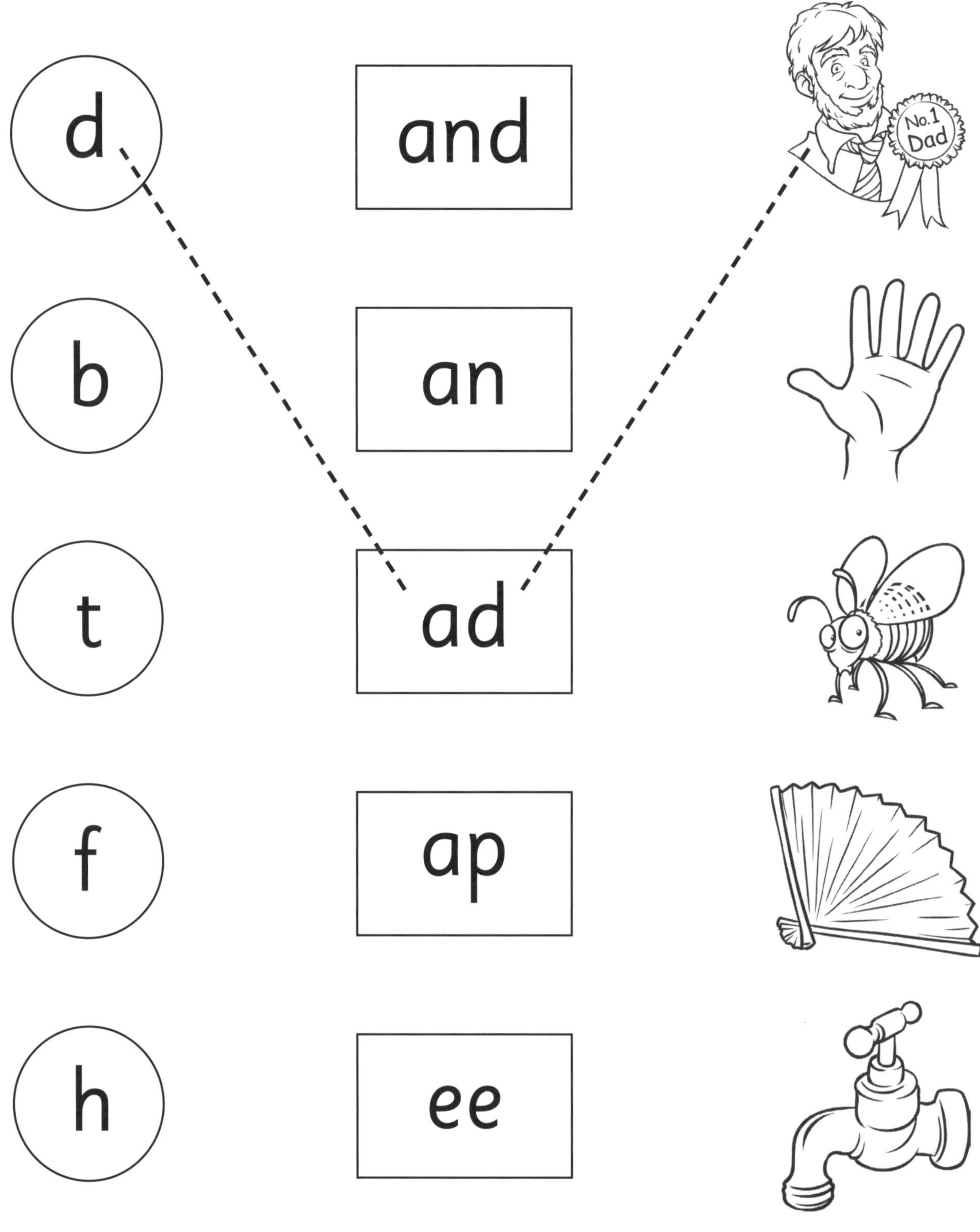

Name

Word families

Lesson 29 • Worksheet 4

Name each picture. Write the word.

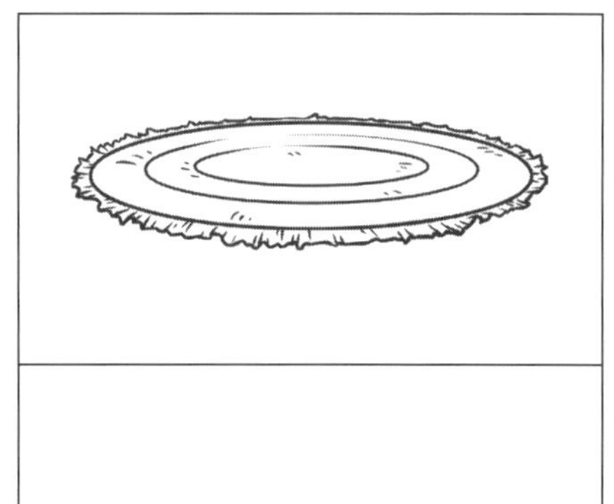

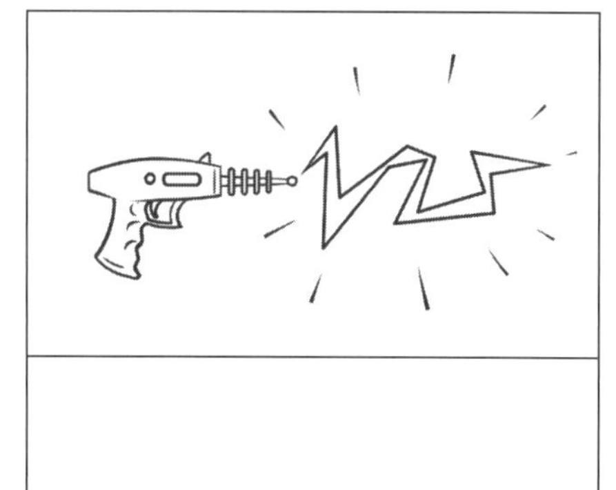

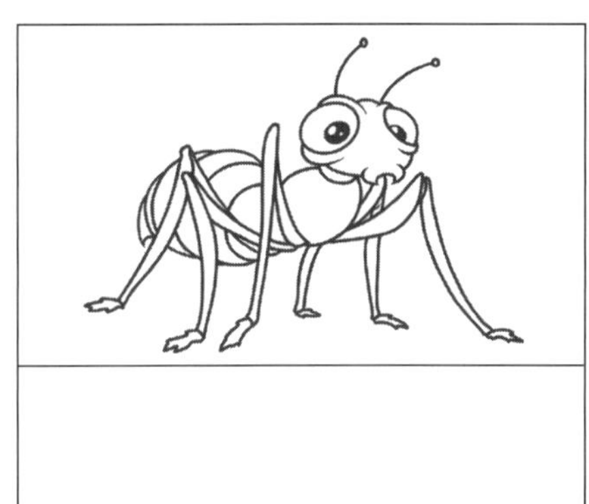

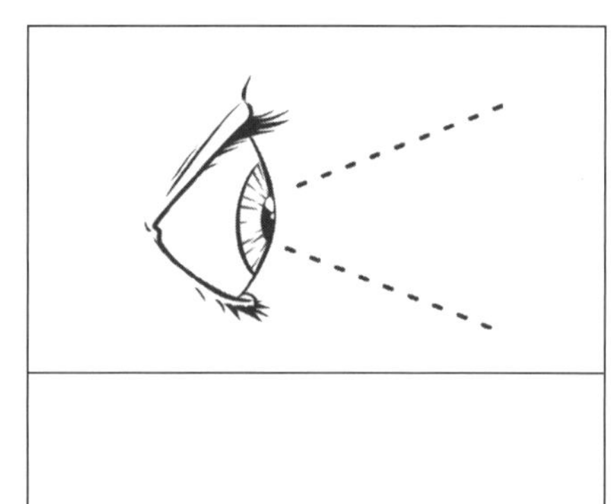

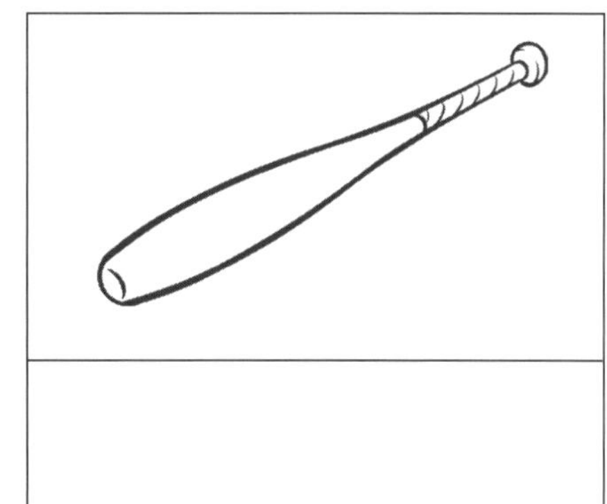

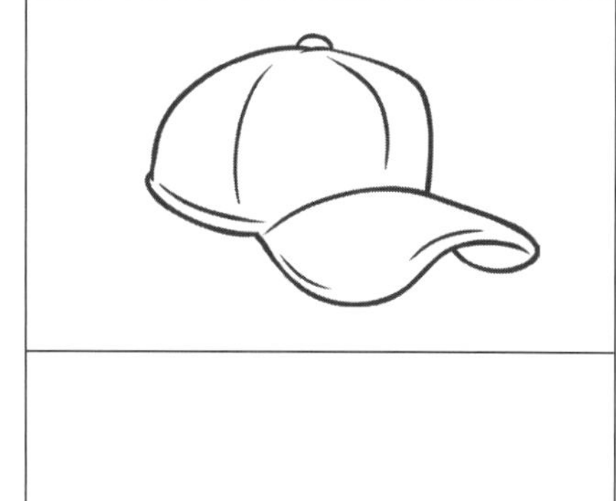

Lesson 30 the letter q

Learning objectives

Children will:
- revise known letters, sounds and sight words.
- identify the sound q.
- read and write q and Q.

Australian Curriculum Content Descriptions

Sound and letter knowledge

ACELA1439 identify and manipulate sounds (phonemes) in spoken words

ACELA1440 identify familiar and recurring letters and the use of upper and lower case in written texts

Creating texts

ACELY1653 follow clear demonstrations of how to construct each letter; learn to construct lower case letters

Expressing and developing ideas

ACELA1758 recognise the most common sound made by each letter of the alphabet, including consonants and short vowel sounds

Interpreting, analysing and evaluating

ACELY1649 navigate a text correctly, starting at the right place and reading in the right direction, returning to the next line as needed, matching one spoken word to one written word

Sight words

I, am, a, an, at, can, see, the, you, and, in, had, is, on, good, bad

Vocabulary words

queen, quilt, queue, quarter, question, quack, quiet, quail

ESL/ELL

Students who speak Spanish may pronounce qu as /k/ instead of /kw/. Practise orally and aurally with queen and keen, quill and kill, and so on.

Extra assistance

The idea that q must always be followed by u is essential for all English language learners. Brainstorm a list of 'qu' words and put the qu in red every time to emphasise that they must go together.

Classroom activities

Letter Pictures

Provide the students with a piece of paper that has a large qu in the middle:
- trace over the qu with a pencil
- draw things that start with qu around the letters and colour them in.

Bingo!

Give students a laminated board with 10 squares on it. Ask them to write a letter in each square from the list q, o, j, d and v (use whiteboard markers). Hold up pictures of items starting with q, o, j, d and v and say the name of the item in the picture. Students put a cross on that initial letter on their board. First one to 10 calls out 'bingo' and wins!

Reading Eggs Lesson sequence	TEACH Content and skills	PRACTISE Children will:	APPLY
Hear: *Animated Lesson*	Revise known letters, sounds and sight words through identification and the song *Running Revision*. Introduce the sound /q/.	identify given letters, sounds and sight words in a group. Identify and read the /q/ sound in isolation.	**Worksheet 1** Phonemic awareness
Write: *Dot-to-Dot*	Reinforce correct letter formation of lower case q.	write the letter q.	**Worksheet 2** Handwriting
Find: *Missing Sound, Mark Your Letter, Letter Grid, Letter Lights*	Identify the correct onset letter to complete the word. Recognise letters in upper and lower case.	choose the correct initial letter to make the word. Locate lower case and capital letters.	**Worksheet 3** Initial sounds
Vocabulary: *Letter Book, Break it Up*	Build vocabulary skills: Recognise key vocabulary. Identify the number of phonemes in a word.	match pictures to words. Identify the number of sounds in a word.	**Worksheet 4** Sight words
Read: *Book*	Read aloud book.	listen, follow the reading and read along.	**Reading Eggs Alphabet book** q

Related Reading Eggs Activities, Interactives, Songs and Books

Reading Eggs Playroom

Alphabet Activities

Book Shelf Song

Books:

Alphabet Song,

Five Little Ducks

Music Café

Running Revision

Reading Eggs Puzzle Park

Alphabet match

Both ways

Read it

Reading Eggs Posters

Reading Eggs Library Books

My Program Books

Alphabet Flashcards

Game 3 – Sound Hunt with q and known letters.

Teacher Toolkit

Targeting Handwriting Interactively

Alphabet Activities

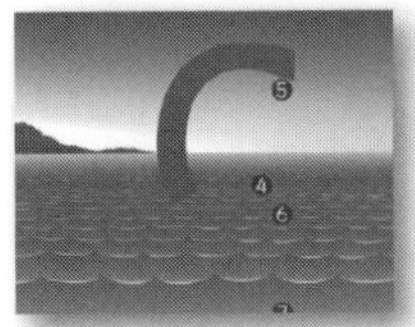

Reading Eggs Apps

Eggy Alphabet

Eggy Sight words

Critter Card

Queenie Quail

Lesson 30 • Worksheet 1

Name

Phonemic awareness

1 Add **q**. Read the word.

 ____ueen	 ____uail
 ____uilt	 ___uack

2 Match each letter to a picture.

3 Colour the letters you know.

a	b	c	d	e	f	g	h	i	j	k	l	m
n	o	p	q	r	s	t	u	v	w	x	y	z

Name

Handwriting

Qq

Lesson 30 · Worksheet 2

1 Complete the balloons.

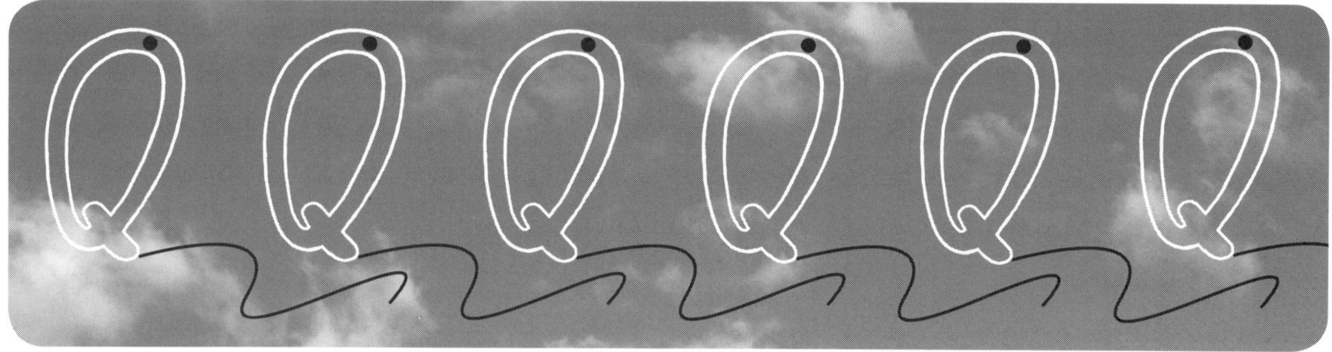

2 Trace and write.

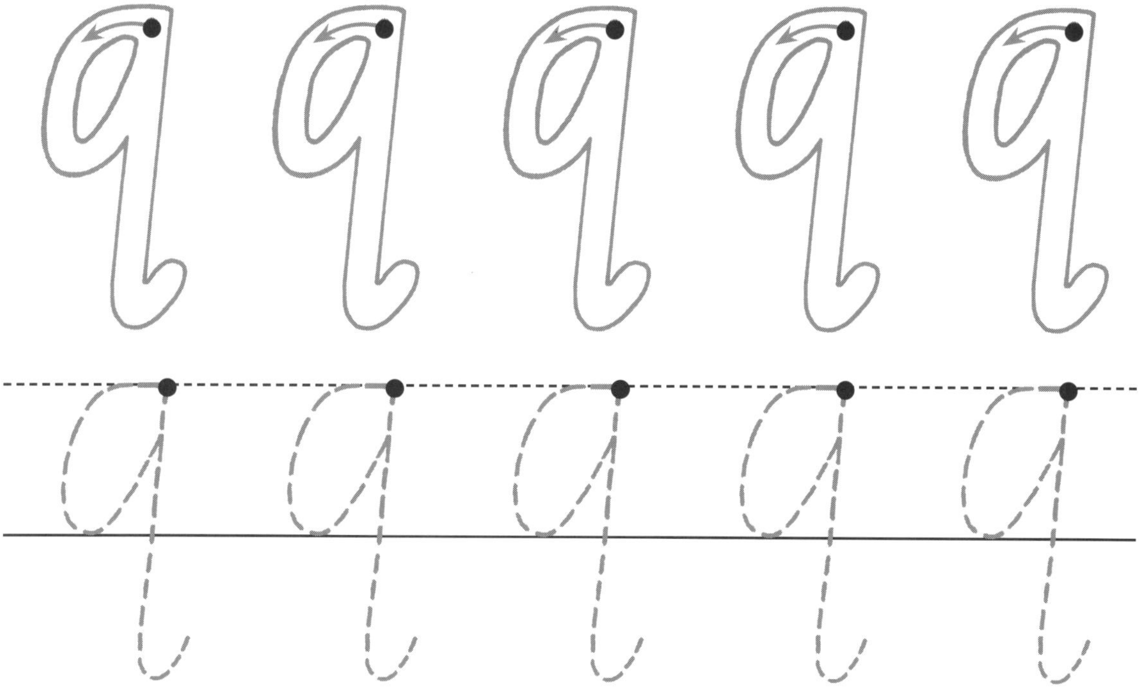

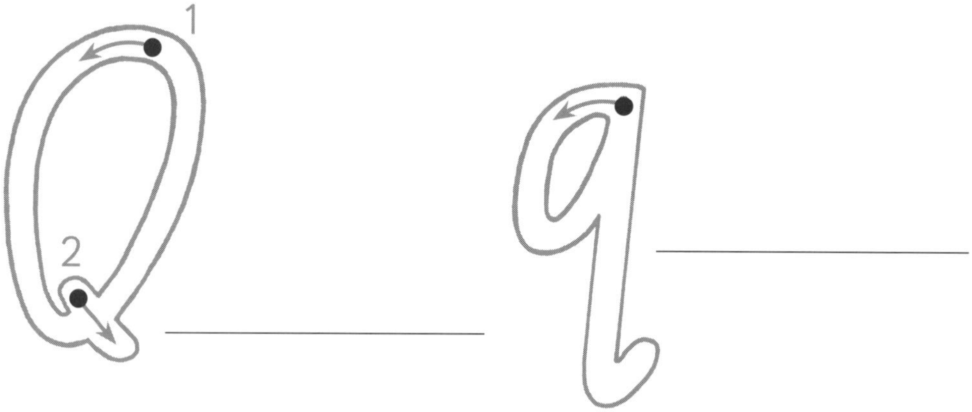

1

2

Circle your best letter.

Qq

Lesson 30 · Worksheet 3

Name

Initial sounds

Colour the pictures that start with the letter.

Name

Sight words

Lesson 30 • Worksheet 4

1 Read and write.

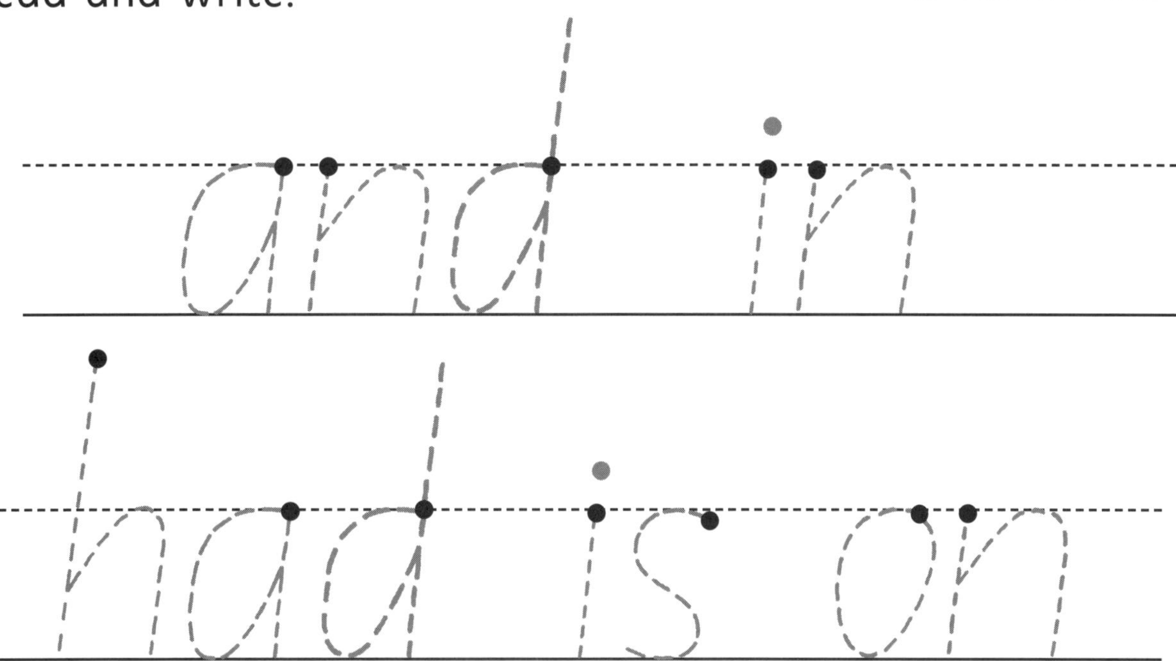

2 Put each word in a sentence.

I can see a rat ________ a cat.

The cat ________ in a tree.

The cat ________ a nap.

The rat is ________ a hat.

The rat is ________ a log.

Reading Eggs Posters

In meeting the demands of the Australian Curriculum we have created a poster series as a teaching tool. These full-colour engaging posters can be used on Interactive Whiteboards and tablets, as well as printed on A3 or A4 for classroom use. The series covers the broad scope of curriculum outcomes including language, literature and literacy. Here is a sample from the series that addresses sounds, sight words and early sentence structure.

Purpose

To provide a solid base to explore sound-letter correlations, sight words and beginning sentence structure. The short vowel sounds are focused on as these form the basis of many CVC words children learn in Kindergarten. As children learn these new sounds, there are also posters to teaching rhyming words and spelling strategies.

Australian Curriculum Content Descriptions

Expressing and developing ideas

Recognise that sentences are key units for expressing ideas (ACELA1435)

Know that spoken sounds and words can be written down using letters of the alphabet and how to write some high-frequency sight words and known words (ACELA1758)

Know how to use onset and rime to spell words (ACELA1438)

Sound and letter knowledge

Recognise rhymes, syllables and sounds (phonemes) in spoken words (ACELA1439)

Recognise the letters of the alphabet and know there are lower and upper case letters (ACELA1440)

Teaching notes

- Use the alphabet poster as a puzzle. Cut each letter into separate squares and ask students to work in teams to put it back together.
- Practise the vowels; play with making new CVC words by adjusting the vowel in each. Create flip books to visually show how changing the vowel creates a new word. As students progress in their sound knowledge you could add double consonant sounds.
- Focus on single sounds and ask students to use recycled materials to build objects that start with the same letter. Create labels for these and display them in an accessible place for students to use during writing.
- Cut the high frequency words into four lists and play 'Word Detectives' to find these words in books you read together as a class. These can also be printed and used for homework. You could also laminate and use them as placemats, then give children playdough to build the words.
- Focus on the rhyming spelling strategy and brainstorm other words that rhyme. Get students to group words together and demonstrate during writing time how to use this strategy.
- Use the sentence poster as a reminder before starting any written work. The simple to follow format can be adjusted to use across the entire curriculum. It can also be used as a checklist at the completion of tasks.

The posters

Alphabet

Vowels

Consonants

High frequency words

Short vowels

CVC words

Rhyming words

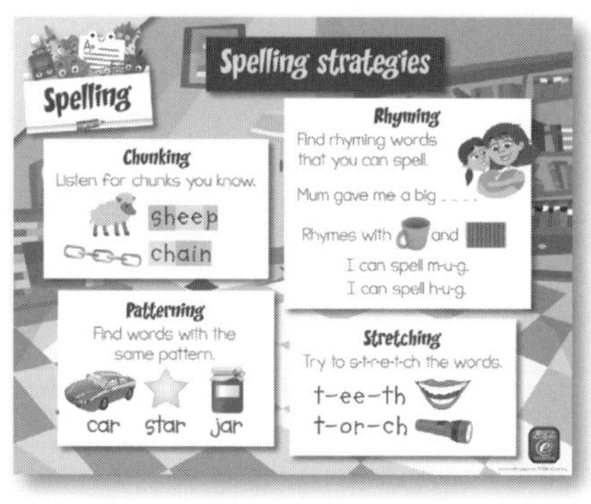

Spelling strategies

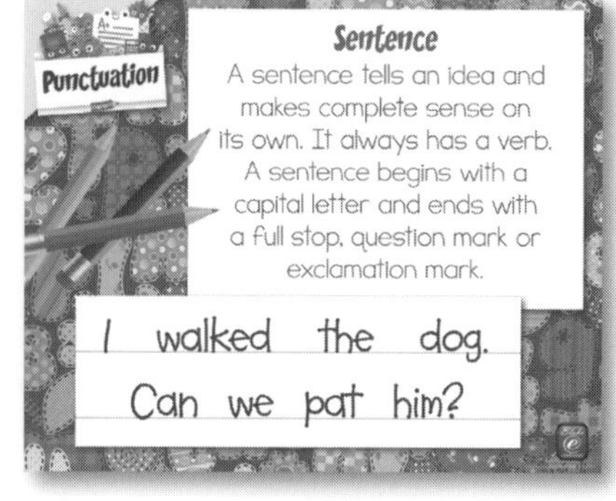

Sentences

Alphabet A - Z

Skills Checklist Lessons 1-30

Name

Lesson	Skills	Check
1	Identifies words which start with the sound /m/. Writes the letter m. Recognises the letter m.	
2	Identifies words which start with the sound /s/. Writes the letter s. Recognises the letter s.	
3	Identifies words which start with the sound /i/ or /ie/. Writes the letter i. Recognises the letter i. Uses the words I and am correctly.	
4	Identifies words which start with the sound /t/. Writes the letter t. Recognises beginning sounds – m, s, i, t.	
5	Reads and writes -at words. Comprehends the words I, am, at. Uses -at words in sentences correctly.	
6	Identifies words which start with the sound /b/. Writes the letter b. Recognises beginning sounds – m, s, i, t, a, b.	
7	Identifies words which start with the sound /k/. Writes the letter c. Recognises beginning sounds – m, s, i, t, a, b, c.	
8	Identifies words which start with the sound /f/. Writes the letter f. Recognises beginning sounds – i, b, c, f. Comprehends -at words.	
9	Uses the words I, am, a correctly. Writes the letter a. Identifies words which start with the sound /a/. Uses -at words in sentences correctly.	
10	Recognises beginning sounds – m, s, i, t, a, b, c, f. Writes the letters a, b, c, f, i, m, s, t. Recognises end sounds – m, s, t, -ap, -at, -an. Writes -at words.	
11	Identifies words which start with the sound /n/. Recognises beginning sounds – t, a, b, n. Writes the letter n. Uses -at words and I, am, a in sentences correctly.	
12	Identifies words which start with the sound /p/. Writes the letter p. Recognises beginning sounds – m, a, b, c, f, n, p. Identifies words which end with the sound /p/.	
13	Writes -ap words. Recognises -ap and -at words. Comprehends and completes sentences. Identifies rhyming words.	
14	Identifies words which start with the sound /h/. Writes the letter h. Recognises beginning sounds – c, p, h.	
15	Identifies words which start with the sound /r/. Writes the letter r. Recognises beginning sounds – m, c, f, p, r.	

Name

Skills Checklist Lessons 1-30

Lesson	Skills	Check
16	Writes -an words. Completes and comprehends sentences. Recognises beginning sounds – m, a, b, f, h, r. Identifies rhyming words.	
17	Identifies words which start with the sound /z/. Writes the letter z. Recognises beginning sounds – p, r, z.	
18	Identifies words which start with the sound /e/ or /ee/. Recognises words which have the sound /ee/ in them. Writes the letter e. Identifies sounds in words.	
19	Uses the words the and see correctly. Writes sentences to go with pictures. Recognises end sounds -at, -am, -an, -ap, -ee.	
20	Recognises beginning sounds – n, p, h, r, z, e. Writes words in correct order to make sentences. Completes and comprehends sentences. Makes words into plurals by adding -s.	
21	Identifies words which start with the sound /v/. Writes the letter v. Identifies words which have the sound /v/ in them. Recognises beginning sounds – a, p, v.	
22	Uses the word and in sentences. Writes words in correct order to make sentences. Writes -and words. Identifies rhyming words.	
23	Identifies words which start with the sound /d/. Writes the letter d. Recognises beginning sounds – a, b, c, n, p, h, r, z, e, v, d. Identifies words which end with the sound /d/.	
24	Uses the words in and had in sentences. Comprehends sentences. Writes words in correct order to make sentences. Matches onset and rime to label pictures.	
25	Identifies words which start with the sound /j/. Writes the letter j. Recognises beginning sounds – i, b, c, n, h, z, v, d, j.	
26	Writes -ad words. Identifies and writes words for pictures. Makes words into plurals by adding –s. Identifies sounds in words.	
27	Identifies words which have the sound /o/. Writes the letter o. Identifies and writes words for pictures. Recognises rhyming words.	
28	Completes sentences using the words is, you and can. Comprehends sentences. Writes sentences. Identifies the words good and bad.	
29	Completes sentences using the words on, in and at. Comprehends sentences. Writes sentences. Matches onset and rime to label pictures.	
30	Identifies words which start with the sound /kw/. Writes the letter q. Recognises beginning sounds – b, c, v, d, j, o, q. Completes sentences using the words on, in, and, is, had.	

READING ASSESSMENT
Lessons 1-30

Name

Read the text.

Sam is an ant.
Sam has a dad.
Sam's dad has the map.

Underline the correct answer.

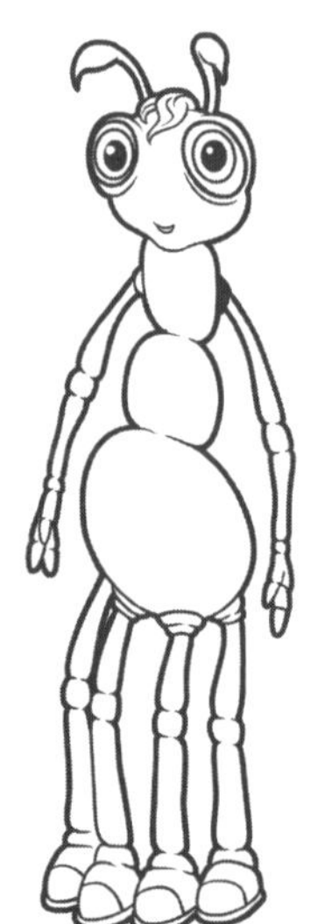

1 What is Sam?
- a dad
- an ant
- a map

2 What does Sam have?
- a dad
- a mop
- a map

3 Who has the map?
- Sam
- Matt
- Sam's dad